CO AZJ 302

# Globalization and Islamism

# GLOBALIZATION

*Series Editors*
**Manfred B. Steger**
*Royal Melbourne Institute of Technology and University of Hawai'i–Mānoa*
and
**Terrell Carver**
*University of Bristol*

"Globalization" has become *the* buzzword of our time. But what does it mean? Rather than forcing a complicated social phenomenon into a single analytical framework, this series seeks to present globalization as a multidimensional process constituted by complex, often contradictory interactions of global, regional, and local aspects of social life. Since conventional disciplinary borders and lines of demarcation are losing their old rationales in a globalizing world, authors in this series apply an interdisciplinary framework to the study of globalization. In short, the main purpose and objective of this series is to support subject-specific inquiries into the dynamics and effects of contemporary globalization and its varying impacts across, between, and within societies.

*Globalization and Sovereignty*
John Agnew

*Globalization and War*
Tarak Barkawi

*Globalization and Human Security*
Paul Battersby and Joseph M. Siracusa

*Globalization and American Popular Culture, Second Edition*
Lane Crothers

*Globalization and Militarism*
Cynthia Enloe

*Globalization and Law*
Adam Gearey

*Globalization and Feminist Activism*
Mary E. Hawkesworth

*Globalization and Postcolonialism*
Sankaran Krishna

*Globalization and Social Movements*
Valentine Moghadam

*Globalization and Terrorism, Second Edition*
Jamal R. Nassar

*Globalization and Culture, Second Edition*
Jan Nederveen Pieterse

*Globalization and International Political Economy*
Mark Rupert and M. Scott Solomon

*Globalization and Islamism*
Nevzat Soguk

*Globalisms, Third Edition*
Manfred B. Steger

*Rethinking Globalism*
Edited by Manfred B. Steger

*Globalization and Labor*
Dimitris Stevis and Terry Boswell

*Globaloney 2.0*
Michael Veseth

Supported by the Globalization Research Center at the University of Hawai'i, Mānoa

# Globalization and Islamism

## Beyond Fundamentalism

Nevzat Soguk

ROWMAN & LITTLEFIELD PUBLISHERS, INC.
*Lanham • Boulder • New York • Toronto • Plymouth, UK*

Published by Rowman & Littlefield Publishers, Inc.
A wholly owned subsidiary of The Rowman & Littlefield Publishing Group, Inc.
4501 Forbes Boulevard, Suite 200, Lanham, Maryland 20706
http://www.rowmanlittlefield.com

Estover Road, Plymouth PL6 7PY, United Kingdom



British Library Cataloguing in Publication Information Available

**Library of Congress Cataloging-in-Publication Data**

Soguk, Nevzat.
Globalization and Islamism : beyond fundamentalism / Nevzat Soguk.
p. cm. — (Globalization)
Includes bibliographical references and index.
ISBN 978-0-7425-5750-5 (cloth : alk. paper) — ISBN 978-0-7425-5751-2 (pbk. : alk. paper) — ISBN 978-0-7425-5752-9 (electronic)
1. Globalization—Religious aspects—Islam. 2. Islamic fundamentalism. 3. East and West. 4. Islam—Turkey—History. 5. Islam—Indonesia—History. I. Title.
BP190.5.G56S65 2011
297.09182'1—dc22

2010022803

∞™ The paper used in this publication meets the minimum requirements of American National Standard for Information Sciences—Permanence of Paper for Printed Library Materials, ANSI/NISO Z39.48-1992.

Printed in the United States of America

# CONTENTS

# ACKNOWLEDGMENTS

I owe a debt of gratitude to many friends and colleagues. I would like to thank Manfred Steger for his continued support and affection for the book project from the onset. I would not have thought of writing this book without his insistence that our conversations about the politics of Islam in the post–September 11 era should have a broader audience. I also thank Terrell Carver for his endorsement of the book very early in the process and for his keen assessment of the book's promise and potential impact. My colleagues in the political science department at the University of Hawai'i, Mānoa, have been uniformly supportive. Michael Shapiro, Jon Goldberg-Hiller, Manfred Henningsen, Noenoe Silva, Ehito Kimura, Debbie Halbert, and Sankaran Krishna deserve a special acknowledgment. Thank you, Jon, for the course release and for your intellectual camaraderie! Thank you, Ehito, for the digital recorder! Among the graduate students, I owe special thanks to Ashley Lukens, Lorenzo Rinelli, Jason Adams, Ozge Tekin, Sami Reza, Rohan Kalyan, and Amir Moheet for either listening to my ideas in their incipient forms or commenting on them after they were written down. Thank you also to Patrick Johnston for reading the entire manuscript carefully with a keen eye to the substance and style.

I want to express a very special note of thanks to three former students, all from Indonesia, without whose help and guidance I would not have been able to pull together the chapter on Indonesia. They are Sofi Encop, Teguh Santosa, and Pramano Tanthowi. Teguh, Pramano, and Sofi accompanied me in Jakarta and Yogyakarta, arranging for interviews with

Indonesia's top political, religious, and academic leaders. They gave generously of their time and personal resources, including driving me around in their own cars. For all they have done, I remain forever indebted to them; these three young and dynamic Indonesians are the sort of organic intellectuals that make the Indonesian polity rich and Indonesian Islam tolerant. Also in Indonesia, the following people, all leaders in their varied fields, shared their insights with kindness and patience, and in the process, enlightened and expanded my horizon: Adurrahman Wahid, Yenny Wahid, Amin Rais, Lilly Zakiyah Machfudz, Nur Rofiah, Bahtiyar Effendy, Moeslim Abdurrahman, Munir Mulkhan, M. Sayafi Anwar, Anies Baswedan, Jamhari, Abdul Muti, Ryad Rais, Shafik Hasyim, Din Siyamsudddin, Rizal Namli, Amin Abdullah, Ahmad Syafii Maarif, Mochtar Pabottingi and Muhammad A. S. Hikam. Dr. Hikam, the former technology minister, had me over for lunch in his house. Moeslem Abdurrahman treated Sofi, Teguh, Pramano, and me to a sumptuous dinner. He was frank and deeply insightful in his observations about Islamism in Indonesia. Din Siyamsuddin and the Muhammadiyah welcomed me to an event on Indonesian Islam while the late Abdurrahman Wahid, formerly of Nahdathul Ulama and the president of Indonesia, treated us to a remarkable lesson in oral history. Finally, the members of the community in Sofi's hometown of Banten educated us on their everyday lives and showed how religion is but one of their many sensibilities and certainly not the only significant one. I would like, last but not least, to thank Mark Hanusz, the owner of Equinox Publishing in Jakarta, Indonesia, for his hospitality and his logistical help. Equinox's English language publications on Indonesia have been particularly helpful for my research. Also, the institutional support provided by the University of Hawai'i, Mānoa, was crucial for the success of the writing phase of the book. A National Endowment for Humanities Summer Grant from the University Research Council enabled my research travel to Indonesia in the summer of 2008.

I would be remiss if I did not thank the Rowman & Littlefield staff, especially Susan McEachern, Carrie Broadwell-Tkach, and Jehanne Schweitzer, as well as others involved in the production process, for their efficient and emphatic professionalism. They facilitated the review process expertly, supervising the outside review that provided excellent feedback on the project's direction. I appreciated the insightful comments that came my way and thank the reviewer very much. All in all, I am deeply grateful to friends and colleagues for insights, guidance, and counsel throughout the various phases of the book. Of course, any shortcomings and errors, although unintentional, are mine alone.

Of the many friends and family members, one has been particularly eager to see the completion of the book. My son Alissandro (Ali), although only eight years old, has been surprisingly interested in the journey this book represents. He has remained curious and engaged, asking many questions and cheering me on all the while protesting that I was staking "sooo long" to finish the book. I take great pleasure in being able to tell him that the book is finally done. As has been promised, he will receive the very first copy. He will share it with his younger sister, Derya, who showed little interest in the book but more than made up for her lack of interest with her random and frequent hugs and kisses. Their mother, and my partner, Clare, has long been used to the drills of a writing project. Quietly, selflessly, and lovingly, she let me have the time (away from the kids) so that I could think. She in turn was supported by her parents, Richard and Patricia, who, in doing their "grandparenting thing" during their visits actually made it possible for me to go to a coffeehouse and write the first draft. Lastly, I would like to express my affection for my parents, Neriman and Cafer, who shaped my attitude on life without prejudice.

# INTRODUCTION

## *Islam, Islamism, and Globalization*

As the world prepared to welcome the year 2010, the Swiss went to the polls and approved a curious law: banning the building of new Islamic minarets in Switzerland.[1] Legendary for its liberalism and tolerance, and made up of many ethnic, cultural, and religious communities, the Swiss vote surprised many and shocked Muslims. Stoked by the fears of a creeping Islamization of their country, the Swiss signed onto a categorically prohibitive measure. They said that the minarets are symbols of a repressive mind-set, a backward religion, and a foreign culture. It is a mind-set that oppresses women and has no place in their European country. Paradoxically, to some people, the outright ban on minarets appeared to mirror the very intolerance the Swiss contended they were voting against. Ironically, not long before the Swiss referendum banning minarets as symbols of a religion that subjugated women, a prominent woman architect in Turkey had been recognized for a brilliant modern mosque she had designed in full, from the minaret to the mimber (pulpit).[2]

Around the time that the mosque in Turkey opened and the Swiss voted in favor of the ban, in Germany a presumably more "tolerant" attitude decided against a total ban in favor of limiting only the height of new minarets. In April 2010, the Belgian federal parliament voted to ban full or partial veil in public spaces. Among the countries that vehemently protested these sorts of measures, Saudi Arabia has been on the forefront. The Saudis, however, have never liked to be reminded that Saudi Arabia forbids the building of any houses of worship other than mosques. More recently, in France, the president, the Parlement, and the French population debated whether or not to ban "Islamic" attire in the country and settled for a partial ban (in government offices and schools) on what is called the full burka, which covers all but the eyes of women. The reasoning: Islamist extremist ideals, symbolized by the attire, clash with the founding "ideals of the French Republic." Again, the world followed with some amazement this strange debate on whether certain religions or religious practices ought to be banned or constrained. However, France was not the first country in Europe to have this debate. That distinction belongs to Turkey, an Islamic country, where Islamic attire, specifically the headscarf, has long been constitutionally banned in government offices and schools. Astonishingly, Turkey has had an Islam-friendly, if not an Islamist, party in power since 2002, which has been unwilling or incapable of removing the ban.

These strikingly confusing if not outright contradictory stories reveal more about the politicization of Islam than about Islam as a transcendental vision. While worldly politics overwhelms unsuspecting citizens' minds, actual religion, Islam in this case and Christianity in others, is pushed into the realm of pure polemics. Only its caricatures are allowed to circulate in the public arena. Conflicts with any religious connotations turn into crises, and crises into catastrophic divides or chasms between peoples and cultures.

Tensions between the West and Islam, at an all-time high since the September 11 attacks in the United States, represent such a chasm, indeed a catastrophic distrust, between the West and the Islamic world. The caricatures of both the West and Islam, obtained in oppositional historiographies, fuel the tensions. Actual histories, in contrast, reveal profound connections and confluences across Islamic and Western civilizations. This globalism of old demands recognition, not only to give a fuller account of the prevalent tensions, but also to highlight the pluralist legacies of earlier encounters still found across Islamic communities. Beyond the Wahhabist Islam that is deployed to caricature Islamic experiences are Arabic and non-Arabic Islamic traditions that remain in step with their times. In that respect, Turkish and Indonesian Islams are especially exemplary and demand greater attention.

Wahhabist Islam, an extremist orientation inspired by ideas of the eighteenth-century fundamentalist Muhammad Ibn Abd al-Wahhab (1703–1792), was first organized into a political movement in the Arabian Peninsula during the nineteenth century by the Saudi clan. In the twentieth century, following Saudi Arabia's founding, it has been exported around the Islamic world, thanks largely to Saudi financing, with the West casting a blind eye to its spread due to Cold War geopolitical interests such as access to Middle Eastern oil and containment of Soviet "Communist" expansion. Wahhabism has become a template for (and has fueled the rise of) hard-line Islamist movements in the Arab world and beyond, in Afghanistan, Pakistan, Somalia, and Yemen.

Wahhabist Islam commands worldwide attention through fear and terror. In contrast, Turkish and Indonesian Islams, which temper religiosity with modern democratic and secular imperatives of globality, receive little notice. This book taps into this nexus of tension born of the Wahhabi movement on one hand and the promise of a pluralist religiosity in places like Turkey and Indonesia on the other. The contrasts are striking. The Wahhabi ideology suppresses rich Arab Islamic histories in favor of its purist revivalist dogma, and rejects any and all achievements of Western civilization. It is governed by categorical prohibitions, terminations, and exclusions in political community. In Turkey and Indonesia, however, Western liberal ideals are generally understood not as alien trajectories to be rejected but as political ideals to be filtered through nominal Islamic sensibilities.

As two non-Arab and unorthodox Islamic countries, Turkey and Indonesia have been central to Islamic histories over the last century. Two modern ideologies—*Kemalism* in Turkey and the *Pancasila* national ideology in Indonesia—imposed on these countries reorganized the political "opportunity structures" for Turkish and Indonesian Islamist movements, thus conditioning the peculiar unorthodox forms they acquired. These ideologies limited religion's role in politics while at the same time they fostered specific religious sensibilities in everyday life in order to support the state. This book examines these multiple legacies in Turkey and Indonesia as it interrelates them with globalization's transnational forces.

Within this nexus, the book develops as a study of the relation and distinction between Islam as a religion and Islamism as an ideology. It argues that contrary to prevailing discourses in both the Islamic and non-Islamic worlds, Islam as a historical religious force was characteristically more pluralistic and flexible than the contemporary Islamist movements allow it to be. The history of what can be characterized as Islam's cosmopolitanism has not been lost, but instead obscured. This book takes a new look at the cosmopolitan traditions in Islam and puts them in critical conversation with contemporary pluralist and globalist orientations. As twentieth-century Islam is being oriented into a series of resurgent Islamist political and cultural movements in the twenty-first century, this study moves beyond the West's convenient caricatures of the East—Near, Far, and Middle—and Islam's suspicions of the West and instead sheds light on the pluralist encounters that have folded the West and Islam together in the past and continue to do so under the conditions of contemporary globalization.

## CHAPTERS IN BRIEF

Chapter 1 locates Islam and Islamism globally and historically within broad areas of tensions, where contemporary Islam is articulated and activated in numerous Islamist movements shaping various political and cultural globalizations. The chapter introduces, defines, and arranges theoretical and conceptual claims in relation to Islam and globalization, treating them both as historical processes and ideological projects. The chapter commences with the historically prevalent Arab Islamist orientations, with particular emphasis on the Wahhabi movement. It argues that even as the Wahhabi ideology has been ascendant in the Arab Islamic world, it has not eclipsed the pluralist and syncretic Arab Islamic experiences of the past and the present. The Arab Islamic legacy continues to resonate in numerous Islamic orientations and traditions. Now more than ever, it is also deeply shaped by them under conditions of intense globalization. Pluralism and syncretism as evidenced in Turkey and Indonesia are perfect examples. They reflect the promises as well as the tensions at work in this interactive Islamic globalism. The chapter focuses on this juncture embedded in the debates on political, economic, and cultural globalization. It draws from the debates eclectically rather than paradigmatically in order to tease out their relevance to Islam and Islamism in global commonspaces.

Expanding on the tensions articulated in the first chapter, chapters 2 and 3 give depth and intensity to the dynamic, rationalist, and transformative histories of Islam based on the premise that those histories are not fictitious but obscured. The Turkish thinker and sociologist Cemil Meric's musings on history guide this return to Islamic historiography. Meric regards rationalism (understood as the work of the human critical faculty) as inherent in the "original Islamic worldview." The thoughts of key Islamic thinkers across the centuries bring such histories to light and enable a study of Islam along temporal, geographical, and sectarian differences. Given the vast and rich Islamic histories, the purpose in these two closely related chapters is to sketch (1) how Islamic pluralist trajectories have animated broad Islamic histories in enduring fashion and (2) how Islamic histories have always interacted and fused with European histories in both conflict and cooperation. The present age of globalization represents not a termination of this nexus but its evolution.

Chapter 4 argues that Turkey is politically and culturally perhaps the most dynamic country in which Islam's past and present are engaged in a critical conversation in light of contemporary globalization. As the inheritor of the Seljuk and Ottoman Islams, Turkey possesses a uniquely rich Islamic legacy and a long-standing relationship with Islam. Turks, who are ethnically non-Arabs, have nearly always occupied a supreme position within Islam. However, Islam in Turkey is made exemplary by secularism, introduced into the Turkish political arena in the late 1920s as the official state policy of the Turkish Republic. Within this secularist legal framework, Turkish Islam has been confounded by a deep popular religiosity, on the one hand, and an intense institutional secularism on the other. After more than seventy years, the uneasy balance shifted in favor of political religiosity in the 1990s mostly around the AKP (Justice and Development Party), which reformulated the core Islamist ideology. "Globalization," stated Prime Minister Recep Erdogan, "is a self-evident planetary commonality; as a common journey, humankind is set on the planetary ship."[3] An inexorable and dynamic cauldron, it presents challenges and opportunities alike. I aim to profile this dynamic cauldron in this chapter.

Chapter 5 focuses on Indonesia as a similarly unorthodox Islamic experience. Like Turkey, Indonesia is pregnant with changes regarding Islam's role in the country. Historically, Indonesia figures as an example of the syncretic reflexes of historical Islams that are suppressed and/or marginalized in much of the Arab Islamic experiences of late. Of the many factors responsible for such syncretism is Islam's historical harmony with Indonesia's archipelagic cultural lifestyles. In Indonesia Islam has always lived in the shadow of a powerful Javanese culture, existing as its supplement rather than forging a metaphysical supremacy over it. Introduced to the Indonesian archipelago relatively peacefully, Islam acquired flexible qualities in light of archipelagic cultural differences. This necessary negotiation of island geography limited orthodox Islam's ability to make deep inroads. Only on Java, except for Aceh, did Islam acquire historical depth and power, and only by being subsumed within the dominant Javanese culture. While this balance remains intact, it is under pressure vis-à-vis the rising tide of Wahhabist Islamic movements.

Still, traditional Islamist movements such as the Nahdathul Ulama (NU) and Muhammadiyah continue to dominate in Indonesia. These movements have remarkably moderate positions regarding the interplay of the sacred and the secular in regulating public spaces. In this sense, moderate Indonesian Muslims, not unlike their counterparts in Turkey, appear willing to think Islam anew under global conditions. Like Turkey's Muslims, for Indonesian Muslims, globalization looms not as a choice to be made but as a reality to be negotiated, accommodated, and appropriated. Islam constitutes a foundational filter through which the global shifts are translated into a national arena.

The final chapter concentrates on the future of Islamism in a globalized world. It contends that the global commonspaces are more definitive of human experiences than they are exceptional to them in ways that clearly implicate and reveal the interdependencies. Political Islamisms have to fit into this interconnectedness instead of aiming to terminate it or stop it at the borders. It is at this juncture of inevitable globalism that critical Islamic capacities beyond fundamentalist ideologies can energize and relate their pluralist histories to the global world. It is true that nowadays, fundamentalist Islamism has injected an extraordinary, if terrifying, energy into the political philosophy of modernity, which remains the prevailing measure of the world. It is also true that in response, pluralist Islam armed with enduring progressive visions is mobilized in the global commonspaces of the world.

A double process of "vanishing-as-emerging," involving fundamentalist Islamism and the Orientalist West, is discernible. The first act vanishes the "diffusionist" conceits of the Euro-West into history, finally accounting for its debts to Islam. The second act vanishes fundamentalist Islamism into the realm of metaphysics, where it becomes one normative compass among many others. Neither negates the political and cultural orientations credited to Europe or Islam. Neither rejects European modernity or Islam as a counterplot. Vanishing should be understood as withdrawing from universal and essentialist animosities, where contemporary conditions of globalization reveal common traces of differences. While it is the last chapter, the sixth chapter is in many ways a beginning for exploring and re-sounding the common traces of differences that might reveal the West as surprisingly "Islamic" and Islam as tantalizingly "Western." It anticipates the coming of a post-fundamentalist age.

Although all the chapters aim to articulate the tensions permeating contemporary Islamic communities around the world, I have never intended the book to have full answers for all possible questions. Further, I certainly do not claim to have given a full history of Islam and Islamism, Arab or non-Arab, nor was that my intention to begin with. If anything, several years of reading in Islamic histories have affirmed my sense of how rich Islamic histories are in politics, philosophy, and arts and sciences and how so very little of those histories are critically studied, let alone sufficiently told and situated within the global history. For this, various parties, Islamic and Western, are responsible. Consequently, for all their global reach and impact in civilizational histories, past and present, Islamic histories have not been sufficiently appreciated, let alone internalized in popular ways as Western histories have been hammered into minds as second nature. While the World consumes the West as the standard or the measure of modernity, it merely cannibalizes its other histories as sundry addenda to the master history. These other histories, including Islamic variations, deserve fuller inventories. I can only hope that this book contributes to such inventories.

I am aware that there is an inherent risk of reifying an Islamic essence in this sort of discourse. So I have tried to avoid enabling or supporting representations that accord Islam or Muslims a singularly distinct or universal essence. I have invoked Arab, Turkish, or Persian Islams in the same spirit as representing distinct historical-cultural traditions rather than absolute and immutable differences. They have all sprung from the same source. Yet they have evolved uniquely, in ways that their differences matter politically. Therefore, in developing an argument that goes beyond simply opposing literalist, prohibitive, and fundamentalist Islam, I have attempted to make this work provoke new thought on Islamic political ontologies. The remarkable robustness of Islamic history has made the task easy. At the same time, the political urgency of developing a rigorous and radical historiography to bring to light diverse Islamic histories has become even clearer. Once in full view, Islamic histories reveal Islam's democratic political characteristics (historically intrinsic to Islam and not foreign to it). They also reveal the incredible narrowness of vision and even ignorance cultivated across the Islamic world about Islam and Islamic histories. The current intellectual challenges that characterize contemporary Islamic societies ought to be seen as the result of the ways in which Islam has been politically appropriated and exploited rather than as the inevitable consequences of Islam's nature. The "genius" of Islam lies not in an unrelenting prohibitive nature but in its overall pluralist outlook in sociocultural matters and its spirit of openness regarding the world around it. Islam is certainly not an all-permissive socio-religious system, but it is also far from being the all-prohibitive ideology it has been turned into in the hands of religious and political ideologues and economic opportunists. Deliberative and emancipatory qualities are as socioculturally essential to Islamic histories as the boundaries definitive of sanctified Islamic outlook. Lest one might be criticized for unduly attributing cosmopolitan characteristics to Islam, one can only point to Islamic histories for evidence, which are clamoring for greater attention. In recovering rich Islamic histories, this work contemplates a future in which Islam recedes into a broader conception of "the political," affirming the political in all its democratic or participatory possibilities.

## OF STYLES AND SUBSTANCE ACROSS CHAPTERS

The book has been shaped by my differentiated access to and familiarity with Turkey and Indonesia. As readers will notice, Indonesia's chapter appears different in style and substance from the Turkish chapter. The chapter on Indonesia relies on firsthand experiences and observations, including interviews conducted with Indonesian political and religious leaders, scholars, and people. While my interest in Indonesia and Islam developed in the post-Suharto era, in contrast, my attraction to politics and religion in Turkey has been constant by virtue of being a native of Turkey. Whereas discussing Turkey has come "naturally" based on the "native" knowledge cultivated over the years, the Indonesia phase of my research demanded a more active engagement, resulting in a discussion immersed in personal observations and formal and informal interviews. In the chapter on Turkey, my customary access to Turkey and Islam situated me both within and without the sites and subjects of my interests. Having lived abroad for two decades, my position concerning Turkey is unique in that I am embedded in the subject matter, but I am not immersed in its daily iterations. As I grew up in Turkey, however, Islam always comprised the sociocultural backdrop to my life, though it was also qualified by disparate influences such as Turkish state secularism, the embrace of Sunni Islam, the dissonance of the Alevi-Bektasi culture, and their similarly complex articulations in the political arena.

I understand fully that as much as my experiences may have allowed new and unique insights, they may have also limited the nature and import of those very insights. I can certainly imagine some limits, while at the same time there may be others I cannot see. Despite this, if, in the end, the ideas and observations in this book provoke few flights of new thoughts or old thoughts in new permutations—considered and inventoried—I will be content.

# CHAPTER 1

# Islamic Globalism Unveiled

On any given day, conversations across the world may invoke Islam simultaneously as a religion of peace, war, love, hatred, greatness, and repression. Yet, it is in the prevailing "Western" discourse about Islam that one finds the most remarkable consistency and unity. In rich and diverse media in the vast Western political and cultural universe, Islam is characterized with uncanny consistency as an archaic and repressive force. Islam appears to inhabit modernity's outlying margins among peoples pushed into a dark and indistinct zone between advanced modernity and historical abyss.

Islam, both its people and the religion itself, appears strange to "Western" people, for more often than not, it is catapulted into visibility through monstrous events perpetrated in its name. Deprived of its manifold histories, Islam figures as an exception to modernity. What

### TEXTBOX 1.1. PILLARS OF ISLAM

**Pillars of Islam as a Faith**

- Belief in Angels
- Belief in revealed books
- Belief in the messengers
- Belief in the resurrection
- Belief in the predestination

**Pillars of Islam as Practice for Muslims**

- To testify that there is only one God (Allah) and that Muhammad is his messenger
- To offer the five compulsory prayers daily (Salat)
- To pay the obligatory charity (Zekat)
- To perform pilgrimage to Mecca (Hajj)
- To fast during Ramadan

*Source:* Adapted from Abdullah Saeed, *Islamic Thought: An Introduction* (London: Routledge, 2006), 3.

is remarkable is that this effect is achieved through simple representations that are large in volume but limited in content. While much has been said and written about Islam as a religion fueling *anti*-modernity, little has been stated to highlight Islam's historical worldviews. The political, philosophical, cultural, and economic "universes" cultivated in and through Islam remain hidden in obscurity.

Reductionist attitudes about Islam are now not only normal but also expected. The most far-reaching effect of this has been the reduction of the political and cultural universes of Islam to an Islam defined primarily by Arab experiences in history. Further still, Arab Islam is increasingly viewed though the precepts and practices of the Wahhabi creed originating in Saudi Arabia in the eighteenth century, which is followed by a negligible fraction of all Muslims around the world. Islam has thus come to be confined to Arab experiences, and Arab Islam has been reduced to a reactionary Wahhabi doctrine of literalism. In this way, not only does the tremendous richness of Arab Islamic histories disappear behind the austere facade of Wahhabism, but also the diversity and pluralism across the Muslim world are obscured.

It is not only "Western" historiography that produces this diminished idea of Islam. Muslims themselves are unable or unwilling to produce and circulate knowledge that shapes contemporary views about their faith. This confluence is instrumental in conditioning how Islam is harnessed to political projects in majority-Muslim countries and the world at large. After the attacks of September 11, 2001, critiques of Wahhabi Islam have been widely expressed, yet very little has been said about the rise of Wahhabi power in the political-economic scramble for the Middle East, beginning in World War I and continuing throughout the Cold War era. This has been a calculated mode of discourse. Anchored both in willful Orientalist historiography and the will to despotism of the "Orient's" modern rulers, it is a mode of inquiry that obscures the political relations through which Europe and the United States actively participated in and shaped Islam's transformation in the Middle East and beyond. In particular, it conceals the role of the United States since the 1950s in catapulting the repressive and violent Wahhabi interpretation of Islam into a global, and increasingly hegemonic, salience. Above all, at the ideological level, it obscures the enduring power of Orientalism as a structure of domination and control.[1]

## ORIENTALISM AS A CULTURAL IDEOLOGY AND A HISTORICAL METHOD

As a cultural and political ideology, Orientalism emerged in the wake of European colonial expansions in the East and Far East in the nineteenth and the twentieth centuries. Colonial expansions had necessitated the knowledge of the lands and peoples to be colonized. However, the knowledge needed had to serve the colonial vision, not complicate or challenge it on grounds of morality or justice. The knowledge needed was the knowledge delivered, which became Orientalism—a civilizational attitude that represented the Orient, primarily the Islamic Orient, as being in the throes of superstition and barbarism and thus designated the "West" as the civilizing savior. Politicians' decisions, capitalists' enterprises, and scholars' treaties, working in unison, operationalized Orientalism, anticipating and legitimizing Europe's colonial projects. In many cases, individuals such as T. E. Lawrence or the celebrated French Arabist Louis Massignon (1855–1922) embodied all three roles. Massignon, renowned for his authority in Arab Islamic studies, also worked for the French Foreign Ministry, just as Lawrence (1888–1935) served the British Crown with distinction and in the process became the legendary Lawrence of Arabia.

The Orientalist designs that followed invented hierarchies across peoples and places in civilizational terms and enforced them through violence and law. Orientalism articulated Europe as the enlightened center of the world, situating the East—Near, Far, and Middle—in relation as clamoring for Europe's light. In this way, Orientalism justified Europe's colonial projects in the Middle East and Asia, bestowing local despotisms with political and practical legitimacy. The Orientalists' claim that traditionalism and authoritarianism represented the Orient's true character and needed reforming in Western light ironically resulted in their validation. In the end, although uneven, the relationship proved symbiotic, supporting imperial interests and buttressing the ruling regimes.

The symbiotic relationship still endures and is seldom questioned in mainstream histories. Most historical inquiries into Islam remain dominated by historiographical and sociological modes that fail to reach beyond "good and evil" formulas anchored in Orientalist paradigms. In "Western" historiography, Islamic histories only appear on the far side of an indistinct haze and are perceived as having little relevance to the *modern thought of humanity*. On the other hand, Islamic historiographies remain captive to the imperatives of the universally repressive state traditions within Islamic societies, particularly in the modern Arab Middle East. They continue to produce romanticized "*ahistories*" that reduce the past to an extra-historical existence, subject to neither time nor geography. The absence of a textured historiography in modern Muslim polities, coupled with the partisan approach prevalent in Western popular historiography, fuels the complicity between "Western" Orientalism and Islamic fundamentalism. This complicity effectively disallows or discourages any sustained and open historical inquiry into contemporary Islamic communities that critically summons the past and the present into the conversation. Unable to invoke and activate continuity beyond a linear chronology, the extant mode of writing history in Islamic communities treats the past ahistorically—either romantically in exaltation or archeologically as something already lost to history. What thus arises is doctrinal continuity without historical memory, lacking any political sense of geography or philosophical sense of history. The Qur'an, for example, stripped of its rich legacy of civilizational experiences from Baghdad to Andalusia, is effectively politicized, subordinating the sacred to worldly interests.

Against this background, contemporary Orientalists, such as Bernard Lewis and Fouad Ajami, can hardly be blamed for issuing broad pronouncements about an entire religion based on selective observations.[2] In this sense, scholarly Orientalists are not unlike religious literalists in their mode of knowledge production. Each employs the Qur'anic and prophetic traditions in order to suggest a particular essence for Islam. Each summons episodes and events in history, not contingently but programmatically, in order to advance a particular political line. Islam thus appears energized as a pure and potentially destructive ideology. Stripped of any mystery or sacredness, it is both antihistorical and antigeographical. Here then arises the paramount challenge in comprehending and communicating Islam's rich and textured histories.

## HOW THE WEST OUTSHONE ISLAM! WRITING POOR HISTORIOGRAPHIES FROM RICH HISTORIES

"Western" historiography has been unwilling and Islamic historiography has been unable to represent Islamic historical worldviews in sufficient depth and detail. While the West has self-consciously developed modernist histories around a global "chain of references extending from Plato to NATO,"[3] Western material and cultural hegemony has rendered Islamic historiography dormant, contributing to the rise of conservative and often violent political and cultural forces within Muslim communities. In the final analysis, it is not the lack of diversity and range in Islamic histories that explains why Islam and Muslims seem inexorably stuck between advanced modernity and a historical abyss. Rather, it is the ways in which the "West" and Muslim worlds perceive and treat those histories that are definitive of how Islam appears today. There are therefore historical and political consequences to seeing modern or contemporary Islam through this or that version without contextualizing the underlying symbiotic relations between Islam and the West. The ascent of Saudi-Wahhabi Islam within the Arab Islamic universe is singularly instructive in demonstrating the consequences.

Emblematic of the symbiosis between Western colonial and state-centric Arab postcolonial interests, no development has been more crucial to the status of political Islam in the Arab world than the consolidation of Saudi-Wahhabi power in the twentieth century following World War I. From the 1920s onward, the convergence of the West's political and economic interests around Saudi fundamentalism not only conditioned Arab nationalist horizons but also narrowed Arab Islamist political imagination. At the nationalist front, autocratic rulers hijacked national agendas into ever illiberal and repressive regimes while Arab Islamist imagination was steadily channeled into symbolic and formalist ideologies. The likes of Gamal Abdel Nasser in Egypt, Hafiz Esad in Syria, and Saddam Hussein in Iraq represented despotism cloaked as secular Arab nationalism, as Wahhabist ideals ruled a state in Saudi Arabia and inspired Muslim brotherhood as a militant supra-state movement.

However, in the years following World War II, Arab nationalism failed to deliver on the rhetoric of political liberation and economic development. Waiting for opportune times, in the 1960s and 1970s Islamists—Wahhabists and the Muslim brotherhood—weighed in, aided ideologically and logistically by the West, to expand the reach of their austere and revivalist Islam. The Wahhabist ideology fed on a simple calculus of a "return" to an "original" Islam. Decades of militant Wahhabist activism, augmented in depth and breadth by an equally militant, albeit clandestine, U.S. support throughout the Cold War, led the Wahhabi orientation to become the main register of popular Islam in much of the Arab world. Arab Islam has come to be seen increasingly through the Wahhabi filter, such that over time Wahhabi ideals appeared to stand for or represent Arab Islamic ideals.

This existential slippage is significant because of the paramount place Arabs hold in Islam's past. Historically, Arab Islam has been treated and emulated as the original and authentic source. Islam was first revealed to Arabs some 1,500 years ago in Arabic and through an Arab prophet, Muhammad. Islamic traditions were and remain steeped in Arabic language and culture and the Qur'an, Islam's holy book, is still recited in Arabic around the world. Further, it is Arab Islam that made Islam into a world religion, along the way conveying Arab history as Islam's master history. In real and symbolic ways Arab experiences have been anchors for Muslims around the world. Wahhabi Islam capitalizes on this historic relation.

As Islam is interpreted and relayed from within the Arab cultural and religious universes, the dominant Wahhabi ideals reverberate through Islamic communities around the planet. They resonate broadly as Muslim and Arab ideals, not as sectarian Wahhabist indoctrination. They thus act as aspirational guideposts, helping to condition the questions asked and the answers given on Islam as a religion and as a political and social regulative regime. In this way, Wahhabi ideals echo extensively in the mainstream Islamic world. Dichotomous in worldview and literalist in praxis, they foment tensions between competing Islamic interpretations within the Muslim world as well as between Islamic and Western worlds. The power of their ideas slips easily into ideas about power, attracting and energizing masses along proto-Wahhabist orientations. Revivalism, literalism, and fundamentalism acquire transnational legitimacy across Islamic societies, becoming idées-fixes—ideas that dominate—while sectarian and ethnic differences are treated as grounds for struggle, where ideas form and explode into the world as movements.

Not surprisingly, when we examine the way that the Arab world and Islam presently appear on the world stage, it is largely through internecine convulsions and violent international eruptions energized by struggles within the orbit of Wahhabi politics. These convulsions and eruptions, however, fuel the uniformist historical, cultural, and aesthetic reflexes supporting the West/Islam divide. Even as they invoke a defense of Islam, they ironically energize the modern Orientalism they claim to reject.

Observers sympathetic to the political-economic "otherness" of majority-Islamic countries argue that the repressive and literalist Wahhabi strand of Islam is a reaction of Islamic communities worldwide who feel besieged by "Western" modernity and capitalism anchored in a Judeo-Christian metaphysics. These observers maintain that much of the Islamic world perceives globalization through capitalism as a Western Judeo-Christian project, a discrete and conditional modernity operating on terms not only alien to Islamic ways of being in the world, but also curtailing Muslims' autonomous capacity for generating Islamic "worldviews." Cast in this light, globalization, more than capitalism, appears as an arrow-like process piercing through Islamic communities, impoverishing them materially and spiritually, and subordinating them politically. As reactions, fundamentalist orientations emerge. For these observers, Western modernity ultimately authors radical political Islam.

Undoubtedly, these claims are not without merit. Yet they are a story partially told, one in need of cautionary interventions. In *Globalism: The New Market Ideology*, Manfred B. Steger[4] distinguishes between globalization as an ongoing material process and globalism as an ideology that strives to capture, organize, and order globalization's trajectory. Globalization and globalism cannot be reduced to one another but instead must be apprehended dynamically in relation to each other. Central to Steger's insight is a nuanced historical sociology that refuses reductionism and easy resolutions.

Viewed in such light, Islam figures as a material and sociological process, while "Islamism" emerges as an ideology that regiments political and cultural agencies in majority-Islamic countries. Similarly, the Wahhabi dominance in Saudi Arabia and beyond is revealed to be a result of the nineteenth-century "Islamism" contemporaneous with European modernity's advent in the Arab world as the regulative ideology of European imperialism—an advent marked by Napoleon Bonaparte's invasion of Egypt in 1798. This historic encounter commenced a new era with powerful ramifications defining our present times.

For nearly a millennium prior to this invasion, Islam had been Europe's alter ego. The "Islam" that Europe first encountered and endured during the first 800 years was a self-confident Islam, not only materially and militarily but also civilizationally. Early Islam regarded itself as a supreme and final way of life. Paradoxically, this supreme confidence cultivated an existential openness, a practical receptiveness to wisdom past and present. The Islamic universe absorbed the Hellenistic and Persian traditions, harnessing them for great leaps in sciences and philosophy from the eighth through the fifteenth centuries, when Islam grew into a hegemonic force. All the same, Christian Europe and Islamic world folded into each other through a crisscrossing transversality.

However, the balance of power organizing these relations began to shift with Europe's "discovery" of the Americas and the rise of extractive protocapitalist enterprises that fueled Europe's "take-off," commenced the Renaissance, and culminated in worldwide modern industrial and capitalist expansion some 400 years later. As Edward Said aptly observed, when Napoleon landed in Egypt with an army of both soldiers and scientists, the moment marked an Orientalist emergence.[5] Although less appreciated historically, it also marked a certain rupture in Islamic confidence, effectively, inaugurating an era of relentless pressures on all forms of openness and pluralism in Islamic geographies. What roughly manifested the triumph of modernity as the dominant affirmative measure for much of Europe translated into a crisis of Islamic cosmopolitanism in the Muslim world.

The Europe that emerged in the wake of the decline of Islamic powers proved supremely confident of its modernity, that is, its own measures of order and progress, and quickly aligned the Islamic world with Europe's needs and desires. Subsequently, Europe's dynamic instincts, now fully energized, erupted into the world's midst as a colonialist territorial expansion—a transversal explosion into the world. That the European transversality was more "arrow-like" than circular, piercing through the world for Europe's welfare is a story already well told. In Muslim memories of this era, what looms significant is that encounters with Europe reduced Muslims to one of European modernity's subordinated and dominated "others." Although historically critical in the development of Europe, Islam was deemed "Oriental" along with other peoples and worldviews and became a "part that had no part" in the Renaissance, Enlightenment, and Modernity. These were all credited to Europe as Europe's own authentic and autonomous projects.

Under duress, Islamic cosmopolitanism nevertheless endured, preserving the traces of its contributions to Europe's modernity in arts and sciences. The works of Muslim luminaries from Avicenna to Averroes recalled not only the rich multicultural societies Islamic political sensibilities enabled, but also the interminable civilizational confluence of the Islamic Orient and Christian Europe, or the West. Paradoxically, as in the past, so in the present Western and Muslim worlds, this unity is instead articulated in civilizational ruptures or chasms. While the West is often fixated on denying Islam's cosmopolitan and pluralist histories, Muslims seldom recognize their own alienation from the infinite dynamism and openness evidenced in historical Islam. Both remain haunted by incomplete histories, which militate in multiple trajectories.

## COSMOPOLITAN ISLAM REDUX

Against this background I want to argue that what early modernity arrested through colonial globalization late modernity currently appears to be releasing as compelling political potentiality, expressed on the one hand as a repressive and intolerant fundamentalist political orientation and on the other as deliberative if still metaphysically inspired political and economic Islamic sensibility. Late modernity is seen as having unleashed Islamic energies from their modern prison-house. While it is clear that Wahhabism embodies the most reactionary and regressive tendencies, what we know much less about are the ways in which Wahhabism fails to represent the full universe of Islamist orientations under conditions of intense global interplay. New globalization is therefore a key to seeing Islam historically anew.

However, globalization is a qualified historical condition defined by new modes of production as well as destruction, not by limitless expansion or an unfettered implosion of ideas, information, and investments across borders and societies. Global flows and networks do not supplant the modern, territorial, and nation-statist forms of identity and exchange. Nor are religions simply pushed to the side as epiphenomenal or unimportant. In reality, Islam, along with other religions, can be said to enjoy a steady expansion from religious into secular civil and political realms. Along with exhilarations in other globally conditioned areas, such as trade and commerce, religions, including Islam, are being transformed—deepened and intensified—without fundamentally casting away the ideas, relations, and subjectivities anchoring the international state-system. Not surprisingly, once regarded as an impossibility because Islam forbids charging interest, Islamic banking has now become mainstream thanks to creative solutions. Islamic identities, too, are dynamically interacting with the flows and networks of new globalism. Flows and networks are channels through which identities are formed and circulated, within countries as well as through them, into the political, economic, cultural, and religious common spaces of the world. They are transnational yet geographically experienced, interlinking national polities through novel technologies without negating the relevance or influence of nationalism. Therefore, I comprehend all that follows in this book under the rubric of Islam as globally developing Islams.

I situate this book in two contemporary variants of Islam—Turkish and Indonesian—in which these global connections, that is, "transversalist" and "syncretic" experiences in Islam, are clear and manifest. Following Edouard Glissant, I understand "transversality" as deep historical relations, extending in multiple directions linking people and places together without collapsing them into one another or treating them as territorially contained and determined.[6] As Glissant suggests, a multitude of relations travels through and shapes local, regional, and national landscapes into what he calls the "commonspaces" of the world. Commonspaces emerge through functional integration without rendering insubstantial the differences that support local or national character. Global capitalism creates such spaces of transversality, as do religions such as Islam and Christianity. The global "commons" of the environment imposes such transversality in time and space. Even the pandemics of yesteryear and the present demonstrate the power of transversal forces that exceed the forces of territorial containment and control. All the while transversality accommodates and cultivates difference and diversity.

I construe "syncretism" as a mode of openness to difference and diversity that produces a coherence of intentions in the commonspaces of the world. In that sense, syncretism is not a result of simple coincidences, but an orientation cultivated in political life through tensions and confluence across ideals. The Turkish and the Indonesian experiences of Islam, more than others, demonstrate these dynamics historically and in the present.

Both Turkey and Indonesia have rich and textured histories in which Islam has been a central locus of enunciation of political-religious formations. Turkey sits atop the legacy of the Turco-Islamic Ottoman Empire. Indonesia has the largest Muslim population in the world today, and is not only non-Arab ethnically but also is geographically peripheral to orthodox Islamic histories centered on the Middle East. Despite their historical-cultural differences, however, these countries played significant roles in Islam's modern history as both non-Arab and nonorthodox experiences.

The Turkish Ottoman sultans were the supreme religious authority over much of the Islamic world as Khalifs from 1518 until the abolition of the Caliphate by the Republic of Turkey in the 1920s. In that capacity, the Turks not only played a central role in Islamic politics, but over the centuries also internalized this primacy as a definitive sociocultural element of Turkish identity, ultimately crystallizing it as a "Turk-Islam Synthesis." This sense of primacy continues to permeate Turkish popular culture and political imagination, which perceives Turkish Islam as exceptional and avant-garde. Similarly, Indonesian Islam created an archipelago-centric Islamic identity, confronting and accommodating, first, Western colonialism and, subsequently, the modern secularist and nationalist Pancasila ideology of postindependence Indonesia.

Feared and welcomed around the world, Turkish and Indonesian Islams fuel exemplary unorthodox orientations. They are feared because they intensify and deepen religiosity in politics, and they are welcomed because they temper religiosity with secular imperatives of globalism. It is this nexus of tension and promise that will interest us in this book, where historical and contemporary political experiences converge into a distinctive politics articulated into global commonspaces rather than remaining anchored in purely religious dogma. Authentic and articulate, Turkish and Indonesian experiences stand in clear contrast to the Wahhabi ideology, which turned Arab Islam into an inarticulate rejection of history. Governed by prohibitions, terminations, and exclusion in political community, in the Saudi-Wahhabi version, Arab Islam has been forced to categorically refute its rich histories in line with a deeply fundamentalist desire for a singular measure. In the Turkish and Indonesian versions, Islam appears a lot more flexible, neither fully internalizing nor completely rejecting the civilizational claims made by the "West."

## NEITHER ORIENTALISM NOR FUNDAMENTALISM

To the West, no matter the version, Islam appears as a counter-hegemonic political field of thought, imagination, conduct, and policy. From the standpoint of liberal, more-or-less secular democracies, the very idea of political Islam is alarming. Recent experiences in Iran, Afghanistan, Pakistan, and Saudi Arabia fuel the fears regarding intolerant, repressive, and "totalitarian" Islamism. Yet, Islamic ideals do not dictate that Muslims refute democratic and pluralist orientations as alien to their religion. In fact, as will be shown in this book, plurality and syncretism have always been elements in the Islamic political imagination, as have the tendencies to control or limit them in Islam's name.

Still, Islam's position in the broader world lies not in the easy claim that it might support an alternative order of one kind or another, but in the possibility that, even through the fears it induces, it might help expand the critical spaces for thinking differently about the world's dominant organizing principles and regulative ideals.

Ironically this critical role is being crystallized vis-à-vis the extremism of the contemporary Islamist fundamentalist movements. For all their complaints concerning how Islam is misrepresented or misunderstood historically, these extremist movements rely on heavily censored knowledge of Islamic histories. Rich and cosmopolitan Islamic histories are the primary victims of their censorship. Fortunately, given the high stakes politically, the more the fundamentalists attempt to sterilize Islamic histories, the more the concerned Muslims push back in order to shine light on Islam's pluralist, progressive, and syncretic histories. Liberal Islam Network in Indonesia, for example, attests to this dynamic. Previously largely ignored in Islamic societies and obscured or denied in the Western imagination, these histories are slow in emergence and still heavily challenged. Yet they still emerge.

More than simple counterweights to fundamentalist movements, these histories also expose a striking parallel between the contemporary Islamist fundamentalist movements and the dominant logic of modern ideologies. Simply stated, viewed in light of the full length and breadth of Islamic histories, contemporary Islamic fundamentalisms are revealed more and more to be and to function as modern ideologies. They mimic or imitate modern ideologies even as they assail them under a religious cloak. Their desire to shape the world in their image only closely mirrors in logic, if not in intent, the sundry ideologies modernity has anchored, from nationalism to capitalism to socialism.

Reflecting an unwavering commitment to a uniform ideological vision of Islam, such a fundamentalist Islam forces all the diverse social, aesthetic, and cultural experiences feeding Islam through a filter preoccupied with the facade of things rather than substance. Signs and symbols pass as content and limit normative or moral possibilities. Captured within the dominant late-modern political model, the majority of the fundamentalist movements imitate the ideological modernity they claim to challenge. Simply put, if in the capitalist moral economy the right and the ability to follow the latest fashion in clothing or technology parades as the core freedom, for the fundamentalist movements, a few rules about the dress code in the Qur'an stand for the ultimate ideal of Islam. Women's headwear or men's beards become the focal point of politics, overriding all other normative political and economic struggles. Nothing else matters as much, neither the abiding Qur'anic interest in social and economic justice nor the Prophet's insistent calls to knowledge wherever the source.

Largely unchallenged within the Islamic thought world, the net effect of this form of Islamic politics in the last half century has been the suppression of historical Islamic diversity in ideas. Yet, however tentatively, the more this form of Islamism is tested and challenged, the more imminent is the relief of the pluralist and progressive histories of which the present Islamisms have only a truncated resonance—truncated not because they summarize or abbreviate these histories but because they marginalize and minimize them. Put plainly, these fundamentalist Islamisms appear more and more as "awful" stories based on "dreadful" historiographies. Under relief, Islamic histories appear in a different light, showing Islamic life-worlds to be fundamentally more about openings, interactions, translations, and transgressions than about exclusions, terminations, stoppages, and prohibitions in human life.

Islam's formative era reflects such dynamic tendencies as having shaped its geographical expansion and ideological diffusion. This era is typically described in the word *fatun*, meaning "opening" in Arabic. In Islamic and Orientalist accounts, however, the word has increasingly signified "conquest" as capture and pure domination. In actuality, the Islamic conquests had a complex and mutually interactive impact on the conquered territories. Undoubtedly, Muslims, too, saw the world as an object of control and appropriation. In this sense, they were not unlike other invaders or conquerors. Yet, unlike many other conquerors before and after the advent of Islamic conquests, Muslims were never driven by a systematic elimination of the existential differences they encountered. The conquest certainly meant an opportunity through which Muslim rulers could expand their rule and influence. At the same time, it also meant an "opening" through which places and peoples were politically, culturally, and economically interlinked in new ways. It is tempting to explain Islam's lightening expansion in the first two hundred years as an "arrowlike" penetration of the societies and communities.[7] However, Islam's spectacular advancement from a tribal movement to a world religion within one hundred years of its birth can be better understood in its cultivation of a pluralist politics—an Islamic humanism—that shaped early Islamic attitudes and attracted multitudes to its milieu. Through this humanist ethos, not only did Muslims regard as valuable the Hellenic, Roman, Persian, and Indian civilizations but they also incorporated them into Islamic civilizational efforts. This receptive attitude, with its complexities and contradictions, is a better key to understanding past and present Islamic polities. The Prophet of Islam himself set the example by calling on Muslims "to strive for knowledge and wisdom if it is in China."

My point is not to attribute, anachronistically, an extraordinary "liberal" acumen to Islamic history. Rather, it is to suggest that unlike the orthodox Islamic and Western Orientalist accounts that characterize Islamic worldviews as a narrow religious ideology of survival at minimum and domination when possible, Muslims channeled their energy and resources into experimentation, learning, and transformation as much as into efforts to constrain human creativity and imagination. More often than not, change was cultivated, not feared or outright rejected in the Islamic imagination.

Then, in this historical sense, "conserving" Islam or being a "conservative" Muslim demands the internalization of the spirit of openness Islam promoted for centuries. For this reason, too, a concern about the fundamentals of Islam has to register the dynamic orientations and attitudes that drove Islamic policy and conduct through much of Islam's emergence as a world religion. The contemporary Islamic fixation with limitations and prohibitions appears at odds with Islamic histories. It is far from reflecting the totality of Islamic histories, especially the Islamic humanism manifested in myriad forms throughout history.

Obscurantism, no matter the reason, does more harm than good to Islam and Muslims in the ever-globalized world. Even if the contemporary reactionary attitudes are due largely to the current political and economic duress experienced in Islamic societies, the duress cannot be a justification for repressive dogmatic politics. Peripheral to modernity and subordinated to the West, most contemporary Islamic societies do indeed make for easy grounds for organizing communities along the logic of interminable or irreconcilable civilizational differences. In fact, many Orientalists and Islamic fundamentalists alike desire or wish for the actualization of such a prophecy so as to be able to speak of diametrically opposed civilizations and their inevitable clashes. Yet, this reasoning highlights only the reactionary tendencies as the locus or center of Islamic/ist experiences and struggles. More alarmingly, it predestines the Islamist norm, either moderate or fundamentalist, as the only form of governance Muslims can be expected to have.

If anything, a return to history, to which many fundamentalist Muslims aspire, reveals Islam as a collection of particular universes shaped through transversal spaces, and Muslims as a kaleidoscope of people who were discoverers and innovators as often as they may have been destroyers, and, as such, essentially all too human. More than anything else, this book revolves around this argument about the humanism that Muslims have articulated and advanced in history. Several caveats inform the argument.

## LIMITS AND CAVEATS

First, this book is not a total history of Islam and Islamism. The book starts with the view that such a project, let alone a claim, is not only entirely unsustainable but also simply futile. Cognizant of this, instead, this book is about how Islamic histories are problematized, that is, deployed to function in the present. Insofar as histories mean "articulated connections" across events and moments, the histories of Islam locate Islam in the world, at once abstractly as an idea and concretely as a practice. They accord it a transhistorical perspective, identity, and intentionality, even as they claim to be historically situated and contingent. Political through and through, they ultimately condition the possible questions that can be asked and the answers that can be given about Islam in time and place.

Second, the book neither assumes nor seeks Islam's distinct or universal essence. Instead, it points to the practices and intentionalities that are deeply imbricated in the development of Islamic identities but also are presently construed as essentially antithetical to Islam. Islamic traditions have always appealed to critical human faculties in comprehending the world; yet this trait is now seen as anathema in mainstream Islam where a broad prohibitionism predicated on narrow formalism has become the currency.

Third, the book does not pretend to offer a full account of the tensions born in Islam's interactions with global capitalism and the modern world but rather argues that Islam finds expression in this world both as a participant and a challenger. Fourth, the purpose of this work is not to rehabilitate something called pluralist Islam, offered to the Islamic world as a form or a trajectory in political governance. Rather the purpose is to develop an argument that goes beyond simply opposing literalist, prohibitive, and fundamentalist Islam. It counters the future of majority-Muslim countries as places where governance is inextricably linked with and defined by religiosity. Lately, in political discourse in the West, it has become fashionable to offer "moderate" Islam as the preferred future for many majority Islamic communities. This discourse focuses on "moderating" Islam. Paradoxically, however, this focus narrows the political horizon to variations within Islamist existence, ultimately privileging political Islamism as the only future. Trying to "moderate" Islamism, these discourses instead end up fueling fundamentalism's ascendancy as the primary organizing ideal socially and politically. Islamist theology, different only in temperament from Islamic theocracy, is offered as liberation.

In the end, this way of thinking reinforces the fundamentalist characteristics of the very Islamist limits to political-economic life-worlds. There are, however, multiple and plural political projects in which Islam would be but *one* of many sources of negotiation of the future, neither the sole beginning nor the inevitable ending. That Islamic populations are supposedly destined to a religious future appears to function as another form of Orientalism, one that cannot see in Muslims an agency sufficient for the complexities of their age and that negates any democratic and participatory potentialities in Islamic societies.

# CHAPTER 2

## HISTORIES UNTOLD
## *The Irresistible Charm of Islamic Cosmopolitanism*

### HISTORICAL INVENTORIES

Around the year 613, alarmed by Prophet Muhammad's growing influence in Mecca, the ruling Quraysh elders pleaded with him to stop attacking the ancestral Meccan gods. In response, Muhammad called on the elders to bear witness that "There is no God but Allah." When the elders refused, Muhammad famously responded: "I will not forsake this cause until it prevails by the will of Allah or I perish, no, not if they would place the sun on my right hand and the moon on my left."

Thus was born Islam as a political movement before it became a religion. In fact, Muhammad's challenge to the establishment, a throwing of the competitive gauntlet in the face of the religions of his ancestors, activated the very first Islamic political movement in history. The political movement that became a world religion has its roots in this original boldness to question the dominant order in preference for Islam's moral vision. From the start, indeed, in order to start, Muslims employed critique and dissent. Islam emerged as an antisystemic movement—a nonconformist project. It not only survived an uncertain founding period by drawing on the power of disagreement and difference, but also expanded through the cultivation of dissent and disagreement. While not always tolerant, nor always pluralist, early Islamic societies managed to integrate cultural and religious differences under the Islamic Ummah, or the community, which constantly fed creative and productive forces in the Islamic realm. In turn, these forces fuelled the socially and economically dynamic visions and traits in Islamic histories, creating a "Golden" Islamic civilization in the few centuries that followed.

This much is undeniable historically, but it remains obscured through historiography—both Western and Islamic. Arabs, as Fatema Mernissi puts it, are too afraid to know about their energetic and radical ancestors for fear of exposing the political inertia characterizing contemporary Arab states. Western specialists, on the other hand, dance to a more orchestrated historiography still anchored in Orientalism. They still declare the West as the civilizational center and list all others as exotic or fearsome supplements or footnotes.

Not surprisingly, Orientalists have largely written Islamic histories around such imagery supplemental to Western histories, thus casting Islam and Muslims apart from or outside of the West civilizationally. At their most generous moments, Orientalists have maintained that Islam developed some progressive qualities spurred by its encounters with Hellenic wisdom, but that these qualities vanished due to Islam's inherently totalitarian tendencies. In the last century, this Orientalist claim has acquired greater depth and authority, disallowing any reasonable arguments to the contrary. Still, the evidence challenging Orientalist claims continues to mount, all showing that the "disappearance" or the "marginalization" of the progressive ideals and forces in Islamic societies cannot simply be attributed to an immutable Islamic essence. Instead, it ought to be traced through the complex set of historical developments, internal and external, that came to bear upon Islam's political trajectories over the centuries.

The historical Islam has had a fundamental impact on what became the West and Western societies. As the Muslim armies "opened" the Iberian Peninsula in the eighth-century conquests, Islam increasingly emerged as the rival civilization against which Europe's indistinct inhabitants began to make sense of themselves as Europe's peoples. The very first territorial European venture—the Crusades—was inspired by the ghostly figures of Muslims in Christ's terrestrial kingdom. During the centuries of encounters that followed in the Mediterranean, first with the Moors and later with the Ottoman Turks, Europe, previously a peripheral geographical landmass within the Roman Empire, was gradually transformed into a political, cultural, and religious center for the world.

Stated differently, the West's history, both as a civilization and as an idea, is thoroughly intertwined with Islam's journeys through the ages, and is thus essentially Islamic. In the same fashion, Islam is Western. These two forces of history, the two historical movements, are interlaced in more ways than imagined, let alone studied. Together, their stories constitute a common "transversal" history. It is from their interactive junctures that the studies of political Islam ought to start if they are to move beyond the familiar rhetoric about how Islam and the West have forever been each other's adversaries. In this way, studies become not only intellectually interesting but also politically compelling. The shared narratives can then make it possible to highlight the progressive ideals in Islamic histories and stress their relevance to democratic movements in contemporary Islamic communities. For the shared narratives to emerge, however, the constituent histories have to be more fully accounted for.[1]

The West's story is well told but remains selective, while the Islamic history is incomplete because by and large it has not been told. The West would like to keep its history reified, while Muslims appear to shun their history or are prevented from exploring it freely. The Islamic historiography of broad brush strokes that chronicles disputations in theology and Muslim conquests as the totality of Islamic history helps to enable the reification of Western history while keeping Muslims in the dark about their own history. The crisis is endemic across the Islamic world but worse in the Arab world. In fact, in *Modernity and Democracy*, Mernissi argues that the Arabs are so afraid of their own history, so fearful of the past, that they even dared something no other great civilization ever tried to do: to deny the past. Yet, she adds:

> Who knows better than Arabs the haunting power of that which is veiled? What memories that are hidden yet continue to haunt the Arab

> minds? What happened to the knowledge of those Muslims who have given their lives to pose and to solve the question that has remained an enigma in the Arab world up to the present: to obey or to reason or to believe or to think. What about those *qadis* or judges thirsting for justice, Sufis thirsting for freedom, and the poets who tried to express their freedom?[2]

From the beginning, contends Mernissi, the existential condition of Islam has been marked by two foundational "trends between *Aql* and *ta'a*, that is, between reason and obedience, or between questioning and forgetting." One has flourished as an intellectual drive that advanced the philosophical foundations of humanity and the other has developed into a desire that aims to limit those very same accomplishments. Nevertheless, together, their creative tension has shaped Islamic history, with reason always occupying as privileged a place in Islamic histories as revelation demanding obedience.

In the very first Qur'anic words communicated to the Prophet Muhammad in 610 CE, Angel Gabriel invites the Prophet simply to "Read." "Read in the name of Allah. . . . Read, Allah is most beneficent; Who taught by the Pen; Taught Men that which they knew not."[3] Later, the Qur'an links this act to freedom of choice in religion. "We are not your keeper," it instructs. For Muslims, therefore, the original act in Islam, the very founding moment, is a call to learning. Islam commands people to submit to "Allah's infinity," yet it demands the submission to be a conscious, knowledgeable act based on *Aql*, not on blind acceptance or obedience. Hence the crucial refrain is that reading involves learning, a coming into possession of the knowledge communicated through the pen, that is, reason. More significant still is the freedom afforded to believers in the reminder that "there is no keeper" in religion, no enforcer, but willful submission. So Islam does not so much demand *submission* but rather *submits* itself for consideration and judgment. It is a proposal made at the tip of the "pen" that creates an unrivalled and unitary source of belief, a pivot from which it is offered up for reading, consideration, and acceptance.

In this spirit, both the Qur'an and the Prophet's *Sunnah* (exemplary behavior) urge Muslims to always seek knowledge and be tolerant in religion, customs, and race. The Al Hujraat Shura in the Qur'an captures these sensibilities unequivocally: "we have created you from a male and a female and have made you into nations and tribes so that you might come to know one another."[4] From the onset, such Qur'anic exhortations cultivated a tradition of inquiry and an ethic of pluralism within the Islamic Ummah, or community. Existential differences were incorporated into the social and economic fabric, not rejected or terminated. The Medina Constitution was the earliest and most remarkable example of Islam's capacity to balance reason and revelation. The Constitution framed a single Ummah out of Muslims, Jews, and Christians while according each group their fundamental rights.[5]

## TEXTBOX 2.1. MAJOR DATES IN EARLY ISLAMIC HISTORY

### The Era of the Prophet Muhammad

| | |
|---|---|
| 570 | Prophet Muhammad born in Mecca |
| 610 | First revelations to Muhammad |
| 613 | Muhammad begins public preaching |
| 622 | Mohammad migrates to Medina (Hijrah) |
| 622 | Signing of the Medina Constitution |
| 624 | Battle of Badr, Muslims defeat the Meccans and capture Mecca |
| 632 | Muhammad dies in Medina |

### The Era of the Rashidun (Rightly Guided Khalifs)

| | |
|---|---|
| 632–634 | Abubakr—First Khalif |
| 634–644 | Umar Ibn al-Khattab—Second Khalif |
| 644–656 | Osman ibn Uthman—Third Khalif |
| 656–661 | Ali ibn Talib—Fourth Khalif |
| 661 | Emergence of Shia (supporters of Ali) and Sunni (those who follow the example of the Prophet) |
| 680 | The Battle of Karbala, Imam Hussein killed, Shia-Sunni schism widens |

Source: Abdullah Saeed, *Islamic Thought: An Introduction* (New York: Routledge, 2006), 1; Mir Zohair Husain, *Global Islamic Politics* (New York: Longman Publishers, 2002); Hans Küng, *Islam: Past, Present and Future* (Oxford: Oneworld, 2007), 95.

Throughout the founding era, from the time of the Prophet, through the reign of the Prophet's companions (the era of the four "rightly guided" khalifs), to the rise of the dynastic Umayyad power in 661 CE, a politically tolerant Islamic ethos enabled Muslims to accommodate existing socioreligious diversity within the rapidly expanding Islamic empire. The resulting civilizational dynamism, in turn, fuelled historically unprecedented transformative forces and visions, including fresh intellectual efforts in arts and sciences.

Barely a hundred years after Prophet Muhammad died, in Islam's dynamic cauldron following the rise of the Umayyads, one of the greatest intellectual shifts in human history began to take shape. The *Mutazila* rationalism promoting *ijtihad* or freethinking, started to form. The Mutazila movement owed its rise to a complex interplay of Islamic thoughts in fermentation in three different forms. These were *Kalam* (Islamic theology) *Falsafah*, (Islamic philosophy) and *Tasawwuf* (Islamic Sufism). Through Kalam Muslim theologians distilled the Qur'an and the hadith into Islamic jurisprudence. Tasawwuf fueled the mystical Sufi movements and produced towering mystics like Jalal ad-Din Rumi. Finally, Falsafah with interest in both philosophy and positive sciences such as medicine, astronomy, and mathematics paved the grounds for the Islamic Golden Age in arts and sciences. In the three centuries following the advent of the Umayyad dynasty, vigorous interactions of theology, philosophy, and Sufism not only radically transformed Islamic thought, but also steered the trajectories of philosophy and science in the world, especially in the West. Let us start with the Umayyads and how their reign helped shaped Islamic intellectual traditions.

## THE RISE OF "REASON" IN THE ARAB/ISLAMIC WORLD: IJTIHAD OR CRITICAL REASON OF THE MUTAZILA FREE THINKERS

The Umayyads assumed power in 661 CE following the reign of Imam Ali, the fourth "rightly guided" khalif after Abubakr, Umar, and Uthman. Instead of relying on the traditions of leadership established by the Prophet and the four Khalifs, the Umayyads founded a dynastic system of succession. While Muhammad had operated with absolute authority as God's prophet and his four Khalifs had been appointed

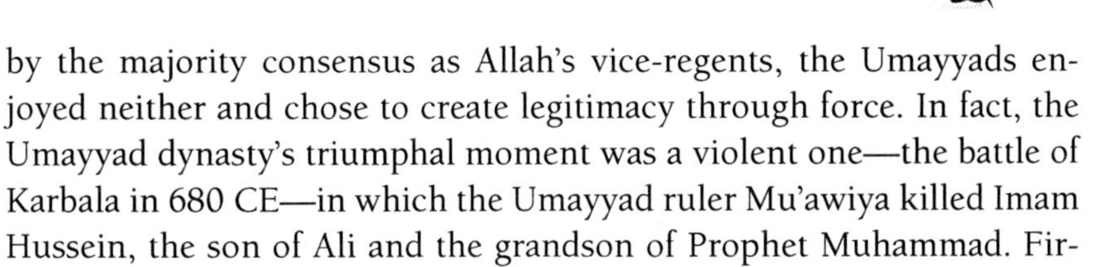

by the majority consensus as Allah's vice-regents, the Umayyads enjoyed neither and chose to create legitimacy through force. In fact, the Umayyad dynasty's triumphal moment was a violent one—the battle of Karbala in 680 CE—in which the Umayyad ruler Mu'awiya killed Imam Hussein, the son of Ali and the grandson of Prophet Muhammad. Firing up the Sunni-Shia divide, this event proved to be the single most poignant marker in Shia Islamic history. It has reverberated in Islamic histories ever since. Every year on the commemoration of the battle, millions of Shias still take to the streets, flogging their bodies with sharp objects until they are drenched in blood. They see these rituals not only as acts of remembrance but also as a manifestation of abiding commitment to the original Shia ideals.

Mu'awiya's victory solidified the Umayyad dynastic rule in a military sense. However, in the theological sense, it polarized the Muslim community further. In power, yet lacking unblemished religious legitimacy, the Umayyads had to invent it politically. And, so they did. After capturing power and declaring himself the khalifah, the Umayyad ruler Mu'awiya engineered a source of legitimacy out of the nascent Muslim clergy (*ulama*). First, he cultivated the ulama as the theological and juridical authority with the capacity to bestow political legitimacy on rulers. Then, he sought and secured their endorsement. This arrangement was institutionalized and subsequently came to underwrite political authority in not only the Umayyad era (661–750) and the Abbasid Empire (750–1258), but also the state-religion relations in the subsequent Islamic societies. As Mohammed Arkoun suggests, while political power struggles fueled the emergence of the ulama class and its authority, the theological-juridical discourse, once created as a field, acquired its own autonomous capacity "to sacralize and transcendentalize state institutions."[6] The alignment furnished a whole repertoire of legitimizing ideas and arrangements for both the Umayyads and Abbasids. The repertoire included calls on the believers to obey the emirs, or the rulers, for the sake of order, even if the rulers are not just, or, as in the Shia theology, to regard imams as infallible as god's khalifs and forbid any dissent.[7] Theology rapidly became a powerful political instrument.

The shift in Islamic thinking raised questions that reverberated in the incipient Islamic community. Although conceived within the Islamic framework, the questions were deeply political in nature. They centered on the key issue of predestination (*qadar*), which had

## TEXTBOX 2.2. THE ERA OF ISLAMIC KHALIFETS AND EMPIRES

| | |
|---|---|
| 661–750 | The Umayyad Era |
| 633 and 635 | Muslim conquest of Iraq and Syria |
| 638 and 642 | Conquest of Jerusalem and Cairo, Egypt |
| 711 | Muslim conquest of Spain begins |
| 732 | Battle of Poitiers in France ends Islamic expansion in Europe |
| 756–1031 | Umayyad Khalifs in Spain |
| 1238–1492 | The reign of Nasrid Kings of Spain in Granada |
| 750–1258 | The Abbasid era in Baghdad / Umayyad Khalifs in Spain |
| 786–809 | Harun al Rashid "establishes" Baghdad's "House of Wisdom" as part of an empire-wide network of centers of learning. |
| 800–870 | Abu Yusuf al Kindi (Alkindus in Latin) known also as "The Philosopher of the Arabs" launches Islamic philosophy. |
| 833 | Khalif al Ma'mun endorses Mutazila rationalism, institutionalizes the "House of Wisdom," and expands the network. |
| 847 | Khalif Mutawakkil ends support of Mutazila rationalism |
| 870–950 | Abu Nasr al Farabi (Alpharabius in Latin) known as the "Second Teacher" after Aristotle, and the first systematic philosopher in Islam |
| 980–1037 | Abu Ali Ibn Sina (Avicenna in Latin), known also as the "Arabic Galen." His *Canon of Medicine* was a required text in medieval Europe. |
| 1058–1111 | Al Ghazali, jurist, philosopher, and mystic, known as the "Deliverer from Error" enters history. His *Refutation of the Philosophers* initiates the decline of Islamic rationalism of the Mutazila philosophers. |
| 1126–1195 | Abu Walid Muhammed ibn Rushd (Averroes in Latin), the foremost Islamic philosopher, known in the West as the "Commentator" for his unrivalled |

| | |
|---|---|
| | work on Aristotelian philosophy. "Averroesism" later becomes an influential school of thought in medieval Europe. |
| 1258 | Mongol invasions: Baghdad sacked, the House of Wisdom destroyed. |
| 1332–1406 | al Hassan Ibn Khaldun, the author of the famed *Muqaddimah*, a history of Islamic societies. Widely accepted as the father of the modern fields of sociology and history. |

acquired the status of a dogma in the hands of the Umayyad-sponsored Muslim ulama. "Are Muslims free to act and thus to contemplate and be responsible for their fate?"

Predestination permitted no fate autonomous from God's will and invested God's will in the worldly order of the khalifs. In this way, Islamic theology came to serve the Umayyad dynasty. But the more the theology demanded obedience, the more the prophetic example of dissent and contest reemerged. Beyond the Sunni-Shia schism, Muslims began to contemplate their dilemmas as scholars and thinkers and theorized disagreement as a portal to extensive rationalism. The brightest among them came together as the "Mutazila," the rationalists, and challenged the instrumentalization of theology in the service of state politics. The Mutazila ideas began to form remarkably early in Islamic history, appearing first in the works of al Hassan al Basri and Wasil Bin Ata around 690 CE and 711 CE respectively. Proliferating theological disputes on creation, predestination, and human agency and their worldly consequences worked as catalysts in spawning the Mutazila scholars and ideas. The details of the disputes are fascinating. However, more important than the details was the richness of the debates taking place so early in Islamic societies. From the onset of the religion, Islamic communities spurred and fostered numerous intellectual movements, anticipating the Mutazila leaps in arts and sciences.

The *Kharijies*, or the Seceders, were among the first groups to make a mark on Islamic intellectual history. While they are generally known for their "disruptive" political role in the early Islamic era due to their opposition to the rule of the fourth Khalif Ali and the first Umayyad ruler Mu'awiya, their real contribution lies in their speculative philosophy. Their relentless Socratic interrogations of the early power struggles has shaped Islamic societies ever since. The *Murijis* were similarly central in their contentions against the conflation of theology and politics. Their deliberations anticipated the revolutionary idea of the "dual nature of truth both religious and philosophical," which the Moorish Islamic philosopher Ibn Rushd would explicitly theorize some five hundred years later. All said, however, it was the Mutazila who stressed the human will and reason as the central expression of revelation, and ran with it.

Some argued that the Mutazila overreached in their reliance on reason at the expense of intuition. Among the skeptics was Ash'ari, whose ideas in his *Science of Dialectical Theology* founded the Ash'ari School. The Asharites emerged mostly from among the Mutazila to scale back the "tyranny" of reason in the Mutazila philosophy. Ironically, in the process, Asharite ideas helped fuel the traditionalist intellectual schools of thought anchored more closely in the Qur'an textually and the prophetic Sunnah as exemplars. The greatest of the traditionalists, al Ghazali, referred to also as the "Proof of Islam," later employed the Asharite arguments against the Mutazila to halt the "rationalist" advance. However, by the time Ghazali's views came into fashion in the twelfth century, the Mutazila had already made an indelible and incomparable mark on history, Islamic and Western, in arguably one of world's most significant intellectual movements. They were to be the stars of the Golden Age of Islam.

The Mutazila focused on reason (*Aql*) and free opinion (*Ra'y*) as integral to religion's work in the world. It is through reason, a faculty divinely gifted to humans, that religion can be applied in the world and thus must be at the heart of deciphering and demonstrating the divine intent. The Mutazila went so far as to theorize that the Qur'an was God's revelation, but it was created (recorded) and organized by humans in time and thus open to interpretation through reason and personal deliberation. Umayyad attitudes galvanized the Mutazila movement around questions of authority, legitimacy, justice, and order. The Mutazila challenged the Umayyad argument of unconditional support for the ruler for the sake of public order. Instead, they argued for cultivating the conditions for a just popular representation. This orientation compelled Mutazila scholars to contemplate agency and dissent in politics without disavowing piety. Moreover, the scholars had to do so without alienating the ruling classes. Working under competing pressures, they invented a novel measure (*khisas*) of politics and theosophy that was politically acceptable to the elites yet remained epistemologically radical in intent. The resulting Mutaliza concept "*Itizal*," meaning "to leave" or "to withdraw" from orthodoxy, opened the gates of freethinking, or *ijtihad*, and in the process gave birth to the Islamic philosophy.

The Abbasid Khalif al Ma'mun (ruled between 813 and 833) energetically adopted the Mutazila teachings as the official state dogma and set off an era of exchange with other civilizations. At the height of his rule, Ma'mun used the Mutazila ideas to repress, even prosecute, competing schools of thought. As I will discuss later, traditionalist theologians, most famously Ibn Hanbal, suffered the brunt of the Ma'mun's austere approach. Notwithstanding this repressive interlude, and independent of the khalif's stance, the Mutazila rationalism spurred an insatiable drive for learning across all religious and ethnic peoples in the Empire. Hunayn Ibn Ishaq, a Christian monk from Syria, for example, had already founded the first rigorous translation school under the patronage of Ma'mun's father, Harun al Rashid (ruled between 786 and 809), the legendary ruler of the *One Thousand and One Arabian Stories* and *Aladdin and the Magic Lamp*. Hunayn Ibn Ishaq only represented the tip of the process of translating Hellenic, Indian, and Persian works of science and philosophy. The process intensified under Khalif Ma'mun's sponsorship. Ma'mun followed in the footsteps of Harun al Rashid, under whose rule the fabled Baghdad House of Wisdom had attracted scholars, scientists, and philosophers from all corners of the Empire. As a result of this sustained commitment to high learning, an unprecedented intellectual network emerged linking up houses of wisdom in Bukhara, Damascus, Aleppo, and Andalus. No knowledge, no matter the origins, was off limits. Cosmopolitanism quickly became the definitive attitude in the Empire's social, political, and cultural life. In nearly all aspects, but particularly in intentionality, the cosmopolitanism functioned as a form of "globalization" in today's parlance. The entire "*Dunia*," or the whole world, was the domain of Islamic *Umran*, or civilization. The Islamic community (*Ummah*) expressed the societal organization of the civilization while a progressive *Asabiyyah* (outlook), in Ibn Khaldun's words, constituted the driving attitude.

The Greco-Roman, Egyptian, Persian, and Hindu influences were welcomed into the growing Islamic realm. The Greek philosophy and scientific knowledge had already been thriving in all of the Near East for centuries. The Alexandrian influence in Cairo, Egypt, was the crown jewel.[8] When the Arab Islamic armies captured the city in 641 CE, they encountered the works of the Greek masters, including those of Plato and Aristotle, for the first time. The city had even cultivated its resident philosophical and scientific heritage, such as the Neo-Platonism established by the Alexandrian native Platonis. The Muslim reaction to the Egyptian and Greek knowledge, already infused with Christian undertones in the hands Coptic and Nestorian monks, was instructive. Instead of rejecting the city's rich Chadic-Egyptian, Hellenic, and Christian heritage, Muslims began to digest and assimilate it, thus spurring the first rough translations of Greek works into Arabic. Among the first "accredited" translations were those of Aristotle's *Organon*, Euclid's *Elements*, and Ptolemy's *Almagest*. Toward the end of the eighth century, during Harun al Rashid's reign, Greek philosophical texts appeared in Arabic translations. Platonic *Dialogues*, including *Republic* and *Laws*, became available to Arab Muslims. By al Ma'mun's reign, commencing in 813, a large body of Greek as well as Indian and Persian works in science, medicine, and philosophy had been gathered in collections that were, in effect, precursors to modern libraries.[9]

Similarly, in the East, as the Muslim armies arrived in Mesopotamia, Persia, and Transoxania in today's Caucasus and Central Asia, they were always accompanied by scholars. As soldiers conquered, scholars quickly followed, studying the Persian art of state, already noted for its support of sciences and arts. Gundishapur, founded by the Persian king Anushirvan "the Just" around 555 CE, served as a center for the "transmission" of Greek and Persian knowledge in science and medicine to the invading Muslims.[10] The Muslims also encountered Indian philosophy, which had long been interacting with Persian and Semitic cultures. In this way, the knowledge of the Indo-Persian philosophy and statecraft met the Roman legal and administrative experience. Muslims further coupled this rich civilizational mixture with their traditional Arab consultative assembly known as the *Shura*. In the process, they fostered an enterprising political and economic culture or, in Ibn Khaldun's words, *Asabiyyah*. This dynamic environment gave impetus to the further transformation of the Islamic paradigm.

Islam's territorial expansion brought about opportunities for the expansion of political and cultural horizons. The geographical expansion worked as a catalyst in the rise of tolerant social conditions, which paved the way for the development of the Mutazila rationalist philosophy. In part because of the fertile intellectual ground already in place in Egyptian, Indian, Greek, Roman, and Persian heritages, but also because of the practical demands of running an expanding Empire, the Umayyads and, later, the Abbasids promoted cross-cultural learning. However, it was the Abbasid period that systematically supported philosophy above and beyond theology, thereby enabling the rise of the Mutazila School. The Mutazila rise was thus both a result and an instrument of Islam's break from its tribal Arab origins into a posttribal movement as it encountered the wider world.

Some Arab historians see the Mutazila movement as a Persian challenge to Arab Islam arriving in the company of soldiers. Failing to mount a military defense, the argument goes, the Persians instead formulated an intellectual offense into the heart of Islamic culture. Persian ideas penetrated the Arab Islamic mind, shaping its orientation and trajectory in the ensuing centuries.[11] In reality, what transpired were the cultures' inexorable interactions more than their head-on clashes. The Arab Islam definitively arrived with a cultural tribal baggage, but it was also a pragmatic movement. Its universalistic ambitions born of its religious drive persuaded the Umayyad and Abbasid rulers to be opportunistic rather then reactionary. As a result, they functioned as Islam's political agents able and willing to learn from others. Ultimately, the demands of an increasingly multicultural empire compelled a spirit of scientific and philosophical eagerness to engage and borrow from the existing civilizations. Rapidly, tribal Arabs turned into urbanites and their desert religion into a full-fledged cosmopolitan ideology. To use the contemporary parlance of world affairs, Arab Islam anchored in the political ideal of Ummah grew "globalist" in civilizational outlook, or *Umran*, within the boundaries of the known world.

It is important to note that the overriding institutional or political framework underwriting and enabling such far-reaching changes remained Islamic. It was Islam's demonstrated capacity for accommodation that had allowed the Mutazila flight to take off in the first place. In return, although nonconformist theologically, the Mutazila discourse never repudiated Islam as the overarching structure of their intellectual endeavors. In fact, many Mutazila philosophers were also devout Muslims who genuinely regarded Islam as a progressive religion. Muslims had already begun to encounter and interact with and absorb different cultures as early as the Umayyad rule. From the onset, the Umayyads welcomed and retained much of the vast Roman and Byzantine administrative knowledge and the bureaucratic structures. Coupling such knowledge with the traditional Arab tribal consultative rule, they succeeded in establishing a hybrid state system bridging Arab tribalism with the Persian and Roman/Byzantine modes of centralized administration.

Under the Abbasid rule, the Mutazila ideas, together with the Kalam of theologians and the Tasawwuf of Sufis, institutionalized these exchanges. The Abbasids involved non-Muslims heavily in political and financial administration as well as educational institutions. They appointed Christians, Jews, and others to prominent administrative positions. They had no litmus test but the specific expertise or qualifications of the appointees. Latin, Greek, and Persian were retained in the business of the Empire and were employed as semiofficial languages until Arabic had developed the relevant imperial linguistic capacity in grammar and vocabulary to supplant them in the Golden Age of Islamic states. Islamic finances remained heavily depended on the circulation of coinage of Latin and Persian origins until the advent of the Islamic mint. In many ways, early on, a certain universalizing historical discourse was at work in Islamic empires, engendering a common political and administrative space without imposing cultural and religious uniformity.

It is to this environment that Mutazila ideas contributed. Employing reason (*Aql*) and free thinking (*Ra'y*), they worked as a catalyst for a new qualitative leap in Islamic arts and sciences. The Mutazila position that reason is not anathema to religion, but rather the divinely bestowed human faculty key to illuminating God's intent, opened the gates of innovation and discovery in Islamic societies. In this way, theology was reined in to serve practical needs in the shifting political and economic conditions of Muslim states. Imperial needs necessitated changes in religious beliefs while Islam's increasing political confidence allowed the changes to take off. This was a momentous shift in the development of the Islamic thought system from its theological-juridical anchors to its political-philosophical trajectory. In some ways, it was a return to the founding tension of Islam that faith is born of knowledge and inquiry. From Sufism to Falsafah, Mutazila attitudes demonstrated that reason is not in opposition to religion and that "disagreement" on matters of faith need not divide and traumatize the Islamic community.

In the ninth and tenth centuries, in which the Mutazila ideas proliferated, Islamic communities exploded in creativity in the arts and sciences. Islamic luminaries entered the history of ideas in force. Al Khwarizmi "invented" *al Jabir*, or algebra, revolutionizing mathematics. Al Kindi (795–866) emerged as the first Islamic philosopher. Al Razi (865–923) was embraced as the master of medicine in the Muslim world and later became famous as "Rhazes" in the West. He was also the Islamic world's next outstanding philosopher who saw philosophy as a means to liberate the soul (mind) from the material limitations of the body.[12] Al-Battani (858–929) advanced trigonometry and astronomy. Known in the Latin world as "Albategnius," Battani's astronomical tables improved Ptolemy's theories on celestial movements of the Sun and the Moon. Translated into Latin as *De Motu Stellarum* in 1116, his work became a source for European astronomy. Ibn al-Haytam (965–1039) revolutionized the field of optics and left us with remarkably accurate theories of how the eye sees and how the light refracts and enables human vision. Al Farabi (872–951) wrote his *Virtuous City* in the ninth century in light of his Islamic Sufi visions, while Al Hallaj (858–922) the Sufi submitted to a torturous death by fire rather than betray the Sufi reason that had led him to "the truth." Hallaj's case showed the limits of enlightenment clearly, laying bare the intensity and the rancorousness of competing ideas and forces. Ibn Sina (980–1037) made a gift of the science of medicine to humanity as the first millennium came to a close. Omar Khayyam, (1048–1131) known to the world as the great Persian poet who a thousand years ago wrote verses that still reach through history and capture the contemporary imagination, also greatly advanced mathematics through his lucid mastery. A towering poet and a mathematical genius in one body, Khayyam graced intellectual landscapes—Islamic and Western. For the next three hundred years, Islamic societies produced knowledge for the world even as they were also bent on subjugating the same world to their will. Muslims were not only "conquerors" and "consumers" but also "producers" and "builders." Their legacies remained obscured or long forgotten in the West, but even more tragically, were simplified, romanticized, and depoliticized in the Islamic world.

Even after the tide turned against the Mutazila traditions, and the Mutazila were banished in the tenth century, the Islamic sociopolitical and ethnico-cultural framework continued to develop, inspiring future generations of Muslims. Nearly four hundred years after the Khalif al-Mutawakkil (who ruled between 847 and 861) terminated the official status of the Mutazila ideas, an Islamic state framework in Andalusia supported the rise of the brilliant Ibn Rushd (Averroes) (1126–1198) who explained Aristotle to Europe's aspiring philosophers and clergy agitating for reforms. The same sensibilities also made possible the training of Maimonides, the greatest medieval Jewish philosopher, who wrote his masterpiece in Arabic. After the Spanish reconquest of the Iberian Peninsula, when the Golden Age of Islam was all but "withering," the Tunisian Ibn Khaldun (1332–1406) wanted to study the causes of the decline. The result of his labor, his masterpiece, was the *Muqaddimah*. With it, Ibn Khaldun not only created the outlines of a new discipline, sociology, but also bequeathed to Europe's historians a template for rigorous historical analysis. Even a less-known figure in the Islamic world, Hasan al-Wazzan (1494–1554), made a big splash in the Western world as a seminal geographer.[13] A Muslim ambassador turned slave in the Papal Court of Leo X in the 1520s, al-Wazzan was not a trained scholar, let alone a geographer. Yet he fulfilled the role so well that he made a name for himself in the Western canons as Leo Africanus, the authoritative medieval geographer on Africa. That al-Wazzan was a "trickster," and not a real geographer, did not matter to his interlocutors. Even his conversion to Christianity under the duress of slavery did not raise any alarm as to the veracity of his intention and knowledge. What mattered was that this ordinary Muslim ambassador-turned-slave-turned-geographer could and did bring so much knowledge and information to the proverbial civilizational table. What mattered even more was that the Islamic Ummah in the "post–Golden Age" period was clearly able to educate a super scholar of sciences, specifically of geography, who came by the sea and brought Papal Europe a flood of knowledge.

However sketchy, this historical perusal is sufficient to raise doubts about the conventional wisdom that, (a) the decline of the Mutazila orientation spelled out the end of *ijtihad*, or independent critical thinking, in the Islamic world, and that (b) the Arab thought-world collapsed entirely, atrophying ever after. While this is the prevailing wisdom, a fresh historical look suggests that both claims are questionable. They both operate through, on the one hand, a combination of historical amnesia, convenient omissions, mischaracterizations, and a native political expediency built into the modern state despotism in the Arab world, and on the other, a partisan Western Orientalism. Both have interest in "fearing history."

In response, I will argue that unlike these conventional historical accounts, the traditions of critical thought in Islamic communities continued to work. They did not disappear but developed along two contemporaneous, even simultaneous, trajectories. On the one hand, they were transmitted to the burgeoning Western intellectual and scientific circles via the Muslim Mediterranean and Islamic Spain. On the other hand, under pressure from the rising Sunni and Shia theological orthodoxies, they took on different forms of reason in the Islamic world. In a two-pronged response to forces of conservatism in ascendance in the Islamic word, the accumulated collective body of knowledge was taken up and developed in the West at the same time that it was being transformed into radical Sufi forms in the Islamic East. I will first deal with the transfer of Arab Islamic wisdom into the West and then take up Sufism as a new form of radical freethinking in the Islamic world. However, any narrative dealing with this history has to start with the cardinal role played by the Mediterranean Sea.

## THE TRANSFER: STAGGERED ENLIGHTENMENT OR HOW EUROPE GOT ITS "GREEK" GROOVE!

The Mediterranean Sea, like the Caribbean Sea of Christopher Columbus in Derek Walcott's poetry, became the place of history, forever linking Islamic-Arab and Christian-European into one civilizational whole. Recall that the Caribbean Sea was where Columbus first sighted land. This is also where Columbus first encountered the natives, whom he regarded as barbarians. The first native to be killed in the meeting of the Americas and Europe lived in the Caribbean, as did the first natives to be enslaved and shipped back to Spain as a gift to the House of Castile. It is in the Caribbean that numerous exotic foods, plants, and animals were first discovered and shipped across the Atlantic Ocean for European eyes and taste buds. In the course of history that followed, tomatoes, potatoes, and chocolate, among other native products, thus lost their American roots and become Italian, Irish, Swiss, or English. The Caribbean Sea was vast, and Columbus's ships were swift. They hauled off the riches of the Caribbean to Europe and beyond. They also conveyed Europe's goods and ideas to the Caribbean and the "New World." Along with material goods, they exported European ideas of progress as well as systems of domination. The natives received them all, suffered and redeemed. We know this history very well and need not rehearse it. In the centuries that followed, the Caribbean Sea thus became "history"—an interactive transversal space of unexpected connections that exploded in all directions in culture, geography, religion, and politics.

The Mediterranean Sea had already been "history" in this transversal sense. It had been the "mother sea" of unlikely connections and convergences—history's playground spanning Europe, North Africa, and the Eastern Mediterranean. The Romans had already declared it as "Mare Nostrum," or "Our Sea." Likewise, Europe's Barbarians, the Vandals and the Visigoths, had treated the Mediterranean as a sea-bridge that connected Africa and Europe, not as a sea barrier separating the two continents. In the same way, in the seventh century, the Arabs came rushing from east of the Mediterranean. When they stopped at the edges of Gibraltar, they did not see a wall of water forever separating the two shores but a waterway reminding them how the opposite shores had been part of the same sea history. They were "European" even before they crossed the strait. They became even more so after they crossed it, settled it, and created al Andalus. In nearly 500 years of active presence in the European civilizational milieu, Arab and non-Arab Islamic influences would consolidate the links further. They were so enduring that, as I shall show later, Islamic arts and sciences continued to inform European minds even after the Muslim dominance on the continent withered. These influences played a considerable role in the rise of the Renaissance, the Enlightenment, and modernity.[14]

The ancient Greek ideas on democracy, for instance, arrived in Europe by way of transcontinental flows of people, commerce, and ideas. That much is not surprising for Europeans. What is surprising is that the ideas arrived "speaking" Arabic in the works of Arab philosophers after a thousand-year sojourn in the eastern Roman Empire. And they came through Spain, not through Greece, after traveling across the Middle East and North Africa. It was through an Islamic political and cultural framework that they entered Western Europe, subsequently orienting and centering the European political imagination on Greek antiquity. It is remarkable that until the seventeenth century, Europeans were talking about Arabs and Muslims in the grudgingly admiring ways Muslims nowadays talk about European achievements. Europeans looked to Arabic as the language of learning, just as the world nowadays regards English as the dominant language in arts and sciences. Yet in the centuries that followed, coinciding with the rise of worldwide colonialism and its global capitalist organization, the material and ideological alignments shifted drastically in favor of Europe. The Arab Islamic legacy was suppressed in Europe's active memory as though the Arab Islamic political culture had played no role in sustaining, enriching, and finally conveying Greek ideas to Europe. Worse than a lack of recognition, the Islamic legacy was all but written out. To this day, the European historical accounts, especially in the public realm, remain largely silent on the role the Arab Islamic philosophers played in transmitting Hellenic ideas that subsequently inspired Western civilization. Even when such contributions are self-evident, the willingness to accept them is hindered by an old attitude wanting to preserve philosophy as the universal domain of an idealized Europe.

Amazingly, this attitude persists not only in the West but also in the Islamic world. It is internalized as a second nature in both. In the West, it is supported by the enduring Orientalist idea that Europe is the paradigm for all humanity. The nineteenth-century French thinker Ernest Renan (1823–1892) was the most passionate and eloquent proponent of this idea. In the Islamic East, the attitude survives because no thought system has flourished free in the Islamic popular imagination since the jurist-philosopher Ghazali's challenge to Islamic rationalism in the tenth century in his *Refutation of the Philosophers*. Ghazali's main argument against the Mutazila philosophers centered on his claim that philosophers overly rely on reason and empirical particularities at the expense of the universal and timeless qualities of the creator and creation. Ghazali (1058–1111) identified twenty flaws in philosophers' reasoning, materializing mostly in physics and metaphysics. He spared mathematics and logic from criticism as sciences that have "no bearing on religion."[15] "Whoever claims," asserted Ghazali, "that theology, abstract proofs, and systematic classification are the foundations of belief is an innovator."[16] Emerging at a time of growing traditionalist apprehension with the Mutazila rationalism, Ghazali's challenge resonated, took roots, and became the refuge of the traditionalists. Among most Muslims, Ghazali was and is still considered as the jurist who restored faith over reason by taking on the towering philosophers such as al Farabi and Ibn Sina. Driven by keen faith, Ghazali regarded his role as "the deliverer from error." He triumphed, but his triumph paved the way for developments that have strained arts and sciences in the Islamic world ever since.

In the nineteenth-century West, Renan became the foremost authority on Oriental cultures. His ideas have since shaped European intellectual attitudes on Arab and Islamic philosophy. Although separated by centuries, Ghazali and Renan were nevertheless kindred spirits in that neither had high regard for Islamic philosophy or philosophers. They both claimed that Islamic philosophers contributed little or nothing to philosophy and science. Referring especially to al Farabi and Ibn Sina, Ghazali called Muslim philosophers mere transmitters of the Greek knowledge, who had accomplished nothing comparable to works of Plato or Aristotle.[17] Renan, on the other hand, dismissed Islamic philosophy altogether as an imitation—a mirage of the Hellenic philosophy. Renan and the like-minded Orientalists were largely responsible for the rise of the dismissive attitude toward the Islamic world of ideas, arts, and sciences. Later on, faced with contrary historical evidence, Renan was compelled to adjust his claims, though he never fully disowned his earlier stance.

Here, however, lies a historical irony. Although Renan was forced to revise his ideas in the nineteenth century, in the Muslim world, Ghazali's claims have remained at work, shaping orthodox Islamic hearts and minds. Paradoxically, the conservative turn Ghazali is credited (or accused) to have started in Islamic thought histories has always been less than hegemonic. As much as it has suppressed ideas in the mainstream, it has also spurred diverse orientations within and without the mainstream. For example, Ghazali's critique of the Mutazila rationalism and Asharite free thinking likely spawned Ibn Rushd's philosophy. At the same time, interpreted more conservatively and transmitted through the chain of conservative jurists, Ghazali's work stirred the ideas of the talented thirteenth-century jurist Ibn Taymiyyah (1263–1338). Ibn Taymiyyah's theological puritanism, in turn, inspired the puritanism of Ibn Wahhab in eighteenth-century Arabia.

In the fourteenth century, Ibn Rushd, arguably the greatest medieval philosopher, decisively and in the best tradition of Islamic debate culture, challenged Ghazali's ideas in his "*Refutation of the Refutation.*" Using the same Islamic history, Islam's sacred texts, and Prophet Muhammad's Sunnah, Ibn Rushd contended that "not only is intellectual investigation not heresy; it is commanded by Islamic law."[18] "Reflect, you have vision," he argued, quoting the Holy Qur'an.[19] Europeans such as Thomas Aquinas and Nicholas Copernicus took heed of Rushd's council—even in opposing him—dreaming of reformation and revolution while Muslims swept them into the wings. The persistent effect on Islamic philosophy has been centuries-long neglect *plus* inhibition. The Orientalists in the West could be nudged enough to see their errors, but the Muslim world, following Ghazali "the Deliverer from Error" himself, has not yet been delivered from the error of rejecting Islam's creative cosmopolitan legacy. The attitude that philosophy and arts are "innovations" contrary to the divine order has limited the development of the original Islamic rationalism. Ironically, Ghazali never intended for Islamic sciences to be targeted with austere measures. He was not an anti-intellectual. After all he was a rationalist theologian—he employed logic and mathematics in his work. He was astutely trained in theology, philosophy, and Sufism. He would have been characterized as a "Renaissance man" in the depth and breadth of his knowledge of arts and sciences had he lived in the twenty-first century. He could not have been any clearer on the dangers of blind submission to any religion.

> Man [can be] loyal to Islam but ignorant. He thinks religion has to be defended by rejecting every science that is connected to Philosophers and so reject all their sciences. . . . He even rejects the theory of the eclipse of the sun and the moon, considering that what they say is contrary to the religion. A grievous crime indeed against religion has been committed by the man who imagines that Islam is defended by the denial of mathematical sciences, seeing that there is nothing in revealed truth opposed to these sciences and by way of either negation or affirmation, and nothing in those truths opposed to the truth of revelation.[20]

Ghazali, of course, has been a symbol, unfairly or not, for the inhibition of the contemporary Islamic thought worlds and the limitation of the Muslim imagination. The traditionalist orientation Ghazali organized as an attack against the Mutazila nearly a thousand years ago continues to shape contemporary political imagination in most of the Islamic societies. Evidencing the enduring legacy of his ideas both anticipated and unexpected, Ghazali's spirit, or specter, still fuels the original clash of ideas between philosophy and theology in Islamic history.

Paradoxically, the resulting Islamic *Salafism* (adherence to the example of the pious ancestors) enabled greater authority to a Salafism of a European kind, that is, Orientalism. By feeding on and propping up Salafism (particularly Wahhabism) as Islamic conservatism in the nineteenth and twentieth centuries, the Orientalist faith in European superiority made European thought-history into universal history. It created a universal intellectual framework within which historians, thinkers, and laypeople, whether Western-Christian or Islamic, all feel compelled to speak. Yet the unity of this framework, ever dependent on obscuring multiple thought worlds, has been under pressure materially and intellectually due to the forces of contemporary political and economic globalization. The current globalization is making possible an awareness of earlier political and cultural interactions that helped shaped the continent of Europe into the civilization now called the West.

There is a growing body of scholarship exploring the links between Arab Islamic philosophy and Christian European philosophy via the Mediterranean Sea. The deeper the reach of such studies, the more factual the links are demonstrated to be. The little that has been undertaken so far indicates the role Islamic philosophy played in the development of European thought first within the circles of theology and then in the form of philosophy. These contributions of Islamic philosophy represent a civilizational movement.

## THE OPEN SECRET: HOW COSMOPOLITAN ISLAM "MOVED" EUROPE

Perhaps the most significant universal Islamic philosopher to enter this center is Ibn Rushd, known as Averroes in Europe. The foremost Islamic philosopher in the Arab world, Ibn Rushd was a rationalist and primarily interested in demonstrative knowledge found in Aristotle's work. Among other important contributions, in his authoritative *Treatise and Exposition of the Convergence Which Exists between the Religious*

*Law and Philosophy*, he asserted that there need not be any clash or contradiction between faith and reason insofar as they constitute separate yet complementary fields of knowledge. Different methods are needed to study and ascertain the truth of reason and faith. Truths relating to creation and laws of existence could be apprehended and transmitted through demonstration, dialectic, and rhetoric. Knowledge by demonstration is best followed by dialectic, or the rational explanation and advocacy of what is known. Averroes classified this to be the field of theosophy (*Kalam*) and attributed certain limits to its purview.

Averroes's main contribution to Western philosophy came in the form of an elaboration and commentary on Aristotle with a precision and clarity that made Averroes the premier Aristotelian philosopher in the European intellectual and theological milieu. His work became so dominant that he was referred to simply as the "Commentator" in Europe. Averroism became a school of thought and spread all over Europe, with centers in many European cities. Hans Küng writes: "Averroes may not have been influential in Islam, but he was in Christianity. If he represents an end point for Islamic philosophy, for medieval Christian philosophy, he represents a beginning."[21] In effect, Turkish thinker Cemil Meric proposes, Averroes's ideas penetrated the European philosophical milieu deeply if unconsciously and ultimately informed the development of modern pragmatism and rationalism. Meric's point, not surprisingly, is that the depth of impact Islamic philosophy had in "renewing" the Western world remains largely obscured.[22]

Küng notes that Renan stated that he could detect Averroism in Western Christian scholasticism and that it subsequently came to be the most dominant influence in its development. Küng also intimates that it was by engaging Arab Islamic philosophy that Western philosophy gave birth to the figure of "the intellectual." The thriving intellectual environment of the late medieval cities and other learning centers in Europe were heralded in Arabic Islamic scholarship in Latin translations. Citing the French historian Jacques Le Goff, Küng suggests that the very identity of the "university professor" was formulated in this period among Europeans grappling with the philosophy of the Arabs.[23] But Averroes was not the first Arab Islamic philosopher to impress Islamic mind-prints on European intellectual landscapes.

Ibn Sina (Avicenna) figures in Western philosophical and scientific horizons as prominently, though somewhat differently. Avicenna's philosophy of Neo-Platonism was based on "the empirical generalization that it is in the nature of human beings to complement one another."[24] In his work on healing (*Kitab al Shifa*), Avicenna noted that "it is necessary for a man to find his sufficiency in another of his species, who in his turn, finds in the former and his like, his sufficiency."[25] Symptomatic of how Arab or Islamic philosophers are treated, Black, the author of such thoughtful words on Avicenna's significance, follows by erasing, unwittingly or not, Avicenna's authority by an anachronistic linking of Ibn Sina to Emile Durkheim, who lived centuries later. "Ibn Sina," Black writes, "extended his argument pursuing a Durkheimian theory on the social function of religion."[26] Instead of being appreciated for their authenticity, in this way, Ibn Sina's ideas disappear into Western history. In contrast with this sort of attitude, during his life, Ibn Sina's attitude toward Greek philosophy, the major source of his inspiration, was one of cosmopolitan curiosity and openness. He treated the Greeks' insights with admiration before pushing them to their epistemological limits and beyond, and he subjected them to an empiricism unlike any organized before him. His cosmopolitanism, in turn, freed him from the intrinsic cultural and temporal limitations of the Greek epistemology. In the end, Ibn Sina was always loyal to his Islamic roots, through which he refracted and articulated Greek insights from Plato, Socrates, and Aristotle for Islamic times and audiences.

Ibn Sina collected his work on politics, culture, and administration under the title of *Kitab al Siyasah* (*The Book of Politics*). He went on to theorize a concept of just governance as an anchor for successful social cohesion and suggested political resistance and rebellion when the ruling class failed to uphold excellence in governance. Avicenna's work in the sciences, specifically in medicine, exceeds all efforts to diminish or erase the significance of Islamic contributions to Western scientific knowledge. Black himself allows the status of genius for Avicenna, "whose work . . . was to influence philosophy and medicine" for centuries.[27]

A similarly meaningful connection, if not an earlier deliberation over similar themes, can be shown to exist in the works of al Arabi and Jacques Derrida, as found in Ian Almond's comparative study of *Sufism and Deconstruction*. The significance of Almond's study lies not in tracing a direct or even indirect connection from al Arabi to Derrida or, as Almond puts it, to cast Jacques Derrida as "Jacques of al Biar." Rather, it lies in showing the ambiguities of ownership over intellectual ideas, declared as categorically and proprietarily to have been invented or as belonging to one or another civilization. Further, its significance arises in recognizing the possibility, indeed the reality, that the questions we see as possible only in one historical era or another may have already been contemplated in the hands of disparate actors of reason. It is in this sense that Almond proposes that the deconstructive thought process is found in al Arabi's work some 800 years before Derrida's thought emerged. His point is not that we need therefore to acclaim al Arabi as a medieval poststructuralist.[28] By the same token, we need not and cannot ignore the historical genealogies through which ideas indeed travel to take their dominant forms in any given period.

Almond, for example, traces Derrida's deconstructive work on mysticism back to Meister Eckhart, the German theologian, mystic, and philosopher, who was tried as a heretic in 1327 and died in mysterious circumstances. He establishes al Arabi as being among Eckhart's primary intellectual inspirations. From this connection arises the issue of not simply attesting to the intellectual or inspirational links between Derrida and Arabi but also deliberating the ramifications of these links for the ways in which histories of thought are recognized, tallied, and credited in modern historiographies.[29] What then is the effect of such a historical genealogy? Is it merely about al Arabi's place in Western intellectual heritage? Or, more than that, does obscuring his influence ultimately deny in the past and the present Islamic capacity for intellectual agency? Absent this debate, Europe and Derrida, or Europe and Renan, effectively and inevitably emerge as the sole universal political and philosophical figures.

The scant work done in the relevant Western histories reveals this issue to be significant precisely because of the extent of the influence of Islamic arts and sciences on European thought histories. That, amazingly, Thomas Aquinas used Avicenna's ideas to combat Parisian Averroism in the theological circles of the twelfth century has to be accounted fully, but it also must be made to count in the most current discussions, which presume unbridgeable intellectual chasms to separate Islamic and Western worlds. What is remarkable here is that the Western theology and Christian-European identities were contemplated and fought over through the competing ideas of two Muslim philosophers. This and other similar episodes are momentous, yet they are treated, if at all, as minor historical footnotes in European intellectual imaginaries. In reality, in Western historical and Islamic-Oriental inventories they indicate historical collaborations and common threads.

In this sense, the ideas of Averroes, Avicenna, Ibn Hazm, al Arabi, Bektashi Veli, and others were never passé, consigned to ancient histories. The Renaissance and Enlightenment were full of their echoes. Ernest Renan, the French Orientalist, is "quoted to have once remarked that great English philosopher and scientist David Hume had said 'nothing (about the causal nexus) more than al Ghazali had already said'"[30] some three hundred years earlier. According to Farrukh, Immanuel Kant's thoughts on time and space can be comparatively discussed in light of the thoughts of Ibn Hazm, who lived more than 700 years before Kant. Farrukh remarks: "It is really astonishing that a Muslim theologian had tackled these problems in the same spirit of objectivity seven and a half centuries before the German philosopher."[31]

Farrukh's words are instructive not because they suggest that Kant owes his creativity to Ibn Hazm or some other Islamic or non-Islamic figure. Rather, they are compelling in demonstrating that some of the ideas readily associated with the Enlightenment and modernism had been contemplated in Islamic societies and shared with others. Indeed, a flurry of studies is suggesting the possible or probable routes through which ideas such as Hazm's might have been transmitted from the Islamic sources to Europe.[32] Who is this Ibn Hazm whose legacy is obscured among all but the most specialized branches of Islamic Sufism? The question of who else has suffered the same fate is not a polemical one, but one that goes to the heart of who speaks and who can be heard through the ages as historical agents.[33]

Incomplete intellectual histories, whether perpetuated by Orientalists or Muslims or both, denude Islam of its rich and complex intellectual legacy. Islam appears parochial and insular as a result. Ironically, this portrayal is consumed readily not only in the West but also in Islamic societies. It has an impact on how Muslims step into the global world as subjects and objects, that is, how Muslims articulate their role and place in the global commons and how others perceive and accord Islam a place and part in the world. All the while, history remains replete with Arab and Islamic figures whose ideas contributed to the development of the previously marginal geography called Europe into the burgeoning ideal called the West.

Translated from Arabic into Latin and European vernacular languages continuously for over 400 years, and studied, fought over, agreed with, or disputed, Arabic/Islamic works heralded the Renaissance and Enlightenment. It is shocking to learn how many Islamic or Arabic scholars had their names Latinized in translations. Ibn Bajjaj became *Avempace*; Ibn Rushd, *Averroes*; al Kindi, *Alkindus*; al Battani, *Albategnius*, Ibn Zuhur, *Avenzor*; al-Betrugi *Alpetragius*; al Razi, *Rhazes*; Jabir ibn Hayyan, *Geber*; al Haytam, *Alhazen*; al Mawardi, *Alboacen*; Ibn Sina, *Avicenna*; Abu al Qasim, *Abulcasis*, and Ibn Tufayl, *Abubacer*. In every field of sciences and arts, Europe was literally inundated by Islamic-Arabic works. Arabic was the lingua franca of the medieval world. Not surprisingly, in an anecdote reflecting the tenor of the thirteenth century, Roger Bacon observed that any study of the sciences would require the knowledge of the Arabic language.

These countless examples reveal the open secret of the modern Western consciousness. Arab-Islamic histories were integral and indispensable to Europe's rise. They folded in the Mediterranean's intellectual streams interactively. Occasionally surreptitiously and sometimes violently following conquests and colonization, they entered Europe and became "European" themselves. But in the process, they also compelled Europe to take on Levantine characteristics. Nevertheless, once unleashed, this interdependence, this dynamic interactivity I refer to as "transversality" emerged as the inexorable arch spanning Islam and Christianity, Europe and the Levant or the Middle East. In the transversal light, civilizational commonspace is revealed unmistakably.[34]

Clearly Arab/Islamic thought animated transcontinental intellectual developments. It was protoglobalist in impact and helped to promote mutual civilizational exchanges through interpenetrating patterns of culture and commerce. It did not exist in any pure form. Instead, it took on a form and function reminiscent of the earlier modes through which it had received the wisdom of the Hellenistic ancestors. Islamic thought became the ancestor thought and the ideas of European philosophy and thus intimately internal to the latter's form, texture, and substance (it formed movements, Islamic in context and political in objective). While the Orientalist discourse, so central to the universalization of European identities, has always obscured such encounters in European history, it has been unable to fully cover over the traces still legible beneath the European palimpsest.

Yet another challenge to the claim that Islamic political and social culture grew barren with the passing of the Golden Age is the monumental work of Ibn Khaldun, who lived between 1332 and 1406. Khaldun lived in an era of the political decline of Andalusian Islamic hegemony and the ripple effects produced in North Africa. He was a government official and traveled widely in both Muslim and Christian lands. His travels exposed him to wide-ranging political, cultural, and social forms. Even after he retired from active public service at age thirty-six, he continued to travel and teach in various places, including Alexandria and Cairo, which was the seat of the Mamluks. His association with the Mamluks led him to accompany a Mamluk expedition against the forces of the Mongol king Tamerlane, whom Ibn Khaldun negotiated with and ultimately advised for a period of time. When Ibn Khaldun wrote his *Muqaddimah*, he was well versed in the political and social forces and patterns at work in the Islamic geographies. What is relevant for our discussion is the vast philosophical and scientific knowledge he had already amassed and the fact that an Islamic milieu, even in decline, had made that possible. *Muqaddima* displays a command of not only the great body of Islamic theology and jurisprudence but also the rich Islamic philosophy, ranging from the rationalist Mutazila to the traditionalism of al Ghazali.

In *Muqaddimah*, Ibn Khaldun examines social and cultural patterns across the Berber society of North Africa with a view to understanding the roots of its societal decline. Khaldun's focus on societal formations led him to formulate a number of concepts entirely novel for his times, in both Islamic and non-Islamic contexts, that yet hold true all through medieval times up to modern societies. The most important of these concepts was *Asabiyyah*, or "group solidarity" born of group consciousness. Ibn Khaldun argued that strong Asabiyyah likely engendered the powerful political force needed in the organization of a durable and capable state. Thus expressed in the hegemonic architecture of the state, Asabiyyah likely facilitated the civilizational development of a society as well. He suggested that the stronger the group solidarity is, the more effective and advanced is the organization of the society. Ibn Khaldun attributed political, economic, and ethical dimensions to Asabiyyah. Strong group solidarity needs to possess and cultivate a commitment to ethical norms for its emergence and consolidation as well as for the creation of enduring political and economic arrangements.

Ethical norms, Khaldun argued, are closely linked to political and economic ones in that they operate interdependently, either promoting or weakening Asabiyyah. Khaldun elaborated and specified Asabiyyah's work by placing it within the urban/city and rural/tribal settings and following their shifts in time. In methodology, he was a historicist and an institutionalist before the terms were coined in the modern sense. The Arabic language, supplemented with Indo-Persian grammar and vocabulary, enabled him to communicate complex ideas with ease. His work was rigorously empirical, anchored in facts and events. Yet it was also attuned to philosophy and theology. This enabled him to abstract patterns and processes in history as being simultaneously sociopolitical and psychological. Ibn Khaldun's work has uniquely contributed to the emergence of both sociology and history as disciplinary fields. Even today, scholars in the West and the Islamic world derive concepts from Khaldun's work in sociology, history, politics, international relations, and cultural anthropology.

As this quick perusal indicates, contrary to the prevailing attitudes among Orientalists and modern Muslims themselves, Islamic societies continued to be dynamic cauldrons of arts and sciences, though under circumstances that limited their systematic expression and the forms in which they were renewed. Against all odds, born of a theological inertia, Islamic societies not only preserved the richly textured scientific and artistic contributions of the Golden Age ancestors, but also advanced their intent in the works of Ibn Rushd and Ibn Khaldun in methodical ways. When inertia weighed so heavily as to make such openly rationalist works difficult or dangerous, these societies innovated further by investing in Sufism as a form of humanist philosophy and art. I turn my attention now to Sufism as a critical political humanism.

## THE TRANSFORMATION: FROM ISLAMIC IJTIHAD TO SUFISM AS POLITICAL PHILOSOPHY

Significantly, the Mutazila rationalism was supplanted by Sufi radicalism. Although Sufism was not known for an emphasis in positive sciences, it retained and advanced the core Mutazila ideal of independent reason. For example, in addition to the conventional Islamic philosophy and sciences, critical schools of Sufism played a particularly central role in preserving and promoting arts and philosophy. Early on in the

Umayyad and Abbasid reigns, Sufi thinkers were already merging philosophy, sciences, and esotericism into an autonomous field of contemplation and criticism of politics. The tenth-century jurist-philosopher al Ghazali, whose systematic defense of Islamic jurists led to the decline of Mutazila philosophy, was also a Sufi who organized Sufi ideas into a respectable form within Islamic orthodoxy. Al Farabi, in his *Virtuous City*, married Sufi transcendentalism to political philosophical utopias in search of an ideal polity. Long before Thomas More dreamed of utopian cities, Muslims were busy building "cities of wisdom" in places like Baghdad and Damascus. Similarly, Ibn Sina, the impeccable empiricist—a towering mathematician and an unrivalled medical genius—devoted much of his life to explaining the illuminist force of Sufi thoughts. Such Sufi ideas have operated as living traditions in the Islamic communities. They functioned as instruments of social and political critique more than they existed as ascetic forms of worship.

For example, under the Fatimid and Seljuk Empires, as well as during the imperial times of the Ottomans, the Safavids, and Mughals, Sufi thinkers promoted critical consciousness around the themes of justice, equality, religious freedom, and economic autonomy. Collectively, these empires span vast geographies from Moorish Andalusia in Iberia to Mughal India in South and Southeast Asia. Together, they also represent a historical period nearly a thousand years long. Particularly from the thirteenth to the seventeenth centuries, they hosted Sufi dervishes who steadily contributed to the rise of an insurrectional discourse in the Islamic Ummah. The Ummah, that mélange of peoples and cultures moored together by Islam, rapidly formed into a borderless domain of Sufi preaching and organizing. Tellingly, the Ummah would expand over to Malaysia and Indonesia in Southeast Asia and sub-Saharan Africa not through violent conquests but primarily "Sufi words." The more the Sufis fused reason with religion, the more successful they were. In the process, they preserved the reason, or *aql*, as being intrinsic and indispensable to Islam.

In Islamic lands, Sufi networks became the highways on which the insurrectional discourse traveled along with the dervishes to reach millions of people. Allegorical stories and poetry were the two foremost instruments, while Sufi master treatises circulated to augment the power of the discourse. Recollecting the power of Rumi's poetry, specifically, the radical substance beyond the rhythm of the words, suffices in helping to comprehend the argument that the Sufi movements played a deeply political role through both the form and substance of their discourse. In many ways, Sufi networks of yesteryear were akin to the network-based political and social movements of the present era. They utilized the "power of networks" to articulate the Sufi discourse of power—syncretist and pluralist in form and content and oriented toward social and economic justice.[35] Rumi's famous words echo these values:

> Come again, come, whoever you are.
> Non-believer, worshipper of fire, a devotee of idols,
> Ours is not a house of despair.
> Come, even if you have broken your vow a hundred times,
> It matters not,
> Come, as you are, come.[36]

The key to the very founding of the networks was Sufi ideas, which were intended for the political and social underclasses spread around the vast Islamic geographies. The Sufi networks emerged as a function of the rich universe of these ideas: networks were vectors before they acquired their autonomous power to shape the depth, intensity, and trajectories of ideas. Rumi shaped hearts and minds in the twelfth century with poetry that was at once esoteric and philosophical-political. Bektasi Veli, a contemporary of Rumi's, contributed ideas that have inspired numerous political movements in the Ottoman Empire over the centuries, including a series of peasant rebellions from the fourteenth to the seventeenth centuries.[37] Veli's ideas have not only survived the test of time, but they have also developed into a worldview known as *Bektashism*. Today, Bektashism is prevalent in modern Turkey as well as in the Balkans and parts of the Middle East as Alevi-Bektashism. Its diverse ideals still inform the contemporary political movements in Turkey, particularly through the populist Sufi poetic genre.

Likewise, Pir Sultan Abdal's poetry embodies not only the remarkable durability but also the enduring political relevance of this Sufi way. Pir Sultan lived in Central Anatolia in the sixteenth century. He was executed on charges of fomenting rebellion against the Ottomans. He was neither the first nor the last in Sufi annals to lose his life to persecution by political authorities. Al Hallaj was the first to be executed in 922 CE for claiming that he was the "truth," while Al Suhrawardi was the most learned Sufi executed in 1119 for the political nature of his teachings. The Prince of Sufis, Ibn Arabi (1165–1240 CE), escaped death, but some considered him "a sheer infidel."[38] In this Sufi tradition, which combined personal asceticism with advocacy for the ordinary people, Pir Sultan's poetry, too, had a deep social and economic justice message against the Ottoman Sunni establishment. However, it was not intrinsically anti-Sunni or Turkish. Rather, it took issue with what Pir Sultan considered to be the repressive status quo dominated by the dynastic Ottoman state:

> The post that is hoisted on this world,
> The heart suffers when toil is not accounted for,
> Who established this rule, let us know,
> Speak heart, speak, for friends to hear.[39]

By Pir Sultan's time, the Ottomans had adopted the Sunni orthodoxy and begun persecuting the Alevis for their alleged sympathy toward the predominantly Shia Safavid Iran. In actuality, Pir Sultan's poetry was a response to the prevalent Ottoman social and economic circumstances. Part of a familiar genre of popular protest, it intertwined Sufi devotional themes with a worldly political ethics and then synthesized them into a social justice discourse. Ultimately, it was and remains an example of how Sufism played a highly political role in Islamic thought worlds.

Alevi or Bektashi Sufism, however, was not the only Sufi stream with deep political interests. The Sunni sects across all of the Islamic Ummah fostered Sufi movements known as *tariqahs* and through tariqahs, Sunni Sufism contributed richly to the development of syncretic Islam. Unlike Alevi Bektashi movements, which were outright dissents in the Ottoman Empire, and thus outside the mainstream, the Sunni tariqahs such as the Naqshibandis operated from within the mainstream and helped preserve pluralist and tolerant instincts in the Sunni thought-world.[40] Their central contribution was one of enriching Sunni *Tasavwuf*, the interpretive fields, along with the Sunni theological *Kalam*, which remained committed to the Salafist ancestral scripturalism. This held true in the Ottoman Empire and beyond, especially in sub-Saharan Africa and Southeast Asia, where Islam arrived in its Sufi forms.

For example, Indonesia, which is a focus of this book along with Turkey, encountered Islam through Sufi *Walis*, or dervishes, who arrived along with Arab merchants and stayed as Indonesian Islam's founding fathers. The Islamic message they ushered in was defined by a pluralistic permissive attitude. Although Sunni by orientation, nevertheless, Indonesian Islam developed Sunni orthodoxy into a syncretic variety, willing and able to interact with the archipelagic geography of Indonesian culture. Individual islands in the archipelago very often developed their unique strands of Islam with their own Sufi masters. With the possible exception of Aceh, almost all, however, had the common trait of accommodating the earlier Hindu, Buddhist, and animistic religions instead of supplanting them. As result, there was never a wholesale cultural and aesthetic Islamic colonization in Indonesia by Arab or Persian forms. The Malay language, for example, remained the dominant vehicle in the development of Islam. The Arabic lunar calendar was adopted through Malay instead of direct importation from Arabic. The Sufi–*Wali* mode made it possible to re-form or interpret broadly the Sunni orthodoxy to a degree that some Indonesian ulama were able to invoke even Buddhism and Taoism as religions of "the book" deserving of respect and protection.[41] What is also remarkable is that al Ghazali, the inspiration for Arab conservatism in the Middle East since the twelfth century, was also the premier theological inspiration, along with Ibn Taymiyyah, for Indonesian Islam. Yet, unlike the latter-day Arabs who turned only to the literalism in Ghazali's work, Indonesian Sufis mined Ghazali's Sufi sensibilities and molded him to their unique circumstances. Ghazali the austere theologian became Ghazali the broadminded Sufi in Indonesia.

Similar cases of dynamic Sufism can be found in other Islamic societies as well. The case of Bediuzaman Said Nursi, whose life spanned the nineteenth and twentieth centuries, is another good example. Nursi reached millions of Islamists in modern Turkey and the world through his *Risale-i Nur*, a political and philosophical manifesto that is Sufi in both style and substance. Its modern political depths and texture, anchored in an Islamic locus or core, have been singularly responsible for the articulation of an Islamist political philosophy, which turned into a formidable political movement in Turkey and beyond. Known as the *Nurcu*, this movement and similar others see themselves as more than mystical and forsaking this world for the rewards in the next. They see their thoughts and ideas as articulating a counterargument to political master texts, as philosophical in contemplation and political in program.

The central point in all of this discussion is simple. For too long in traditional thinking, Sufi thoughts and practices have been categorized as *apolitical*, or politically irrelevant. The history of Islamic philosophy and political thought has to be reconsidered in light of Sufism as a sui generis Islamic thought system. Casting Sufism as nothing more than a metaphysical indulgence has largely been the work of modern Orientalist dogma rather than a historical consensus among Muslims themselves. In fact, in contrast, Sufi movements have always operated as containers of political reason in Islamic societies. They have been at work in most of the radical, indeed revolutionary, episodes in Islamic history since the time of the Mutazila. Although not always "progressive," they have always been politically influenced, if not politically influential. As a result, Islamic annals are full of the names of Sufi masters or leaders who led or supported radical and even insurrectionary movements. Sheik Bedreddin of Simavna[42] was a fifteenth-century example of the political character of Sufi movements in the Ottoman Empire. Bedreddin inspired a series of peasant rebellions in Ottoman Anatolia on account of the political repression and economic exploitation of the peasantry. The rebellions were quelled and Bedreddin subsequently hanged. Yet his story registered anew Islamic Sufism as a radical political philosophy. In the very same Anatolia, only in the twentieth century, Said Nursi became the modern reincarnation of Sufism as a political orientation. Ultimately, both Bedreddin and Nursi fed on the same dynamic, traceable to the founding tension in Islam, as Mernissi reminds, between "questioning and obedience" and between "reason and imitation."

In short, Orientalists might perceive and represent the Sufis as steeped in the supernatural and/or the transcendental. Sufis, however, have always regarded their path as "transformative" in this world. Time and again, any close reading of Sufi histories shows that Sufi ideas and thoughts represented socially situated and politically organized movements in the Islamic world. These ideas operated through a political and socioeconomic reasoning that was deeply informed by but was by no means limited to or captured by theological-religious reasoning. Further, Sufi thoughts ought not to be detached from the social histories in which they emerged. Their histories, particularly their social and psychological dimensions, reveal the diverse forms through which Sufi thoughts are articulated into political streams. Without regarding Sufism as political, it is not possible to comprehend the political in Islam.

Long before the Ottoman or the Safavid-era Sufi lines, Arab-Islamic streams, for example, had already developed a thorough humanist philosophy by employing what can be regarded as an illuminative rationalism. This rationalism moved beyond the Hellenic logic to get at the "sociopsychological" realities that had been previously reduced to the realm of the imaginary or the unconscious.[43] Able to exceed the real/imaginary divide, Sufi Muslims worked instead to infuse them together under the rubric of "Illumination" and challenge the positive literalism of both the Sunni and Shia orthodoxies. Sufi thought organized by figures such as Ibn Arabi and Ibn Hazm in Andalusia and Rumi and Bektashi Veli in Anatolia functioned as political and philosophical lines. "The thought of Ibn Hazm,—so agile, incisive, daring and modern—remains not only poorly known but also poorly utilized."[44] Given the influence Ibn Hazm's ideas exercised directly and indirectly in European philosophy, the neglect becomes more troubling. Therefore, if Ibn Hazm's thought system appears incommensurate with the logic of modern positivism, now dominant in both the West and the Islamic worlds, the conflict indicates not a failure for Ibn Hazm's thought but a systematic impoverishment of modern political thought enthralled by pure positivism. In the end, Ibn Hazm's knowledge informs about the social, cultural, and psychological dimension of power and powerlessness more than we are led to believe. It reveals the social history that made Sufism both necessary and viable.

Historians have long studied the conditions and reasons for the rise of the rigid theological attitude at the expense of Islamic philosophy and Sufism's filling the lacuna left by the marginalization of philosophy. Arkoun's outline is instructive: The Arabs developed numerous sciences, from mathematics to astronomy to botany to pharmacology to geography to zoology. Their knowledge benefited the West, as Arab Islamic works were disseminated into the West from the eleventh century on. In the case of philosophy, however, Islamic advancements were halted in part because of the new social, political, and economic insecurities facing the Arab Islamic Empire. Beginning in the eleventh century, the Ottoman Empire came under heavy pressure from the Mongol invasions as well as the Crusades in the East and the *Reconquista* in Andalusian Spain in the West. These mounting challenges threatened the network of great Islamic cities from Damascus and Baghdad to Cairo and Cordova through which Islamic sciences and arts were organized and supported. As the empire grew more vulnerable, the intellectual concerns shifted from innovation to preservation. Philosophy in particular was forced to give way to conservative theology. In the narrowing field of political freedoms, illuminative rationalist movements, especially Sufism, emerged as alternative forms of social inquiry without explicitly declaring a political intent. In short, social and historic uncertainties and threats created a defensive intellectual aura. Sufism became the radical conduit that could survive the resulting conservatism and channel the anxieties and aspirations into movements.[45]

That the illuminative streams were not the "ruling" ideas cannot be construed to indicate that they were not influential or that they did not command significant following. Historical research readily reveals that Sufi thought systems were quite dominant socially and psychologically between eleventh and seventeenth centuries. However, more revealingly, that they have rarely been marked as ideas that historically and politically mattered demonstrates a preference for a historiography among or about Muslims that is either state-centric, unable to look beyond the privileged official histories of Muslim societies, or steeped in an Orientalist perspective. An unwillingness to see Muslims as historical agents of the European Renaissance, Enlightenment, and modernity remains—the three epochs of intellectual achievements that Europe and Christianity claim as their products, their historical heritage, and their patrimony.

What is even more remarkable is how Muslims themselves have internalized much of the Orientalist claims about their own historical character through their officialdom and as part of their popular imaginaries. Political despotism arguing that the repressive nature of regimes reflects the character of the Muslim people—Arabs, Turks, and Persians—is prevalent. A former Turkish president, Suleyman Demirel, famously suggested this to be the case in the 1990s when he was asked about the limitations of democratic governance in Turkey. Under constant pressure, Muslim Arabs or other Muslims, similarly hopeless about their potential as human beings, ally their fears with the prevalent modern Islamic state and sacrifice their hopes at the altar of "Islamic" tradition. They remain entranced by the West and modernity and are afraid of their own history. They experience neither meaningfully or critically, for the former is forever exalted as an ideal for Arabs or Muslims while the latter remains an unworthy project so long as the fantasies of the first dominate the mind.

All the same, from the eleventh to the seventeenth centuries, the period during which the Islamic world allegedly atrophied intellectually, the Sufi ideas proliferated as ideas of resistance and insurrection against the oppressive reign of the ulama and the ruling elite. This shift was especially notable in Ottoman-era Anatolia (modern Turkey) and the Balkans. A list of Sufi masters whose ideas still guide masses in Turkey alone would be as long as the aforementioned list of Islamic philosophers and scientists from the Golden Age. Ahmet Yesevi, Bektasi Veli, Jalal ad-Din Rumi, Yunus Emre, Pir Sultan Abdal, Karacaoglan, Seyh Bedreddin of Simavna, Abdal Musa, Karaca Ahmet, and Hubyar Sultan are distinguished sources of wisdom for millions. Of these figures, perhaps the most influential is Bektasi Veli's thinking organized around his famous dictum: "*Eline, beline, diline sahip ol.*" "Mind your hand [deeds], your waist [desires], and your tongue [words]!"

It was not a coincidence that critical Sufism became widespread in the Ottoman era in the Muslim world. Let us remember that the Ottoman Empire was geographically expansive. With Anatolia at the center, it stretched into the Balkans, Ukraine, and the Caucasus in Europe and Asia and enveloped Yemen, Saudi Arabia, Egypt, Sudan, and much of North Africa. At its zenith, it was a "world empire set on half of the inhabited world." Given its size and might, the Ottoman influence was definitive of Islamic trajectories in the Sunni world.[46] Under the Ottomans, Islamic philosophy experienced no significant advancement. In fact, in the 600 years of Ottoman rule, between 1299 and 1919, only a handful of authentic Ottoman intellectual figures emerged, many coming in the eighteenth and nineteenth centuries. From the onset of the empire, the Ottoman aspirations were not philosophical, though they were not actively antiphilosophical either. The Ottoman Turks had a more practical orientation. They were at heart a martial society whose military might had found a powerful compass in Islam. Anchored in the Islamic faith and spurred by military efficiency, Ottomans emerged as an unstoppable force from the thirteenth century onward. Eventually, they dominated Anatolia (and later the Balkans) like their forefathers the Seljuks had done for 200 years before them.

Moreover, the Ottoman political and administrative sensibilities were formed in a time when the debate between philosophy and theology in the Islamic world had already been settled in favor of the traditionalist theology. By the time the Ottomans swept through Anatolia and into the Balkans, and subsequently into North Africa, Islamic philosophy and philosophers in the tradition of al Farabi or Avicenna had been pushed either underground or westward, away from the political centers of Islam in Anatolia or Persia. The last refuge of the Islamic philosophy became the Andalusian Islamic states in what is today southern Spain. Under conditions of austere theological purity, a traditionalist Islam was fused into the Ottoman political culture. What remained of Islamic philosophy and rationalism in the traditional heartland of Islam took on different forms, particularly the Sufi forms. With few exceptions, these Sufi streams developed largely outside of the state framework. In this way, they acquired a relative autonomy from the state as well as developing a capacity for political independence. This independence of the mind anchored in the autonomy of their everyday networks led to development of a post-medieval brand of Sufism as an alternative Islamic political philosophy.

In the end, Sufism developed into a thought form beyond its early esoteric character. It became the philosophers' salvation in the Islamic world, when Islamic philosophy was out of fashion and Islamic *Kalam*, or theology, was in ascendance. Combining *Tasawwuf*, philosophy, and *Kalam*, Sufism enabled the cultivation of a thoroughly political thought field—so much so that a procession of Islamic thinkers through the ages—Avicenna, al Farabi, al Gahazali, to Ibn Rushd, Ibn Khaldun, Sheik Bedreddin, Khayr al-Din, al Afghani, Said Nursi, to name a few—were as deeply shaped by Sufism as by theology, philosophy, or other sciences relevant in their lives.

The Sufi legacy has to be comprehended through the historically appropriate lens of philosophy of science and not the provisional lens of modern European hegemony. Viewed through a time-sensitive lens, Sufis figure as Islamic political philosophers in their own right. Further, as with Islamic philosophers, they are revealed as ancestors to Western traditions in the same ways the Greek philosophers are so readily assumed to be. It is in this sense that I raise the Islamic intellectual legacy as being active in the West and in the East. My purpose is not simply to argue that Muslims continued to produce intellectual luminaries even after the Islamic Golden Age. Instead, it is to highlight the legacy left by Ibn Sina, Ibn Rushd, and Ibn Khaldun as being simultaneously Islamic and Western. This legacy is of a common intellectual-civilizational history connecting Euro-West and Islamic-Orient. Re-viewed in this transversal light, Ibn Rushd's or Ibn Khaldun's legacy is relieved from historiographic captivity as purely Oriental, medieval, and Islamic. Instead, each is revealed also as Occidental, modern, and European. When in the 1970s Iranian thinker Ali Shariati wrote that for the West, "thinking" in the Islamic world is seen possible only as theological, never philosophical, he was striving to contest a well-established prejudice against seeing, say, Averroes as a universal philosopher, equal to the likes of Immanuel Kant, or Avicenna as the father of Western medicine more than Galen, the celebrated Greek medical doctor.

The more we study relevant histories, the more we discover Islamic thought bridges to Europe. Islamic mind-prints abound in European traditions—not Islamic as in religion but Islamic as civilizational makeup. Hassan Ibn al Wazzan, whose Oriental Islamic body and mind as Leonus Africanus in the Court of Pope Leo X in 1518 literally became the bridge between Renaissance Europe and Islamic North Africa, bespeaks of the same forces that interpenetrated across religious and civilizational divides. Different historical inventories of the Islamic world reveal dynamic societies capable of producing and preserving critical knowledge. The consensus that civilizationally Islamic societies are inherently lacking in critical disposition is simply a hegemonic idea historically nurtured through struggles and sustained by a complex architecture of political and economic powers. This consensus about Islam and Muslims is not innocent, nor is it forthright about Europe and its peoples. It obscures convergences not only in history but also in identities. Even as the European West and the Islamic East were charting different cultural trajectories, differences themselves nearly always have had common traces. The directions of the prevailing winds of influence or inspiration shifted, but the winds themselves were never dormant.

For nearly 700 years from the eighth century until the fifteenth century, Islamic thought worlds contributed to the common civilization with Europe, inspiring European ideas of the Renaissance and Enlightenment. Beginning in the sixteenth century, the winds of influence changed course by way of worldwide European colonialism, culminating in modernity as the new revolutionary condition in politics and philosophy. European modernity interacted with the Islamic world, triggering new intellectual trends among Muslims. This time, Muslims were on the receiving ends, having to negotiate with the intrepid forces of modernity, with capitalism as its worldwide driving force. Contrary to the prevailing perceptions, the responses in the Islamic thought world to what quickly became the modern capitalist world system were rich and varied. These responses ushered in the next stage in the transformation of the Islamic thought world. The political Sufism of old, with its locus in Islamic empires, was not fully sufficient to comprehend the empires of new that treated the entire planet Earth as their domain. Crucially, Sufism was not jettisoned as old, but activated anew in multiple directions, and it paved the way for modern Islamic thought. Many of the scholars who were to shape modern Islamic intellectual trends had themselves been shaped by Sufi sensibilities running deep in the Islamic milieu. It is this transformation and beyond that I examine in the next chapter.

# CHAPTER 3

# ISLAMIC INTELLECTUAL LEGACIES
## *Modern Amnesia and Political Philosophy*

When Napoleon Bonaparte invaded Egypt in 1798, accompanying his armies were tens of scholars and scientists who went on to write a twenty-three-volume masterpiece on the Egypt of the pharaohs and the great pyramids. Their multivolume masterpiece not only initiated modern Egyptology but also started off the modern obsession with ancient Egypt.[1] Curiously, however, their interest in ancient Egypt was always expressed in contrast to Islamic Egypt. It conveyed a certain fundamental point with urgency. The ancients, it suggested, were everything that Muslim Egypt was not—daring, enterprising, and ingenious. Monuments to boundless human aspiration, the pyramids of the ancients had fallen into ruins just as the Muslim-Arab mind had under Oriental Islamic despotism. The classical Egypt of the ancients had to be rescued from "the present Oriental barbarism" that had enveloped it, and must be given its rightful place in the annals of great civilizations.

Of course, Europe was to do the job. As a souvenir, the French sent an ancient Egyptian obelisk to Paris for display. In 1801, the British, making inroads into the Middle East, forced the French out of Egypt. As for the obelisk, it still stands in Paris, a sad testimony to Orientalism as a cultural ideology of modern colonialism.

For all its military setbacks, French Orientalism, like its British counterpart, excelled in "defining the Arab Islamic mind" as backward and repressive. This characterization of the Arab Islamic mind as being "out of time" and "out of joint" proved not only enduring but also highly instrumental in fulfilling the goals of European colonialism. It enabled Orientalism to justify European expansions under the conviction that the Arabs and Muslims were not up to the demands of a dynamic new world. In the following century, Europe emerged as the "master" of the world and also as a model for emulation. Under European "supervision," the world became "whole" again, fashioned through capitalism and modernity. Among the unanticipated results of this new globalism were the encounters between Islamic intellectuals and the newly forged ideas of modernity streaming out of Europe. Like the earlier ancestral exchanges, which had defined both Europe and the Islamic Arab world, these exchanges, too, proved intellectually definitive of peoples in their paths.

If the Islamic Arab world had fallen asleep at the civilizational wheel, thus lagging behind Europe by centuries, Europe's colonial expansion abruptly woke them up to the new realities. All forms of Islamic intellectual traditions—theology, theosophy, Sufism, and even philosophy—were energetically dusted off, stirring fresh intellectual movements. As European modernity penetrated the Islamic East with colonial and capitalist interests in mind and intent on obscuring and dismissing historical Islamic contributions to the arts and sciences, it also played a central role in birthing the conditions of a modern Islamic thought world.

The grounds for the intensification of Islamic intellectualism had always been ripe behind the appearances of an Islamic world in decline. Islamic thought streams, while not flourishing along the European axis, had remained active. Even today in the Arab world, when all appears dominated by conservative or fundamentalist tendencies driven by a certain artificial, politically induced fear of history, many struggles are being waged for a progressive realignment of the current state of affairs.

Such struggles have always been central to Islamic histories, as have the repressive tendencies, shaped by the two founding tendencies in Islam, reason and obedience.

Recollect that the Qur'an began instructing people "by the pen." The Prophet of Islam originally preached "change" as the essence of revelation. Muslim philosophers theorized reason as an agent of change and called reasoning a duty for all Muslims. Even the traditionalists like al Ghazali and Ibn Taymiyyah were advocates of "demonstrative" knowledge. For example, Ibn Taymiyyah, for all his opposition to Islamic philosophers, advocated for a compromise between extreme edges of various thought streams. He characterized the compromise as the *wasat*, or the "center." Yet over time in Islamic cultures, the concept of wasat came to mean ordinary or average instead of the creative and dynamic compromise or center Taymiyyah had in mind originally. In the political sense, striving for wasat increasingly signified a preference for the status quo. Over the centuries, internal Islamic fundamentalist and external Orientalist colonial forces have nurtured this meaning—so much so that even Ibn Taymiyyah, for all his traditionalism, is now criticized by radical Islamists for his audacity to seek the "center" or "compromise" in religious matters.[2] In an ironic fashion, that Ibn Taymiyyah is not conservative or Salafist enough for many contemporary fundamentalists demonstrates the narrowness of the horizons ordinary Muslims have to negotiate with. In short, Muslims have not stopped thinking. Rather, they have been scared from thinking or scared into silence. In fact, in these times, the very act of "thinking" beyond the status quo has become dangerous across countries such as Saudi Arabia, Egypt, Iran, Iraq, Afghanistan, the Sudan, Algeria, or Pakistan.

This collusion has a more recent genealogy than typically assumed in circles that attribute conservatism to Islam's nature. In a sense, it can be traced back to the political reform movements in Muslim societies as the seventeenth century gave way to the eighteenth century. The Ottomans, the Safavids, and the Mughals were no longer the uncontested powers over their dominions. In the case of the Mughals, after Akbar the Great's "enlightened" rule lasting more than half a century ended in 1605, with his successors Jahangir and Shah Jahan, the builder of the famed Taj Mahal, the Mughal Empire atrophied. While Akbar's ruling motto was "peace for all," his grandson Shah Jahan's ambitions turned to monumental building projects without sufficient funds. He

## TEXTBOX 3.1. THE ERA OF ISLAMIC "ETHNIC" EMPIRES

| | |
|---|---|
| 1299–1924 | The Ottoman Era |
| 1332–1406 | al Hassan Ibn Khaldun, the author of the famed al *Muqaddimah*, a history of Islamic societies, considered the father of modern disciplines of sociology and history |
| 1453 | Ottoman Turks capture Istanbul; control the Mediterranean. |
| 1492 | Columbus sails West for India and lands in the Caribbean. The last of the Moorish kingdoms extinguished in Andalusia, Spain |
| 1492 | Jews and Muslims expelled from Spain |
| 1566 | The Ottoman Sultan "Suleiman the Magnificent" dies. His death marks the decline of the Ottoman Empire. |
| 1839–1876 | The Ottoman "Tanzimat Reform Era" culminates in the 1876 Constitution—first for the Empire. |
| 1502 | Shah Ismail's reign gives rise to Persian (Shia) Ottoman (Sunni) rivalry. |
| 1502–1737 | The Safavids of Persia/Iran. Shiism becomes the official religion of the Empire. |
| 1795–1925 | Qajar dynastic period |
| 1803–1824 | Russo-Iranian wars usher in European colonialism. |
| 1901 | The British granted the first oil concession in Iran. |
| 1905 | Constitutional Revolution |
| 1526–1858 | The Mughals of India, the Alid (Shia) Islam serves as a source of inspiration. |
| 1556–1605 | Akbar the Great expands the Empire and founds the hybrid *Din i-Ilahi*, the "Religion of Divine God," which contains elements from Islam, Hinduism, Jainism, Zoroastrianism, and Christianity. |
| 1601–1757 | East Indian Company arrives, securing trade concessions and competing with other European powers such as the Dutch and Portuguese. |
| 1651 | Shah Jahan has Taj Mahal built in memory of his wife Mumtaz Mahal. |

| | |
|---|---|
| 1658–1707 | Aurangzeb turns his back to Akbar's policies of tolerance and imposes strict Sharia on the Indian subcontinent with majority Hindu population. |
| 1798 | Napoleon invades Egypt: Orientalism emerges as cultural ideology of European Imperialism. |
| 1757–1858 | The British East India Company rules on behalf of the Crown. Also called the "Company Rule" |
| 1858–1947 | "The British Raj," the British Crown rule (with the native rulers of princely states) covers India, Pakistan, and Bangladesh. |
| 1918–1923 | The Ottoman Empire collapses—end of Islamic Empires |

nearly bankrupted the empire. Worse yet, he steadily moved away from the liberal policies of his grandfather. When Aurangzeb (1658–1707) followed him to the throne, the Mughal Empire was at its height geographically, yet economically it was on the brink of collapse. As a remedy, Aurangzeb turned to fundamentalism, seeking salvation in religious purity. The ensuing repression of the majority Hindu population weakened the empire economically. With its people uninterested in the well-being of the empire, the Mughal rule became increasingly vulnerable to Europeans, who had already been encroaching on India, Southeast Asia, and China. The decline vis-à-vis Europeans knocking on the door not as guests but as conquerors started the process for reforms. The reforms were too little and too late. The age of European mastery had arrived decisively in Asia via India.

The Safavid reforms were compelled by similar dynamics minus an enlightened leader of the caliber of the Mughal Akbar. Safavids had their "great" leader in Abbas I (1588–1629). However, Abbas was no liberal in religious matters. He promoted a doctrinaire Shiism as the official ideology of the state in the tradition of the earliest Islamic rulers from the Umayyad and Abbasid eras. The competition with the Sunni Ottomans sharpened Safavid sectarian commitments. While the empire expanded, intellectual horizons gradually narrowed. As with the state of the Sunni faith in the Ottoman Empire, Shiism in the Safavid state service lost its moral compass and turned into a spiritual overseer of the imperial decline. Only with the fall of the Safavids in 1722 and the rise of the Qajars in 1789 was Shiism able to refocus its message as a voice of dissent in Islam. By the end of the eighteenth century, European colonialism had put the Qajars under duress as well. Although never directly colonized by European powers, the Qajar Iran increasingly came under Russian and British pressure in the nineteenth century. A series of military defeats by the Russians, coupled with economic and commercial concessions granted to the British and the French, changed Iran's character from an independent power to an economic colony in the making. The 1872 concession to the British Baron Julius Reuter (the founder of Reuters News Agency) for exploiting minerals and forests, followed by the tobacco concession granted to the British Imperial Tobacco Corporation in 1891, culminated in the Tobacco Rebellion of 1892. The Shia clergy played a major role in the rebellion, thereby coming to the realization of its organizing capacity and of Shiism's potential as a revolutionary ideology. In such a fluid environment, anticolonial ideologies began to proliferate. Among those were the Shia militant clerics cum ideologues who harnessed the Shia self-image of the revolting subjects to religious and political movements both reformist and revolutionary. The 1906–1911 Constitutional Revolutionary period crystallized Shiism's transformative power so long as it eschewed capturing power for the clergy's sake. Indeed, what became apparent in the Constitutional Revolution of 1906–1911 was the progressive role of the Shiism of the masses in contrast to that of the clergy, which succeeded in coalescing with the nationalists, the *Bazaari* merchants, and the urban intelligentsia to mark the rise of Iranian modernity.[3]

Clearly, the idea of reforms came to the fore in all three Islamic empires in an era marking Europe's ascent and Islamic empires' decline. However, given its direct contact with Christian Europe, no case was starker than that of the Ottoman Empire. The Ottoman story is therefore emblematic of the intimate dance of politics and religion. Once a powerful empire that had ruled over "half of the inhabited earth," beginning in the sixteenth century, the Ottoman Empire entered into a period of decline. Heralding the decline was the unsuccessful Ottoman siege of Vienna in 1683, which effectively ended the empire's expansion in Europe and exposed its vulnerabilities. After the siege, the Ottoman armies went on a losing streak in wars against the Russians in the Balkans and in the Crimea. The empire began to unravel in Europe, with similar troubles brewing in the territories in North Africa. These losses prompted the Ottoman administrative and political elite to ponder the causes of the precipitous decline of fortunes. How could this be so after Suleiman the Magnificent had confidently declared himself the "Shadow of God on Earth" destined to rule as the King of Kings? Had God forsaken the empire? Many devout Ottomans among the royal and religious classes thought so and called for the return to Salafi traditions. However, others began to think that rather than God forsaking the Ottomans, in the delusion that they were God's chosen subjects, the Ottomans had lost sight of what had propelled them to the heights of power in the first place when they first converted to Islam: an openness to knowledge and opportunities around them and an enterprising attitude in political, economic, and military fields.

Beginning in the ninth and tenth centuries, the Turks' conversion to Islam had proved to be a brilliant move for their political future. From serving as slave/mercenary soldiers under the Abbasid, Eastern Roman, and Persian empires, Turks rose to establish the Seljuk Empire in the tenth century and the Ottoman Empire in the thirteenth century. Their conversion to Islam, the most dynamic force in this period, had been the catalyst in the emergent Turkish power in Anatolia and Mesopotamia. As the Turkish tribes spread deeper into Anatolia, they encountered a thousand-year-old mosaic of the Byzantine world, rich in peoples, cultures, and religions. This historic convergence afforded the Turks fertile grounds for accumulation of power. They rose to their prominent position by creating a syncretic political, cultural, and religious mentality, or what Ibn Khaldun called the Asabiyyah. By the reign of Suleiman the Magnificent in the 1520s, the Ottoman Turkish Asabiyyah had created an empire that stretched across the lands once controlled by the mighty Roman Empire. However, the Ottoman dynamism proved short-lived. It withered as the Ottoman Sultans adopted the Islamic Sunni orthodoxy in the sixteenth century. The Ottoman Asabiyyah was increasingly shaped by the Sunni theology rather than by the enterprising frontier ethos that had propelled the Ottomans from a small tribe into a vast empire.

The more the Ottomans embraced the Sunni orthodoxy, the more they turned their back to the syncretism of the age that had served them so well. The Sunni orthodoxy, coupled with a desire to preserve the territorial gains and the resulting mercantile economy, made the Ottomans averse to change and enterprise over time. Religiosity distanced them from the outside world beginning in the sixteenth century. Within the orbit of Europe's ascending power yet intellectually insulated from it, the Ottomans stagnated while European powers expanded overseas. First to fall within Europe's control was the Americas, whose riches Europe appropriated and harnessed to its industrialization. Later, along with Asia and Africa, the Ottoman as well as Safavid and Mughal territories were brought into Europe's sphere of interest. With rich oil reserves in the Caucasus, Iraq, and Arabia, the Ottoman Empire made a particularly attractive bounty for the emerging world capitalist system. By the twentieth century, the Ottoman Empire was ripe for the taking and the Europeans moved in with enthusiasm.

When the Ottoman intelligentsia asked if God had forsaken them, this was the material background. It was in response to a similar dilemma beginning in the eighteenth century that the Ottomans had initiated a series of reforms aimed at altering Islam's role in the empire. The *Nizami Cedid* (the New Order) in 1793 under Sultan Selim III and the 1839 *Tanzimat-i Hayriyye* (Beneficial Reforms) of the Sultan Abdulmecit were not antireligion but intended to fashion a reform-friendly Islam.

In the wake of these reforms, in the 1900s, the policies of the Young Turks grew more secularist in orientation yet retained an ambivalence toward religion. The Kemalist reformers who followed the Young Turks in the 1920s, however, were certain in their objective: the subordination of religion to the nation-state. The towering character of Mustafa Kemal embodied the modern skepticism toward religion. But there were also the likes of Jamal al Din Afghani and Said Nursi, for whom piety superseded any other sentiment in the polity. A new clash of ideas was in the making in what became the Turkish Republic. After the republic was founded, the Alevi-Bektashis, who occupy a unique place in Turkish Islamic imaginaries, joined in. Yet, despite their differences, all these constituencies converged on the same horizon shaped by the nationalizing forces of modernity and the transnational impulses of the Islamic Ummah. One of the first persons to operate in this horizon was Jamal al Din Afghani.

## HEAD ON: COLONIAL GLOBALIZATION AND THE ISLAMIST VISION OF JAMAL AL DIN AFGHANI

Jamal al Din Afghani is an incomparable figure in modern Islamic history. He was born in Iran in 1837 and died in Istanbul in 1897. Afghani is considered as one of the earliest modernist Islamists. He represented the modern reformist movement in ascendance in the Islamic world, but he refused to renounce traditional Islam as a source of cultural and political identity. As a young man, Afghani traveled the length and breadth of the Islamic world at a time when Islamic states and societies were under duress from or already colonized by European powers. Like many Islamic intellectuals Afghani's formative experiences were the product of this transitional era. Afghani and his peers grew up thinking they inherited Islamic patrimony, characterized as being brilliant, golden, and glorious in civilizational achievements. The Umayyads, the Abbasids, the Seljuks, the Mughals, the Mamluks, the Safavids, and the Ottomans evoked pride in their minds and hearts then, as they do today among Muslims. At the same time, to Afghani's eyes, the present Islamic states and societies seemed in disarray, being conquered and turned into mere shadows of their former selves. Afghani's reaction to these conditions, formulated during his years as an itinerant scholar, teacher, and agitator, was neither a revivalist Islamism nor a nationalist modernism, which were then the dominant movements against the European colonial expansion in the Islamic world.

Afghani's ideas differed from, for example, the nineteenth-century Wahhabi puritanism, then active in North Africa and Arabia, advocating a return to the Islam practiced during the time of the Prophet Muhammad and the rightly guided ancestors, or the *Salaf*. His ideas also stood in contrast to the modern nation-statist model that was in ascendance in all of Europe, in Ottoman Turkey, Iran, and British India. In contrast, Afghani was a syncretist in the traditions of the Mutazila philosophers as well the Sufi mystics. Well versed in theology, jurisprudence, and philosophy, he agitated against the British in Afghanistan and India, but he was also able to debate the father of the romantic French nationalism and the prolific Orientalist Ernest Renan in Paris in the 1860s. Characterized as a restless genius, Afghani later taught in Cairo in reformist circles but also managed to advise the Ottoman Sultan Abdulhamid on the possibility, indeed the desirability, of a pan-Islamic polity—a kind of transnational Islamic Union.

Afghani was open to new ideas. For him, Europe and modernity needed to be seen not as exemplars for imitation but as a wake-up call for Muslims who seemed to have lost the original spirit of Islamic *umran* (civilization): forward-looking, creative, flexible, tolerant, and syncretic in outlook. Therefore, in Afghani's mind, Europe and modernity stood not as an object of desire or imitation but as a large cautionary "tale" demanding the renewal of the progressive and syncretic Islamic spirit. In a syncretic orientation, "receiving" modern reason from Europe is not perceived as imitation or incorporation of a foreign element, but is rather the restoration of a basic historical Islamic mode of openness to humanity's achievements through the filter of Islamic tenets. The Sunnah of the Prophet Muhammad, full of examples of his openness to difference, is a testimony to this Islamic intent. Didn't the Prophet of Islam once say, "Seek knowledge even if it is in China"? In this light, in Afghani's universe, knowledge conveyed across peoples and civilizations need not be seen as defeat by or assimilation into the European cauldron; rather, it was part and parcel of the Islamic tradition in reason and freethinking. After all, it was the Islamic scholars who transmitted the Hellenistic wisdom to Europe after having enhanced it as Islamic. Demonstrating such syncretism, in his response to Ernest Renan, Afghani echoed Renan's suspicion of religious dogmas yet also fearlessly articulated his own suspicions of modernity. He endorsed individual reason and freedom of conscience as keys to progress but refused to dissociate them from the mysteries of revelation. Put differently, in Afghani's mind, religion and reason were interlocked in that they employ different forms of reason for the common purpose of cultivating *Umran* or civilization.

In many ways, Afghani was an enigmatic figure who freely expressed admiration and criticism for both Western and Islamic societies. However, the real significance of his ideas lies in his grasp of the nineteenth-century globalism that linked together the world's places and peoples, with Europe as its center. European colonialism was the engine. Afghani's hostility to Europe was a reaction to what he considered a worldwide European oppression of Muslims. In Afghani (along with a number of his contemporaries, such as the Egyptian Ahmed Tahtawi, the Ottoman Young Turks, and Khayr al-Din al Tunisi), the Islamic intellectual world acquired a requisite depth and breadth in the knowledge of this new wave of globalization. While Afghani was a firebrand activist thinker and philosopher, al Tunisi was a levelheaded Ottoman statesman-scholar. He was well educated in the classical Islamic sense, but he also lived in France for two years. He was a border figure that managed to span the Islamic and European worlds. He caught on to the fact that connections and transitions across places and people define periods or even ages of history. Columbus's voyage defined Europe and the Americas. Likewise, the "Middle Passage" of enslaved Africans on their way to the Americas changed Africa, Europe, and the Americas.

Historically and politically aware, al Tunisi urged Islamic societies to take seriously the transitions and connections through which Europe was reshaping the entire world. "We are a part of that world, yet wield very little control over it." He understood clearly the unequal economic exchange and how it leads to a steady decline by economic means of even a power like the Ottoman Empire. "We receive none of the increased value resulting from the manufacturing process, the basic means of creating abundance [accumulating capital]. . . . If the value of imports exceeds the value of the exports ruin will unavoidably take place."[4] The folding-in of the globe whose farthest distance is now connected with its nearest makes this self-evident, argued al Tunisi. Using Islamic sentiments as a cheer for engaging the West, he advocated learning from European achievements in sciences and politics. For him, such mode of knowledge acquisition was fully in line with the Holy Sharia. When the Sharia was strong, he noted, it exerted influence on Europeans, who benefited greatly. Now was the time for Muslims to learn talents and skills from Europeans without the paranoia of losing their faith.[5]

Ultimately, al Tunisi as well as Afghani regarded the prevailing ideas underlying this emergent globality as Western yet also within the Islamic traditions. After all, for them, the Islamic contributions to the Renaissance and Enlightenment had heralded Europe's rise. The next generation of Muslim thinkers took up this line of thinking and solidified Islamist modernism as an intellectual trend. Muhammad Abduh in Egypt, Said Nursi in Turkey, Taha Hussein in the Sudan, and Muhammed Iqbal in India-Pakistan are some examples. In the age of modernity consumed by a drive for exclusionary roots, whether expressed as nation-building or the invisible hand of the market, Islamist modernism would not fare well as a pluralist movement, which is by definition an assemblage without a single logic or a unified orchestration. Instead, Muslims inspired by the revivalist Wahhab, and later the antimodernist Qutb, would turn inward even as they looked outward. While nationalist modernists had turned to Europe for ready-made enlightenment, fundamentalists saw European enlightenment as distinctly and abjectly European. Refusing to see them as part of the legacy of the ideas to

## TEXTBOX 3.2. THE COMING OF THE MODERN ISLAMIC AGE

| | |
|---|---|
| 1703–1792 | Muhammed Ibn Abd al Wahhab, the father of Wahhabism, the inspiration for Saudi Arabia's brand of Islam—puritanist and politically antimodernist. |
| 1838–1897 | Jamal al Din Afghani, the father of Islamic modernism, advocates Pan-Islamism as an anticolonial movement. Afghani and Muhammad Abduh, the eminent Egyptian modernist, publish the Pan-Islamist newspaper *al Urwat al Wuthqa* (*The Indissoluble Link*) in exile in France. In Paris, Afghani debates Ernest Renan, the father of European nationalism. |
| 1868 | Khayr al-Din al Tunisi publishes "The Surest Path," an early modernist manifesto remarkably "globalist" in its conceptualization of world politics. |
| 1918 | World War I ends, ushering in twentieth-century European colonialism in the Middle East. Britain controls Egypt, Sudan, Trans-Jordan, Palestine, Iraq, and the Arab Gulf. France controls Syria, Lebanon, Algeria, Tunisia, and Morocco. Italy settles for Libya and Ethiopia. |
| 1911 | Said "Kurdi" Nursi gives his "Damascus Sermon" at the Umayyad Mosque. Organizing his sermon around "Six Words" or parts, Nursi examines the reasons for the decline of Islamic civilization and articulates an Islamist political vision. |
| 1918 | Saudi Arabia "founded" with Britain as the kingmaker. The British military officer T. E. Lawrence foments Arab nationalism against the Turks and finds fame as "Lawrence of Arabia." |
| 1923 | Republic of Turkey founded; Mustafa Kemal becomes the president. |
| 1924 | Turkey becomes a constitutional "secular" republic." |
| 1925 | Sheik Sait Rebellion in Turkey. Rebellion suppressed and Sait hanged. |

| | |
|---|---|
| 1925 | Said Nursi, accused of involvement in the rebellion, is exiled to Isparta. He completes the *Risale-i Nur* collection. His thoughts are a challenge to twentieth-century nationalism in defense of a transnationalist Islamic vision. |
| 1928 | Hassan al Banna founds "Muslim Brotherhood" in Egypt. The Brotherhood spreads across Arab countries. It aims to establish an Islamic order through social, economic, and charitable institutions. Banna was executed in 1949 for inciting terrorism. |

which the likes of Ibn Sina, Ibn Hazm, Ibn Rushd, and ibn Khaldun had directly or indirectly contributed, they rejected Enlightenment ideals unequivocally.

Paradoxically, the nationalists failed not in rejecting European ideas but in treating them as purely and exclusively European in origin and superior in achievements. They received and incorporated them into their respective Islamic societies to promote modernity and civilization on par with Europe. For instance, in Turkey, after the commencement of the republican era in 1923, "Avrupalilasmak" or "Europeanization" literally became the national goal.

Interestingly, what has been at work in both orientations is only the modern instrumentalist logic of the West. Modern ethical, cultural, and aesthetic forms have been either ignored or downplayed as strange or foreign or received en masse without the underlying normative sensibilities. Therefore, instrumental logic has been seen as that which makes the West materially superior and desirable for the nationalists or spiritually lacking in the eyes of the fundamentalists. In each case, only a caricature of the West was constructed and considered. In Turkey, for example, Kemalism saw Westernization as modernization and modernization as applying instrumental reason, at times absurdly, requiring people to wear Western dress, or alarmingly, inventing a new Turkish history and a new Turkish language. Paradoxically, the Islamist resistances to Kemalism share in this commitment to instrumental logic, though drawing on different sources for inspiration. They declare their Islam to be the truth and the only truth in Turkey and beyond. Even then, they deny the plurality of truths within, embodied most prominently in Turkish Alevis. Arab Muslims, it appears, are not the only ones afraid of their own histories.

Relief for the Islamic minds might be found in uncovering and identifying with transversal the historical inventories of which they are unconscious parts. Fundamentalism as well as nation-statism in Islamic countries betrays the rich historical Islamic legacies—religion in one and reason in another are constructed into relentless "anti-politics machines." They have to be historicized. One figure who attempted it more than any other since Afghani, Abduh, and Nursi is Ali Shariati of Iran in the 1970s. Shariati, although an Iranian Shia, quickly rose as a trans-sectarian thinker and modern philosopher and wielded widespread influence among the young and restless in the Islamic world.

## (AUTONOMOUSLY) I THINK, THEREFORE I AM (MUSLIM): ALI SHARIATI AND THE ISLAMIC THOUGHT WORLD

Educated in religious schools in Iran, Ali Shariati went on to receive a doctorate degree in sociology from the Sorbonne in France. After Shariati's return to Iran, his ideas developed in the context of the Shah Reza Pahlavi's regime, at once a "modernizing" force and a despotic authoritarian government. Iran's alignment with the United States and NATO during the Cold War era compounded the tensions between the modernizing character and the repressive instincts of the Shah's regime. Increasing U.S. support for Shah Reza Pahlavi deepened Iran's status as a client state, consolidating its authoritarian character. Opposition to the Shah increased in the 1960s and 1970s with religious clergy, the Bazaari bourgeoisie, and urban intelligentsia as the vanguard. In due course, the opposition culminated in the 1979 Islamic revolution that overthrew the Shah and catapulted Ayatollah Ruhollah Khomeini onto the world stage as an Islamic revolutionary who had come to head a state.

Shariati wrote in the environment leading up to the revolution but died before the actual revolution. Although a Shia by faith, his ideas resonated widely across the Islamic societies shaped by similar political-economic and discursive cultural forces at the height of the Cold War era. His intellectual vision appealed to many Muslims as well as secular intellectuals. He was as interested in a critique of capitalism as a dynamic yet exploitative force as he was in a critique of traditional

Islamic theology as a conservative movement. With ease, he enlisted the Western history of social philosophy and Islamic history of thought and theology into brilliant yet accessible political critiques of both. In his *Islamic Liberation Theology*, Hamid Dabashi calls Shariati's project the most "revolutionary" in its intention to make Islam worldly, that is, rescue it from nativism and renew its cosmopolitan worldliness without worrying about the West.[6]

Interestingly, in spite of his command of wide-ranging socio-philosophical and political-economic fields, to many around the world, Shariati is known mostly as an Islamic thinker. In a way, this is not surprising, since Shariati was self-consciously vested in his sociocultural milieu super-dominated by Islam. At the same time, his status as a renowned Islamic thinker, as opposed to a renowned thinker, sociologist, or philosopher, is a result of the Orientalist attitude in the West. Orientalism in the West still makes it difficult to see universal scholars in philosophers or sociologists who hail from the East—both Near and Far. The human subjects who articulate to universal conditions and themes beyond their immediate milieu appear strange in the Orientalist mind-set since universal knowledge is seen as a reserve of Euro-Western minds only. Such is the Orientalist conceit still at work in Euro-Western modernity. Of course, this conceit is not so much openly stated anymore as it is maintained in praxis. Insofar as Shariati is read under the rubric of Islamic or Oriental thinking or Middle Eastern or Eastern philosophy, his ideas are held in the thrall of their Euro-Western counterparts, which stand for the universal ideas.

Shariati is fully aware of this position. He is not particularly troubled by it, nor does he himself actually think in "thrall" of the Western corpus. Instead, he traverses both the West and the East, the Orient and the Occident, and reads them as distinct yet related, separate and overlapping, distanced from one another and yet also in each other's close historical proximity. He calls upon Descartes, Gide, Balzac, Nietzsche, Marx, Camus, and Sartre, among others, not in order to "center" them as universal luminaries but rather to relate to them Islamic political, cultural, and religious histories. His is a genteel reminder, that, just like the respective histories, European and Islamic ideas are intimately interwoven. Even the religious dogmas—Judaism, Christianity, and Islam—have been fellow travelers, if not coconspirators, in making a single Middle Eastern God into universal force in human life.

Shariati engages the Western tradition of thought but often pushes it into the wings of his discussions. It is as though he wants to show how it is possible to think and talk without relying on Europe as the center. Clearly, Western thought continues to inform and inspire him even as it remains in the wings and held in thrall of Islamic traditions. In this way, Shariati's work does not "de-center the West," but instead reveals its links with the rest. Situated in rich layers of history, in Shariati's discussion, Euro-Western ideas are thrown into relief, erasing the conceits of superiority and exceptionalism, and are made to help, not dominate, other sources or traditions.[7] Shariati accomplishes for the West in the Islamic Levant what the Afro-Caribbean writer Edouard Glissant dreams for the West in the Americas: rescue the West from its own conceit and captivity.[8] Once in relief, Shariati then embraces Euro-Western ideas as his own and does not reject them as foreign or un-Islamic. By the same token, he simultaneously treats some Islamic traditions (for example, as developed into Sharia) as strange and un-Islamic and challenges them.

It is fascinating to see how Shariati calls on Albert Camus' dictum that "to revolt is to become human" (I revolt, therefore I am) in order to theorize the concept of historical humanity in Islam while in the same breath assailing the sense of the human in the West as having already been alienated into an instrumental form away from the revolting political subject. The insinuation is that the Western subject has largely ceased to revolt. This idea is echoed later in Paul Virillo's argument that the Western subject has become a *mort-vivant*, or a zombie, unable or unwilling to challenge the dominant political-economic ethos that treats them like soulless machines, mere factors of production. Ultimately, Shariati is interested in "a revolt of the mind" in Islamic minds, not against Islam but against its official history insofar as it has imprisoned Muslim societies into a Byzantine labyrinth of power.

> What is needed is an intellectual revolution and an Islamic renaissance, a cultural and ideological movement based on the deepest foundations of our beliefs, equipped with the richest resources that we possess. In a word we need Islam. Only those who are the children of their age can revitalize the history of their people—the history which is fossilized in the past, is dead or frozen rigid, and has ossified the life of its society and prevented it from being alive.[9]

Shariati observes that the West has never given up religion, nor "reformed" it but rather distilled it into its soul as a civilizational source. "Christianity," he wrote, "was the cause of retardation but was transformed into a builder and energizer of Europe. Unlike what we have been told, this reformation was a not a negation of religion that created the Western civilization but the transformation of a corrupt and ascetic religion into a critical, protesting and mundane Christianity."[10]

Shariati embraces religion as a historically enduring force, hence as a kind of ideology, which has the additional force of mystery and magic. "Religion is an amazing phenomenon that plays contradictory roles in the life of human beings. It destroys and revitalizes, puts to sleep and awakens, enslaves and emancipates, teaches docility and revolt, etc."[11] In short, the history of humanity is the history of the struggle of "religion against religion and not religion against atheism." In an echo of Afghani and Abduh, Shariati contends that religion and reason inhabit the same spaces of thought and praxis. His departure from them is in the audacity of his voice declaring religion to be a historical orientation more than an ongoing divine expression.

> The history of Islam is a story of the contradictory roles of religion among various social classes. It is the history of the war of Islam against Islam and even the war of the Qur'an against the Qur'an. . . . Always and everywhere the logical and progressive Islam, and Islam of motion and movement, has been outmaneuvered and defeated by the Islam of stagnation and compromise.[12]

Shariati was not afraid of History—a dangerous attitude in the twentieth-century Islamic world. This historicism made Shariati an inspirational figure in both Iran and beyond in the 1970s up to now. In the end, it may have cost him his life too, as he died in mysterious circumstances in England. Many believed that the Shah's intelligence operatives poisoned him. He was quickly replaced by a similarly inspirational though not a revolutionary figure, Abdulkarim Sharoush, who too advocated "unfortunate" ideas that ran afoul, this time, of the Islamic Republic. He, too, ended up in exile, in Germany, and he too lives an uncertain life.

For now, it suffices to state how intellectuals like him and Shariati are not anathema in contemporary Islamic societies because intellectuals as free thinkers are not anathema to historical Islam. Rather, they have been made scarce or silenced under modern states in an ongoing collusion of religion and politics. In the past, the collusion of the ulama with the emirs made free thinking a dangerous occupation. In the present, a collusion of modern state form with capitalist class interests turns Islam into a specific Islamist movement, assigning voice and agency to some and silencing others. Who speaks for Islam cannot be fully determined in this way, but who can be heard as the voice of Islam can be and has been limited. The coming of age of Saudi Wahhabism as a dominant ideological stream is a perfect illustration of Islamic piety sacrificed to the gods of politics and capital in this material world.

## THE ANGLO-AMERICAN SAUDI WAHHABISM

The Wahhabi Islamism was brought into prominence in the Cold War era and in the geopolitics of oil. Its "islam" is not innocent. If it were only about religion, it would be tenable. It is not simply brutal and repressive toward ideas. It is intolerant toward Islam itself in the sense of silencing or banning Islam's rich, albeit discordant, history. It recognizes Ibn Wahhab the revivalist as the authentic Islam, yet violently negates the ideas of Islamic figures like Ibn Rushd. Ibn Wahhab's doctrine narrowed the Islamic horizons in the name of returning to the original Islam, while Ibn Rushd's ideas spanned the world in the spirit of the Prophet Muhammad's encouraging Muslims to learn from every corner of the world. In rejecting Ibn Rushd, the Saudi-Wahhabi puritanism rejects Muhammad's legacy as a messenger of Allah, most merciful and beneficial, and turns the message into an unforgiving ideology. It rejects history in favor of a story of existence—past and present—based only on a historiography of fear and fiction.

There is more to the Saudi-Wahhabi Islam than just self-directed repression. If it were only this, it could be contained and ignored. Instead, Saudi Wahhabism has become a global ideology striving for hegemony over other Islams. Contributing to its meteoric success has been the geopolitical significance of Saudi Arabia as the world's largest oil producer for the global markets. For years since the 1970s Saudi oil money has financed the Wahhabi ideology in support of U.S. and Western Cold War geopolitics. Mutual interests have suppressed feelings of mutual distrust or even mutual disgust. Saudis have gotten American protection and massive oil wealth while the Americans have secured a steady supply of oil for the energy-starved capitalist markets plus a political ally in the rabidly anticommunist Wahhabi Islam. The relationship has flourished functionally and institutionally in the global order from the Saudi role in OPEC and OIC to the Saudi financing of the Wahhabist Afghan Mujahedin against the Soviets as well as the Contra rebels against the Sandinistas in Nicaragua.

Wherever Saudi money went following Cold War designs, so did the Wahhabi creed as a theological anchor. In that sense, the Wahhabi Islamism is more "Western" than Oriental or Levantine, layered into the global political order through the Anglo-American hegemony. Its powerful Western allies help to secure its puritan ideology under the facade of state sovereignty in international relations. And in return, the Saudi state strives to supply the global system with an Islam that is acquiescent, emptied of its historical capacities for transformation and change.

The net result has been the birth of a kind of Anglo-American-Wahhabi Islam. Together with the Islamic Brotherhood, the most widespread fundamentalist movement in the Arab countries, Wahhabism shaped the countenance of Islamist ideals in the majority Sunni world. It may be accurate to suggest that had it not been for the historical confluence of Anglo-American material interests and Saudi theocracy around oil, Wahhabi Islamism would have been long consigned to the dustbin of history as a local fundamentalist movement. It may still suffer such a fate, as the efforts to push it into the wings of Islamic imaginaries have intensified lately. Ironically, these contemporary struggles against Wahhabi Islamism and in defense of pluralistic Islam were activated due to a monstrous Wahhabi-Islamist eruption in recent history—the al Qaida attacks of September 11.

Turkey and Indonesia are among the places where these agitations are encouraging political thought and praxis that are not afraid of their respective histories. Such ideas are leading to what previously had been unthinkable or only thinkable at the risk of one's life. Turkey presents a fascinating case. Arabs received Islam through conflict and negotiation as an indigenous religion. Turks stumbled upon Islam as they penetrated Islamic lands as invaders and soldiers of fortune. For nearly a millennium before encountering Islam, they had their own indigenous religion—shamanism. But shortly after the first encounters, they began to negotiate away the pluralistic deity system of shamanism with the

## TEXTBOX 3.3. ISLAMIC MODERNITY IN THE TWENTIETH CENTURY

| | |
|---|---|
| 1954–1966 | Sayyid Qutb emerges as the ideologue of the Muslim Brotherhood in the 1950s and 1960s until his execution in 1966 on charges of terrorism and sedition against the state. Qutb's *Milestones* advocating jihad by all means necessary becomes a "classic" among the radical Islamists. Saudi-Wahhabism and the Brotherhood's ideals reinforce fundamentalism in the Arab world. |
| 1945 | Turkey adopts multi-party electoral system. Islamist political movements support the Democrat Party, catapulting it to power in 1950. |
| 1950–1960 | Democrat Party (DP) era. Secularism eased to accommodate religious practices. The DP era ends with the 1960 military takeover. Islamist movements, working through *Tariqahs*, cast their lots with conservative parties. |
| 1960 | Said Nursi dies. The Nurcu Movement's influence expands. |
| 1964–1978 | Ayatollah Ruhollah Khomeini is exiled from Iran to Turkey for his Islamist and anti-Shah activities. Between 1965 and 1978 he lives in Najaf, Iraq, where in a series of sermons he outlines his book *The Islamic Government*. Forced to leave Iraq by Saddam Hussein, he goes to France in 1978. |
| 1968–1977 | Ali Shariati gives his lectures on "Approaches to the Understanding of Islam" at the university at Husayniya-yi Irshad Center in Tehran, Iran and is set to become one of the most original philosopher-sociologists. His work was influenced by Franz Fanon, and anticipated Edward Said's *Orientalism*. |
| 1977 | Shariati dies in England under mysterious circumstances—only two weeks following his departure from Iran due to threats against his life. |

| | |
|---|---|
| 1979 | Khomeini returns triumphantly to Iran after the overthrow of the Shah and presides over the consolidation of the Islamic Republic of Iran. |
| 1979–1989 | Soviet Union invades Afghanistan and the Islamic Mujahedin resistance to the invasion begins with Saudi financing and U.S. assistance. Radical Sunni Isamism around the Muslim world flourishes with Saudi financing and within the purview of U.S. geopolitical interests. Osama bin Laden recruited by the Saudi and U.S. intelligence agencies to organize and finance the Arab Mujahedin groups in Afghanistan. |
| 1979 | The Islamist General Ziya Ul Haq takes over power in Pakistan. |
| 1980 | Turkish military coup d'état; the Turkish-Islamic synthesis comes into fashion through the military rule. |
| 1989–1990 | The Cold War is over! The Soviets withdraw from Afghanistan in defeat. The Soviet Union collapses, and Eastern and Central Europe is liberated. |
| 1990–2001 | Islamic Mujahedin spawn copycat armed movements across the Islamic world from Algeria to Pakistan and India. Political Islam is on the rise in Egypt, Yemen, Turkey, and Malaysia and Indonesia as well as in the Islamic diaspora of North Africans and South Asians in Europe. |
| 1990 | Historian Bernard Lewis publishes "The Roots of Muslim Rage" in the *Atlantic Monthly*. On the cover of the magazine depicting the "enraged Muslims" is a fiery-looking portrait of Mehmet the Conqueror, the Ottoman Sultan whose forces captured Istanbul from the Byzantines in 1453. |
| 1993 | Samuel Huntington follows up the theme with *The Clash of Civilizations* identifying Islam as the new threat to the West. |
| 1993–2000 | American interests are targeted by a new terror organization called al Qaida—"the base." |
| 2001 | On September 11, Islamist terrorism arrives in the United States. |
| 2001– | Islam in the post–9/11 era: "Islamisms" challenged, Islamic histories arouse renewed interest around the world. |

monotheistic allure of Islam. These negotiations have been ongoing in Turkish culture since the first conversions, engendering a uniquely Turkish Islam, at once orthodox and syncretic. Between Islamic orthodoxies and Turkish cultural mores, Islam among Turks acquired and retained diverse characteristics after the Ottomans adopted the Sunni orthodoxy as the official Islam and imposed it vigorously over the Ottoman subjects. Ironically, the Ottoman official fervor in support of Sunni Islam spawned a similarly energetic opposition to hegemony of any sort of orthodoxy. Alevi-Bektashi ideals as well as Shia and Sunni Sufi tariqahs embodied the unorthodox movements. As a result, throughout the Ottoman era and the modern Turkish Republic in the twentieth century, Turkish Islam has been politically dynamic. It has agitated in light not only of Islamic traditions but also of Western histories in which Turks were integral players for nearly 700 years. It is in the vortex of such rich histories and overlapping destinies that Turkish Islam has been conceptualized and articulated.

## CEMIL MERIC'S SYNCRETIC PALIMPSEST

Cemil Meric, more than any other Turkish intellectual, embodies the richness of the history in which Turks negotiate their Islamic identities. His intellectual journey demonstrates the paradigms as well as the paradoxes and ironies of Turkish Islam. Paradigmatically, Turkish history with Islam engendered a broadly understood Turkish Islamic identity. It also accorded Turks a central place in light of the Ottoman leadership of the Muslim Ummah. Paradoxically, the protracted involvement with Islam brought no particular uniformity or clarity regarding the role of Islam in the polity. To this day, Turks remain arrested by the struggle to clarify the role Islam should or should not play in the political community.

Meric's life mirrors these tensions. Meric was a child of an era of turbulent transformations. He was born in 1916 in Hatay near the northeastern Mediterranean city of Antioch. The Ottoman Empire was disintegrating and World War I was in progress. His family had migrated to Hatay from Greece after the Balkan Wars of 1911–1912. At the war's end, Meric was still living in Hatay, occupied by the French during the war. Meric was educated in French schools, and after finishing high school, he studied French literature and language at Istanbul University. After completing his studies, he worked as a French teacher in rural Anatolia as well as a translator for the education ministry. During this period, he wrote essays for various literary and political magazines and began to translate French authors into Turkish. Among the authors Meric translated were Victor Hugo, Honoré de Balzac, and Emile Zola. It was during his tenure as a professor at Istanbul University that his literary works developed political consciousness, whether in translating the Western canon or in writing about them in the Turkish context. He developed an interest in Western philosophy, which he mastered during his years at the university.

In his brief autobiographical sketch entitled, "Leaves" (Yapraklar), he wrote how his early political leanings were those of a Marxist:

> I cried out that I was a Marxist at a court twenty-four years ago. It was a rebellion born of hopelessness, a sort of defiance, a desire to be left alone. . . . I wanted to belong to some community after spending my life amidst difficulties. I did not have class-consciousness, and faced with the cruelties of the real world, my dream world collapsed in on itself. How could all the injustices [in the world] be the conscious work of God? I went from having faith to suspecting the existence of a divine creator and from suspicion to non-belief and finally to materialism.[13]

The journey started anew for Meric when a student he encountered on a bus in Anatolia told him after trying to make sense of his work on French literature: "You are not one of us." Meric realized then that even his Marxism was without roots. "I realized," he wrote after, "I was declaring myself a Marxist, yet I had not even shaken a worker's hand."[14] With a sense of rootlessness in his mind, Meric's intellectual compass turned to Turkism. He read literature on Turkism, including the writings of Yusuf Akcura, a founding figure for Turkish nationalists in the early twentieth century.

His interests in nationalism and modernity compelled him to read further in European history, but also to look beyond Europe. He encountered India. He wrote:

> I discovered Asia through India. Asia as seen from Europe, through European eyes. What I mean is that my intellectual guides were still European. My first teacher was Romain Rolland. I looked deeper in European thought in order to understand the contemporary European civilization. Meeting Saint-Simon and Proudhon. Yet the magic was

> already gone. Until India, my word had consisted of several dozen echoes, all from the European hemisphere. I added the knowledge of India to my being. Yet even India was an escape. . . . I stood at the edge of precipice with the words "you are not one of us" in mind. I realized that, since the Tanzimat Reforms, the destiny of the Turkish intellectual was conditioned through two acts—[being] deceived and deceiving [people in Europe's thrall]. Not knowing Europe was catastrophic, but knowing Europe led to alienation from one's one country [culture]. How do we break free from this dilemma? I realized that as the society is Westernized, intellectuals have to be Turkified (in the sense of Easternization). I started work along these lines. Spinoza had died at age forty. Nietzsche went mad at age forty-four. I had found my way at age forty-four.[15]

What makes Meric instructive for our book, unlike many others in Turkey, is that his new path did not mean turning his back on all that he had been previously. Instead, he put the elements in conversation with each other. This turned out to be the brilliance of Meric in ways that made him an enigmatic figure for Marxists, Socialists, Turkish nationalists, ultranationalists, and Islamists alike. No single group has been able to fully claim his legacy. Nor has any group dared to actively disown him. His ideas traveled in all directions in Turkish political and cultural landscapes. His central contribution came in the form of a call to be unafraid of Turkish and Islamic histories.

He argued, however, that learning Turkish Islamic history was not for the purpose of constructing an artificial or a dogmatic history but for remembering the dynamic role Turks and Muslims had played in history and can now play anew without disappearing into Western universalism. Almost half a century before Mernissi observed that Arabs are afraid of their own history, Meric had sensed a prevailing fear of history, a rising antihistory sentiment, in the new Turkish state's modernization and Westernization drive. In fact, the Turkish Republican State had already invented a new Turkish history, called the *Turan History Thesis*, which built a modern Turkish identity on ideas of racial distinction and superiority. "One Turk is better than the rest of the world" and "How happy he who says he is a Turk" became the operative thinking for the nation. Islam's role was reduced to minimum in the stories on Turkish history, in effect, mirroring the institutional subordination of Islam to the new Turkish state.

For Meric, such a manipulation of history was unnecessary at best and at worst culturally and politically devastating. Along with a fear of history, it represented a fear of "thinking beings." "The monument I want to protect (preserve) is [this thinking] human being," Meric protested. His struggle appeared twofold at this point. First, Westernization is a total alienation if it is an absolutist project demanding social, cultural, and aesthetic capitulation to the West. For him, this is tantamount to a civilizational "murder" of Turks and Muslims as agents of history. It is not only a denial of one's past but also a denial of one's future since it commands a total civilizational subservience to the West. Second, the Turkish Ottoman and Islamic histories represent a certain civilizational accumulation that should be valued and affirmed. Wholesale approaches either fully embracing or completely rejecting these histories miss the point that civilizations interact, share, and learn together. For Meric, then, capitulating before the West intellectually as if it is the ultimate civilizational destination for all humans is against the very dynamics of history. What needs to be done is to relate/communicate the "thinking" Turkish and Islamic subjects to the West—in effect, to interact, share, and learn together with the West, not to be subsumed into it.

Meric was not immune to hyperbole in both linguistic and substantive forms. The flourish of his language aside, at times his ideas rely on civilizational exceptionalism that he finds so objectionable in European hands. Of course, his preferred civilization was Turkish and Islamic. For example, toward the end of "Leaves," he writes: "Turkish Islamic civilization relies on high morals and sacrifice. The ideals it has cultivated are more valuable than literature, philosophy, and science. I want to be the voice of this selfless (*mazlum*) civilization . . . tirelessly and without anger, for the real art (knowledge) does not divide but unites." These are the kinds of words that confused liberals and Marxists and confounded yet attracted Islamists and Turkish nationalists to Meric's works. Yet in the next paragraph, talking about his new book project, Meric takes back what he gives by promising to locate everyone, "Our people," the "Western thinkers," "the Russian Intelligentsia," all in the same cave, that is, "Plato's Cave."[16] Ultimately, Meric's work was driven by a desire to converge "our peoples" and "theirs" in the commonspaces of history to learn civilizations anew in the same cave. Even when in another book he wrote that the "light comes from the East," his was an invitation to such a project in the spirit not of a termination of dialogue but of a renewed dialogue across civilizations through active and honest thinking:

> Thought is a bridge, thinner than a single stem of hair and sharper than the cutting edge of a sword. Crowds cannot cross over. Countries have lived ignorant of one another. Neither Asia nor Europe knew each other. Al Biruni strived for naught to tell his contemporaries about India. Continents are closed off to each other. Even neighbors are strangers to one another. Each house is like a compartment that moves toward the unknown. Marx's mother did not understand her son, nor did Cromwell understand Milton. Saint Simon states that "the path to infinity is laid through the madhouse." It is a dangerous sojourn, the madhouse. Many sojourners chose to stay there with madness. Nietzsche, Holderlin, and Comte all quarreled with madness through their lives as if with a capricious lover—now together and now separated.[17]

Meric laments throughout his work that for all its wonders modernity promoted alienation among human beings. He offered "thought" as remedy to this malady, but his is an active organic thought that is born in the freedom to learn and speak through one's own authentic experiences without being slapped with various stereotypes such as backward, uncivilized, or barbaric. It is in this sense that Meric demands critical thinking from all in the East and the West. Condemning others' ideas, others' cultures, others' religions, and others' humanity has to give way to encountering others actively. Spurred by such an orientation, he refutes the charge that "conservatism" simply equals "backwardness"—a charge leveled against the Ottoman Turks, Arabs, and other non-European cultures in their preference for their cultures. By this logic, Meric contends, all those past reformers in the Ottoman Empire, from the Koci Pasha to Resit Pasha, should be charged with backwardness since they militated against their present conditions as being unable to conserve the Ottomans' previous accomplishments. In the West, he argues, the same charges can be leveled against Dante, who detested his era; against Balzac, who wrote in light of the two repressive forces, the Church and the King; and against Dostoyevsky, who was enamored of the past. Meric grows more rhetorical to drive his point home: "Dante is backward-looking (reactionary). Balzac is backward looking (reactionary), Dostoyevsky is backward-looking (reactionary)! Retrograde (backward) or Progressive. Freedom of thought begins by the throwing off the yoke of this vocabulary—thus materializes the freedom of thought and the honor of thought."[18]

Nowadays, he notes, Turks suffer from same affliction of thinking that they are backward. "First, they became ashamed of the Ottoman and Turkish history. Later, their shame turned into forgetting: 'We are European,' they asserted. 'Asia is a land of leprosy.' The European friends took pity on them and whispered into their ears. 'No, you are just "underdeveloped."' Our luminaries accepted this death sentence proudly as if it was a medal of excellence."[19]

It is through these ideas that Cemil Meric worked to perform a task in Turkey not unlike what Edward Said achieved in Arab histories. Meric recovered and re-sounded Islam without in essence becoming an Islamist or a fundamentalist, and reanimated Turkish history without growing into a retrograde Turkish nationalist. He occupies a significant place in understanding the syncretic and pluralistic reflexes of Islam *a la Turka*.

# CHAPTER 4

# Crossroads of Global Islam and Islamism in Turkey

Turkish Islam is storied. It has deep roots in the traditions of the Seljuk and the Ottoman Empires as well as in Turkey's modern republican era. Historically, two elements elevate Turkish Islam to a special status. First, Turks are ethnically non-Arabs. Second, they have nearly always occupied a distinguished position within Islam. Starting in the early sixteenth century and over the course of the next four centuries with the conquest of much of the Middle East and North Africa, the Ottoman Sultans acted as Khalifs, the highest religious authority for Muslims. Together, these dual elements accord the Turkish Islam a special status in the Muslim world. Moreover, two additional elements bear analysis.

What makes Islam in Turkey distinct in the modern sense is a third element injected into the Turkish political arena in the late 1920s, that is, secularism as the official state policy of the Turkish Republic.

Named after Turkey's founder Mustafa Kemal Ataturk, the Kemalist secularism has since served as Turkey's organizing ideology. Within the Kemalist legal framework, Turkish Islam has been confounded between the religiosity of the majority Sunni Turks and the draconian institutional secularism supported by the political and military elite. A fourth and historically understudied element shaping Islam in Turkey is the Alevi minority constituting about 20–30 percent of Turkey's 73 million people. Only nominally Shia in the doctrinal sense, Alevis of Turkey have long been immersed in Sufi traditions, and as such, have played a quietly powerful role as a natural bulwark against the Sunni orthodoxy. They also have acted as arbiters between modernity and Islam. For more than seventy years, an uneasy balance prevailed across these elements of Islamic heritage, modern secularism, and the Turkish nation-statism.

In the 1980s, the balance of forces began to shift in favor of political religiosity, catapulting Islam beyond the confines of private spheres into the institutional political arenas. The protracted power struggle finally culminated in the spectacular electoral victory of the AK Party (Justice and Development Party) in 2002. Socially moderate Islamist yet economically deeply liberal, the AK Party has since ruled Turkey decisively, winning two more popular elections convincingly and electing its own Abdullah Gul as the president of Turkey in 2008. It remains remarkably popular for a political party that has been in power for the last seven years. It continues to attract the majority of Turkey's socially conservative masses to its ranks. Paradoxically, though not surprisingly, for its consistent appeal to a democratic ethos and implicit anti-statist and militarist stand, it also elicits considerable support from the Turkish left intelligentsia. Its impact on post–Cold War Turkish politics has been so compelling that the AK Party has become the embodiment of the shift in the traditional balance of forces.

This shift reflects in part the dissolution of the Cold War, which gave fresh impetus to the Islamist ideologies around the world. It is also due to the rise of the so-called Anatolian Tigers, the new bourgeoisie hailing from Turkey's conservative and pious hinterland and wanting its fair share in decision-making circles. Coinciding with a full-fledged implosion of flexible capitalism around the world and the new "opportunity structures"[1] created in attendant transnational networks, the changes in the position and the character of Islam in Turkey have been profound. The changes have set the country on a course on which the future of political Islam is being negotiated. The course of action is laid through the interplays of national and global processes in revelation and reason, infinity and efficiency, and theocracy and democracy. Seen as a test case around the world, Islamic dynamism in Turkey contains elements both of greater pluralism through careful integration into the global system and of a possible collapse into parochial religious literalism. Much depends on (a) what the Islamists make of the new "opportunity structures" before them, (b) how the military and political economic elite negotiate and accommodate the Islamist desire for folding their values into the participatory democratic regime—an element that might very well mark the end of the old balance—and finally (c) how the Alevi minority reacts to the developments.

The Turkish case is certainly unique. However, it is also a harbinger of similar formations in much of the Muslim world. It is for this reason that it is closely watched as a possible model for inspiration and even for imitation. For example, a 2007 report in the *Financial Times* noted a widespread interest in the Arab world in Turkish experiences in democracy, pluralism, and Islam. Aspiring Arab democrats, the report suggested, are watching the developments in Turkey with both concern and hope. Turkey's neighbors in the region are not the only interested parties. Countries as far away as Indonesia and Malaysia display growing interest in Turkey as a possible model of a pluralist Islam. Conversations with Indonesian scholars and politicians, including with former president Abdurrahman Wahid and the former head of the Muhammadiyah movement, Amin Rais, reveal an abiding interest in the developments in Turkey. The Islamic Ummah as a transversal, that is, interactive social and political, community of Muslims became apparent in my own interviews in Indonesia. Large numbers of Indonesian intellectuals, Islamist and secular, have indicated that they study Turkish experiences for lessons, both inspirational and cautionary.

This interest intensified following the April–May 2007 constitutional crisis in Turkey, which exploded into the open during the appointment for Turkey's president. Abdullah Gul, a stalwart of the ruling AK Party and the then foreign minister in the government, fell short in his bid. However, the process was seen as deeply flawed, as it unfolded under the shadow of an online military press release expressing suspicion of the commitment of the AK Party to secularism and democracy "beyond mere words." In response, the AK Party called for snap general elections. In July 2008, the party produced a resounding victory in elections, winning more than 340 of 550 seats in Parliament. Gul was renominated and elected as the president. Since then, Gul has established himself as a moderate, staying above the political fray and striking a conciliatory tone in his public role. Anticipating the delicate, if not explosive, political balance, the AK Party, under the leadership of Prime Minister Recep T. Erdogan, has taken great care to solidify its secular constitutional credentials. Always carefully operating within the secularist framework and frequently appealing to the Turkish nationalist ethos, the AK Party has nevertheless revolutionized politics in ways unseen in Turkish Republican history. The AK Party itself has a fascinating history, with roots in the Turkish Islamic imaginaries on the one hand and deeply influenced by contemporary globalization on the other.

The AK Party represents a decades-long evolution of Islamist political movements in Turkey. In ways I will explain below, it is quite traditional in outlook. At the same time, it displays a refreshingly cosmopolitan and globalist attitude. More than the embodiment of an inward-looking traditionalist Islamist movement, the AK Party appears as a reformulation of the core Islamist ideology in Turkey, moving away from the traditional separation between the West and Islam, or between *Dar al Islam* (Realm of Peace) and *Dar al Harb* (Realm of War). The AK Party leader and Prime Minister Erdogan articulated the shift best in the party program in 2004:

> The central imperative for global governance is the recognition of human solidarity based on civilizational diversity. The dialogue between civilizations is key to a just and an acceptable system. . . . Progressively in greater solidarity following various catastrophes, humanity has been striving to produce and institutionalize common values. The countries that are unable or unwilling to integrate with the world, to internalize universal values, and to develop human rights, democracy, and the rule of law are being steadily pushed into isolation. . . . [In this environment] the preservation of indigenous identity requires not isolation from the world but coordination [with it] based on universal values. . . . In today's world, what is needed is the development of a global consensus around human rights and freedoms as fundamental values for all, with democracy as the indispensable political regime.

> Globalization is a self-evident planetary commonality, as is the common journey humankind is undertaking on this planetary ship.[2]

Erdogan's prologue to the party program, as the program itself, reads like a discourse on globalization theory and praxis. Globalization is construed as inexorable, presenting both challenges and opportunities. It creates fundamentally new horizons. Within the global juncture, for AKP intellectual cadres, the West no longer represents an unqualified civilizational externality to Islam. Rather, it is perceived as a transformative civilizational (though not axiomatically civilizing) force that also operates in Islamic communities. The West, as a civilization and as an idea, induces a mélange of ambivalent responses and emotions that oscillate between suspicion and hostility and sublime admiration. The AK Party's attitude has evolved to be less categorical since its establishment in early 2000. Paradoxically, the AK Party's own liberal evolution has activated more consciously Islamic sensibilities in the public realm beyond the traditional rituals of devotion. Turkey's secular constitutional regime continues to limit the political openings for the AKP ideologically. At the same time, as many observers have noted, the AKP's growing flexibility is not a simple function of external pressures and constraints but also a result of authentic internal dynamics reflecting the party's desire for agency in the broader world. In other words, although the AKP has not been forced to change and has not escaped the hold of the circumstances under which it has had to operate, it has also been genuinely, and largely unexpectedly, responsive to the shifting opportunity structures at the junctures of political and economic changes. In the process, the AK party has reshuffled the political positions in Turkey, where ironically it now appears as the most transformative and liberal force in the country.

Erdogan's words in May 2007 further attest to new thinking. In an address to the International Press Institute delegates in Istanbul, Erdogan chose striking words to define the character of Turkey as a state. "Turkey," he stated,

> is advancing rapidly to a higher level through its economic and democratic development and the historical reforms it has undertaken. As those who follow Turkey closely will know, it is a very different country than the Turkey of the 1970's, 80's and even the 90's. Turkey, thanks to the reforms we have undertaken, has become an economy

> open to the world, an open society. Using the terminology of the Internet, I call this a state that is on-line on a 24-hour basis. Turkey is, to a large extent, an on-line country in an off-line region. In a difficult region, where uncertainties and conflicts reign, it is an island of prosperity and stability. The Turkey of today integrates with the world and benefits from this integration, and also transfers these benefits to countries around it and plays a leading role.[3]

What made these words even more remarkable was Erdogan's claim that his AK Party was indexed to human happiness for which all else—democracy, secularism, and religion, is construed as instruments: "all systems are means; democracy is a means, secularism is a means. Religions are means as well. What is the aim then? The aim is the happiness of the people."[4] Erdogan's central point appeared to be that neither democracy nor religion is an end in itself but only a means to human happiness. At once situating the political discourse in an infinite field of humanity and diffusing all political differences into a search for human happiness, Erdogan reshuffled the conceptual canvas of modern governance. In effect, he asserted Islam as a mode for seeking human happiness, just as legitimate as secularist and democratic modes when circumstances warrant. He did so by presenting Islam not as an externality to *laïcité*, or secularist democracy, but as a collaborator or partner striving for the same ideal. In this light, in Erdogan's political imaginary, Islam thus appears as part and parcel of a democratic outlook. It emerges as a core sensibility in the organization of the fundamental ethical principles in modern societies though it is presented in a way that eschews any categorical public role constitutionally. In the indistinct zone between the ethical-religious public reason and political-economic public reason, Erdogan's imaginary quietly activates Islam as a deep organizing ideal or intentionality.

Two larger geopolitical changes in the 1990s undoubtedly played a significant role in the formation of the AKP thought in contrast to repressive, even terrorist, orientations embraced by Islamist movements elsewhere. The first was the ascent of the Islamic worldview following the collapse of the Soviet Union and the associated discrediting of the secular socialist ideology. The second was the slow reactivation of the protoglobalist religious and philosophical instincts in Islamic histories. These instincts had long been suppressed or rendered dormant under modern Islamic states governed by secular military, political, and economic elites.

The first development freed the Muslim intellectuals from the hegemony of secularist ideas. It also ushered in an era of uncertainty, a time of emergency in thought and conduct. Yet the emergency necessitated and supported the second development, that is, a resurgence of Islam's syncretic qualities in Turkey and in some other Muslim societies. In Turkey, these developments amounted to catalytic formations. Initially, the AKP responded to the historical ambiguities pragmatically. It managed to articulate a sufficiently cosmopolitan vision in concert with global shifts while casting its vision against the background of the earlier Islamic cosmopolitanisms experienced in Baghdad and Andalusia as well as in the Ottoman Empire. Unlike many who have been characterizing the increasing salience of the Islamist movements as antimodern and, as such, outside of modernity historically, AKP activists and sympathizers managed to frame a worldview that is attuned to the globalization of capitalist modernity, not outside of or against it.

In the AK party program, modernity is treated with nuance, aiming to resolve the paradoxes and predicaments of orienting the party's political compass simultaneously through reason and revelation. Comprehending modernity more as a process—modernization—than as an already finished product, the party program welcomes modern ways of life as signaling a triumph of rationalism. On the other hand, it also qualifies and challenges modernity for its "negation of intuition" (read: the sacred) as a mode of knowledge. This refrain is not employed to reject or displace secular-scientific reason. Instead, it is deployed as a philosophical debate aiming at the recuperation of the legitimacy of "intuition" as a source of knowledge—a different, not an alternative, source. The AK Party program draws on an astonishing pantheon of thinkers from the East and the West, from Greek antiquity, the Islamic Renaissance, English institutionalism, and French postmodernism. Socrates, Averroes, Rumi, Peyami Safa, Descartes, Michel Foucault, Alain Tourane, Anthony Giddens, as well as Václav Havel, among others, are called upon to argue that ultimately "to be modern need not mean the displacement of intuition from the public space. Instead, it should aim for a dialogue between reason and intuition."[5] In Erdogan's words, "Perception of 'conservatism' in the AK PARTY is: a modernity which doesn't exclude tradition, universality which accepts locality, rationality which doesn't reject spirit and the change without going into radicalism."[6]

Islam's historical encounters with the "West" inform and support the vision of convergence. Due in no small measure to overlapping histories, many Islamic intellectuals came to see themselves as fellow travelers in modernity's eruption into the capital-driven globalism. Neither a simple obstructionism nor an outright rejectionism defines their outlook. In this way, the AKP represents a continuation of the evolution of Islamic worldviews in which cosmopolitan movements had always been central. The AK Party's orientation works as a radical flight into history and the future simultaneously.

There is no doubt that the AK Party's vision is deeply informed by Islam and its history. Yet, the party is publicly silent on the ways in which Islamic history inspires its ideology. The primary reason for the silence is the constitutionally secular and modern ideological framework of Turkey that is poised to sanction religious political parties. In 2008, the AKP barely survived a Constitutional Court case to close it down on charges of antisecularist sedition activities. In some ways, the AK Party, which is the first "Islamist" party to survive a constitutional closure case, grew stronger out of the challenge. On the other hand, the consensus among the political observers was that the Court's nuanced decision was the final warning as to the "red lines" of the secular system never to be crossed. This suppressive environment makes the AKP into a curious political formation, which finds much of its raison d'être in Islam ideologically, yet is unable to articulate and own it historically. Therefore, beyond broad appeals to Islam as a spiritual anchor or a traditional compass, the AKP vision is stated generally in modern and liberal democratic terms. Its historical lineage in Islam is silenced while its Islamist instincts are referenced through modern imperatives of a global world and of economic interdependence.

Of course, the AK Party is not the first party or movement in Turkey or the larger Islamic world to operate under an Islamist umbrella yet downplay its Islamic roots or to appeal to Islamic emotions while it institutionally moves away from its religious base. Modern reformist movements have been at work in Islamic societies in the last two centuries. Egypt under Muhammad Ali, the Ottoman *Tanzimat* era in the eighteenth century, and the reign of the Young Turks in the early twentieth century are some examples. Similarly, individuals such as

Jamal al din Afghani, Muhammad Abduh, and Said "Kurdi" Nursi were leading intellectuals in reformist Islamic orientations in the nineteenth and twentieth centuries. Contrary to the general perception that the Islamic world atrophied intellectually in the previous centuries, the majority of Islamic societies continued to experience varied discussions, influenced by internal and external pressures, during the consolidation of colonialism into world capitalism and the ascent of the nation-state system as its political anchor. This new orthodoxy subordinated the practical force of Islamist movements and individuals to a secularist set of political deals that promised unprecedented material development and spiritual fulfillment.

## SECULARISM AND RELIGIOSITY IN MODERN TURKEY

In the new Turkish state, established in 1923, secularism became the official ideology, in theory disentangling and separating the state from Islam. On the surface, and by a considerable genuine desire, Islam was relegated to the private sphere, to languish as a spent force vis-à-vis modernity. The goal was to institute a "guided Islam" by consolidating all religious matters under a new department: *Diyanet Isleri* (Department of Religious Affairs). Although an ordinary political organ within the secular state hierarchy, Diyanet Isleri enjoyed full authority over Islamic affairs, shaping not only Islam's everyday administration but also its character as a religion in Turkey. In this way, the calculation went, Islam could be put at a distance from the state yet still be controlled by the state.

However, this logic proved neither fully secular nor fully modern. Its rationale as well as its method was traceable to some of the earliest state traditions in Islamic history, where an Islamic doctrine defined by the ulama was deployed in support of the state and in return the rulers promoted the Islamic doctrine in question. As discussed in an earlier chapter, the original deal was struck during the Umayyad era with the ulama empowering the Sunni Muslim rulers as khalifs (viceroys) of the community of believers. In the Ottoman Empire, likewise, Ottoman sultans appointed Sunni *seyhulislams* and, as a quid pro quo, they demanded their blessings giving religious legitimacy to their rule. The Safavid Persian Empire had a similar policy in support of Shia Islam, which became the official state religion and still retains its predominant status in modern Iran.

In the Turkish Republic, even as the state professed to secularism, paradoxically, the Sunni tenets inherited from the Ottomans as a state tradition prevailed in the Diyanet Isleri. Further, the new policy terminated the relatively pluralistic ethno-religious ethos that had characterized the Ottoman attitudes vis-à-vis non-Muslim peoples of the empire. Throughout, even as the Ottomans had promoted Sunni Islam and suppressed the Shias, Alevis, and various other Sufi creeds, their treatment of non-Muslims was informed by the Qur'anic injunction to treat them as the "people of the book."

To be sure, the Ottoman tolerance was calculated. The Ottomans installed an elastic yet effective balance between the Qur'anic dictations and their administrative and organizational needs in dealing with Christians and Jews across the vast empire. Their toleration of non-Muslims, who comprised nearly 40 percent of the empire's population in the sixteenth century, was as much by necessity as by religious conviction. Still, when needed, the Ottomans did not hesitate to treat non-Muslim minorities with harsher methods.[7] However, they saved the harshest of treatments for Muslim minorities. They tolerated absolutely no challenge from Muslim minorities such as Hurifis, Alevis, and Melamis. As discussed in chapter 2, from the sixteenth century onward, gradually and steadily, the Ottoman establishment embraced the Sunni orthodoxy of the Hanefi school. As the Sunni creed took on institutional identity within the empire's organizational and administrative structures, the Ottoman tolerance (*hosgoru*) dissipated toward syncretic Islamic ideals and traditions. Syncretic Islamic movements organized in Sufi networks had been the backbone of the Seljuk and Ottoman expansions in Anatolia and the Balkans. Sufism, with its liberal and pluralist religious orientations, became the primary target of the Sunni Ottoman establishment. This is "perplexing," as noted by Karen Barkey, because "the Ottoman state emerged at the cusp of networks that bridged heterodox with orthodox Sunni Islam and various forms of Christianity, and the foot soldiers, colonizers and early ideologues supporting the state were the Sufi Sehys and dervishes."[8]

The Sufi networks supplied an ideological anchor for Ottoman military expansion for nearly 200 years between the fourteenth and sixteenth centuries. However, once firmly established in the Balkans with Istanbul's conquest in 1453, and in the Middle East with Sultan Selim's defeat of the Persians and the Mamluks, which resulted in the capture of Cairo in 1517, the Ottoman attitudes toward pluralist outlook, or *Asabiyyah*, began to change. Sufism, with its "fluidity of movement" and syncretist ideology, appeared increasingly as a source of instability and thus a threat to the emergent political and administrative structure. Having assumed the leadership of the Islamic community (*khalifat*) from the Arabs following Selim's victories, the Ottomans adopted the Sunni schools of legal and cultural orientation ever more explicitly. Specifically, they adopted the Hanefi teachings, representing a less strict orientation among the four Sunni and lone major Shia schools of legal and theological orientation. Although Hanefist, the Sunni orthodoxy the Ottomans came to embrace was already dissimilar to the formative Islamic orthodoxies—both Sunni and Shia—that had given rise to and supported Islam's innovative Golden Age in the ninth and tenth centuries. Rather, the Ottomans adopted a Sunni orientation akin to one which al Ghazali had popularized in the eleventh century, which, having been further purified of innovative and syncretic traits, was conservative in outlook.

Given the overwhelming dominance of the Ottomans in Islamic history from the fifteenth century to the nineteenth century, this preference for Islamic conservatism proved crucial in the development of Islamic societies. In these three centuries ushering the medieval era into modernity, the Ottomans embraced the orthodox Sunni theology and promoted it until the disintegration of the empire in World War I. In this way, they adopted and refined the Umayyad formula of alignment between state and religion, where religion was marshaled to legitimize the state but remained subservient to it.

When the Young Turks, including the Kemalists, appeared on the historical stage in the early twentieth century, they inherited not only the conservative Sunni hegemony in form and content but also the ancient alignment between religion and the state. As the Kemalists began to create the new republican state, they relied on the same reasoning, albeit under the new rhetoric of secularism. In theory, the state and religion were separated. In practice, the state and religion grew intertwined in new and "modern" ways. Paradoxically, the resulting secular state was no improvement over the Ottoman arrangements regarding the rights of Christians and Jews as "people of the book." Nor did

## TEXTBOX 4.1. ISLAMIC MAHDABS (SCHOOLS OF LEGAL THOUGHT)

### SUNNI MAHDABS

*Hanefi*: Born of the ideas of Abu Hanifah al Nu'man ibn Thabit (699–769), originally the Hanefi School was associated widely with the emphasis placed on reason much more than other schools of law. It is considered a moderate school. Abu Hanifah left considerable scope for freedom in decisions in law around the Qur'an and the Sunnah. Although bearing the Sunni limits in theology, Hanifites have been regarded as representatives of free thinking and the use of dialectic, and have appeared tolerant of "interpretation of Islamic law." Today, this school is dominant in Turkey, Egypt, Central Asia, China, and South Asia.

*Maliki*: Founded on the ideas of Abu Abd Allah Malik ibn Annas (716–795), Maliki schools rely heavily on the Qur'an's text and the Sunnah and refrain from interpretation and inference in applying Islamic Sharia. Today, the Maliki school is strong in North Africa and sub-Saharan Africa.

*Shafi*: Following the ideas of Muhammad ibn Idris as Shaf'i (767–820), this school promotes a moderate and eclectic brand of Islam that tends toward the continuity of tradition as well as change through independent thinking, or Ijtihad. It employs analogical reasoning in interpretation. Presently, it is predominant in Egypt and Southeast Asia, particularly in the Indonesian archipelago.

*Hanbali*: Organized around the thoughts of Ahmed Ibn Hanbal (780–855), the Hanbali school is the most conservative and literalist of the Sunni Mahdabs. It is known for its strict interpretation of the Qur'an and the Sunnah. Originally, Ibn Hanbal's ideas were developed in opposition to the popular Mutazila rationalism and independent thinking. Most famously, Hanbal's opposition to the Mutazila claim that the Qur'an was created not revealed landed him in an Abbasid prison. However, under another khalif, Hanbal's ideas gained much legitimacy and following. The Hanbali school developed into the most puritanical and literalist tradition in Islamic history. The founder of the contemporary Wahhabist fundamentalism, Abdul Wahhab, was heavily influenced by the Hanbali

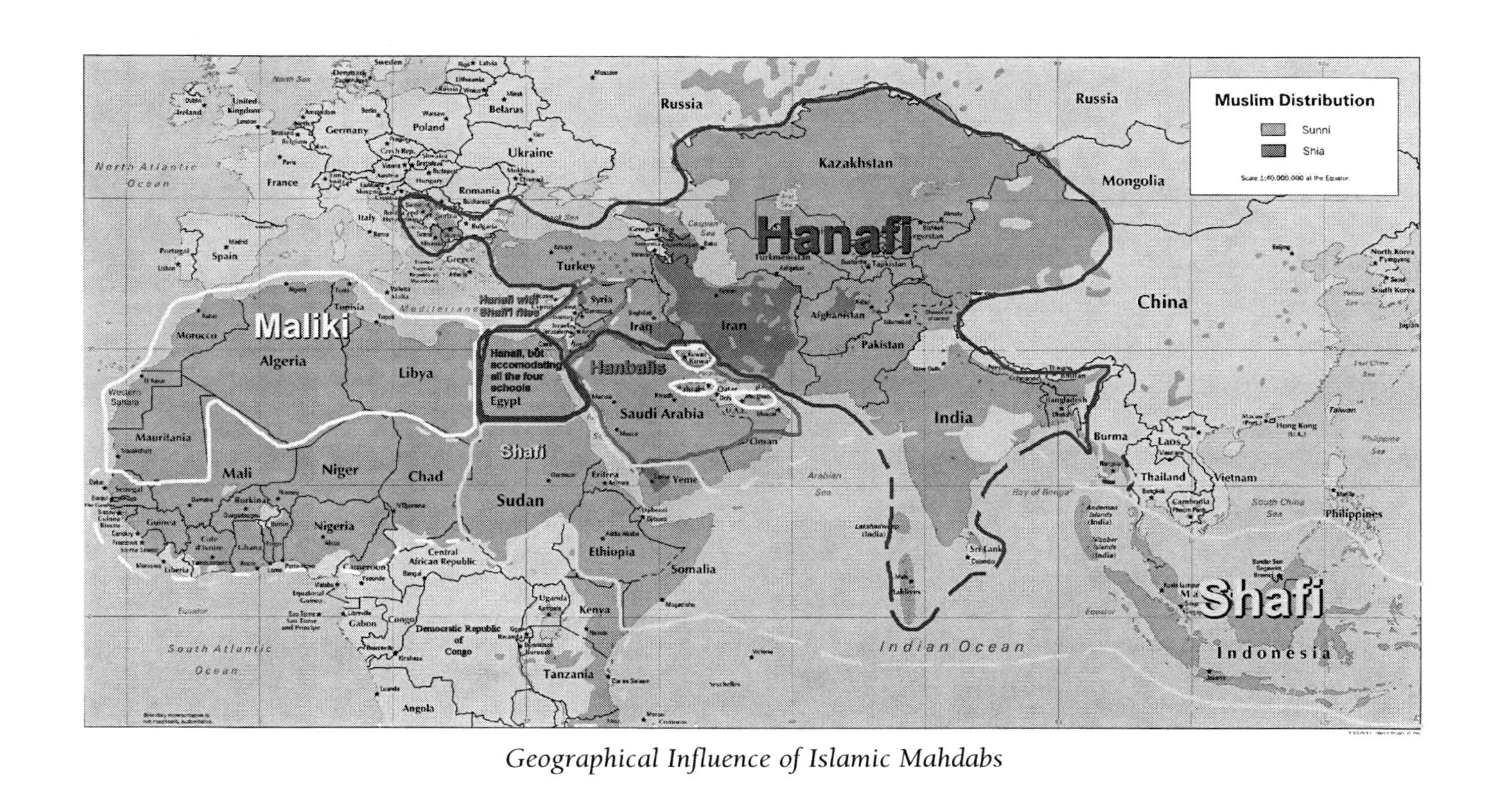


*Geographical Influence of Islamic Mahdabs*

position against innovation (*bida*) in religion. Today, the Hanbali school is practiced primarily in Saudi Arabia and Qatar as well as among the many Islamic fundamentalist movements around the world.

### Shia Mahdabs

*Jafari*: The major Shia school named after the Imam Jafar as Sadiq. In effect, it differs little from the Sunni Mahdabs in that it, too, considers the Qur'an as the first source of Sharia and the Sunnah as the second source. Its departure from the Sunni Mahdabs is found in its reliance on the interpretations of a succession of Shia imams who are regarded as the rightful inheritors of the legacy established by Prophet Muhammad and the Fourth Khalif Ali. Shia imams are seen as infallible and having the true knowledge to interpret the Qur'an and the hadith authoritatively. Jafarism developed its legal system through the Umayyad and Abbasid eras. It was consolidated during the Safavid and Mughal empires. In the present, it is followed primarily in Iran, Iraq, Azerbaijan, Syria, Turkey, Pakistan, and Afghanistan. In Turkey, Jafarism is followed among the Alevi Bektashis, though not all Alevis consider themselves to be of Jafari Mahdab.

secularism usher in an era of secular freedom for Muslim minorities such as the Alevis.

Under the new republic, thanks to the 1923 Lausanne Peace Treaty between Turkey and the Allied Powers of World War I, the non-Muslim minorities retained some religious freedoms. Muslims, however, became subjects of the new secular state. For the new rulers, a secular state did not mean freedom for all religions or allowing a benign diffusion of piety among people. Nor did it mean that the secular state would keep an equal and impartial distance from various religious orientations. In actuality, the historical bonds with Sunni Islam had the effect of privileging Sunni theology socially and institutionally while narrowing the political space for other creeds, especially for the Alevis. Time-honored habits of Ottoman statism (*devletcilik*) colluded effortlessly with the modern nationalist zeal for shaping a uniform identity, Turkish in ethnicity and Sunni Muslim in theology.

As sociologist Kadir Cangizbay argues, the Turkish Republican revolutionaries wanted to control everything in the new Republic.[9] Their treatment of religion did not escape this desire. The ruling logic, as Cangizbay put it, was indeed economical: If there was to be a place for religion in modern Turkey at all, the state would determine its shape and place.[10] In the end, these revolutionaries remained captive to the very choices of the ancestors they were so critical of in matters of politics and religion. Unconsciously or not, they fell in line with the Sunni orthodoxy as the religion for the masses even as they were trying to control its influence among the masses. Almost as if in a magician's trick, the new Turkish Republican elite promised *laïcité*, a separation between religion and the state, but instead conjured up a quasi-religious system that privileged Sunni Islam over the entire population.

In this way, contrary to the widely held belief that the Turkish Republican secularism repressed Islamic practices indiscriminately, the new Turkish "secular" state can be argued to have shielded Sunni Islam while actively retarding the development of Alevi and Sufi orientations. Undoubtedly, Sunni Islam paid a heavy price for its elevation to preferred status within the Kemalist establishment. In return, it was subjected to draconian controls through state institutions. It was deprived of a capacity to develop autonomously beyond the uniform one-size-fits-all Islam the Kemalists had in mind. Alevi-Bektashi and some heterodox Sunni Sufi sects and movements, however, with their informal networks targeted and captured by the state, either withered or went underground. While Alevis and Bektashis withered, recalcitrant Sunni Sufi formations that did not fit in with the system, such as the Naqshibandis, Sulaymancis, and Nurcus, turned to informal, and often clandestine, networks.

This was not an unintended effect but a result of political choices made to advance the modern Turkish statism-cum-nationalism. The preferential treatment, cultivated beneath the austere veneer of a secular modern polity, became manifest in the mass revival of the Sunni faith and institutions in the 1950s under the reformist Democrat Party. Ironically, the Young Turks like Mustafa Kemal, who may have indeed seen religion as an impediment in the transformation of the Ottoman Turkish society into a modern nation, ended up facilitating a stealthy Islamization of the state and society in a new political-economic distribution of Islamic ideals through the society. Distressingly for the

Islamic faith, the Islamization that the Republican secularism ushered in had a limited theological horizon reflecting the limits of life under an authoritarian and uniformist regime. It was as orthodox in its Hanefi theological beliefs as the Republican secularism was modernist in its zeal to determine the place of religion in society.

Clearly, this argument goes against the grain of the conventional claims about the secular nature of the Republican government. Although the ruling political and military elite would like to pretend that secularism took organic roots in the country, the Islamists maintain that the secular regime was forcibly imposed on a deeply religious people. And, as a result they rightly argue, millions of pious Muslims in Turkey still suffer the consequences, unable to freely practice their Islamic faith. The ban against wearing headscarves in educational and state offices is a poignant instance of the curtailment of religious freedoms. The truth spans both claims.

The Kemalist secularist regime was not a bolt out of the blue. A gradual secularization of the Ottoman political culture had already begun with the Ottoman efforts at reform in military, education, courts, sciences, and administration. Furthermore, the Young Turks' rule in the 1910s under the *Ittihad ve Teraki Cemiyeti* initiated a series of modernizing reforms elevating the role of modern scientific reason in the empire. As a graduate of one of the reformed military academies, Mustafa Kemal himself was a beneficiary of the earlier modernizing efforts. Not a devout Muslim, Kemal was nevertheless steeped in Turkish Islamic ethos and understood the power of faith in the collective consciousness of the people. During the war of independence, in which he emerged as the charismatic leader, he enlisted the support of religious orders and official clergy. Both during and after the war, when opportune, he employed religious imagery and discourse. Even as the secular state institutions were being created through reforms, Kemal never openly denounced the Islamic faith but rather worked to bring it in line with the modern nation-statist ideology in ascendance in Europe and beyond. That the Sunni Islamic traditions previously upheld by the Ottoman Empire as supreme not only survived the Kemalist era but also reemerged dominant following Kemal's death in 1938 indicates, if not the complexity, the permissive attitude of the Kemalist secularist orientation toward the Sunni traditions. In other words, Sunni Islam was handled with a velvet glove, albeit a tight one-size-fits-all kind, while other Islamic sects, including Alevis, were put under severe duress. Periodic Alevi rebellions between 1922 and 1939 were crushed ruthlessly and without compromises that, if given, might have supported an Alevi renaissance along with the Sunni revival in the 1940 and 1950s.

The point here is not that the Kemalist secularism was a renunciation of religion, as Islamists claim, or that it programmatically melted religion into the state. Rather, it linked religion to the state hierarchically, subordinating the religion to the state. The linkage was also a separation, but not an ironclad separation between the state and Islam. Rather, it was a "spanning-across." Ultimately, the state had to be administered, that is, peopled, by political and military elites. The vast majority of the Turkish elite have been imbued in everyday Ottoman Sunni sensibilities even if they have subscribed to the state's formal secularism. It is quite revealing that no more than a handful Alevis ever exercised high political power in the Kemalist state throughout its history. Not surprisingly, in the current parliament, there are only two openly Alevi parliamentarians among the 330-plus AK Party deputies. This is likely not intentional or deliberate. However, it is not accidental either. Instead, it reflects conscious or unconscious preferences and choices even if they remain publicly unstated. Nevertheless, from the founding of the Republic onward, the authoritarian nature of the Kemalist regime went without questioning. The single-party system, coupled with the charismatic authority of Kemal, who was named "Ataturk" or the Father of Turks, after the victorious war of independence, turned Turkey into a vast field of Turkish nation building and statecraft. Turkish history and the Turkish language were reinvented in support of modern Turkish national identity. The Turkish state borrowed criminal law from Mussolini's Italy and civil law from the Swiss tradition, and its constitutional framers were well-versed in the knowledge of the prevailing one-party systems of the time in Europe and the Soviet Union.

Following Kemal's death in 1938, this alignment came under heavy pressure. The discontent with the regime's desire to govern all aspects of life increased. The single-party system controlled by the Republican People's Party (CHP) began to hemorrhage during World War II. The first of the dissenters were not radical Islamists, but pious "free-marketers" in a state dominated by central economic planning, the doctrine of import substitution, and Soviet-style industrialization. Led by Celal Bayar, Adnan Menderes, and Fatin Rustu Zorlu, the "reformers" invoked pluralism as their philosophical call and found in Islam a productive ally—Sunni Islam of course. They established the Democrat Party (DP) in 1946 and contested in the first multiparty elections the same year. The DP won sixty-one seats, the first ever held by any opposition within the Parliament that had previously been a rubber stamp for the policies of a small ruling elite. The 1946 elections imploded the Kemalist alignment, introducing new actors to the political field, in which religion was increasingly summoned both as an instrument in politics and as an end in itself. The subordination of Islam to the state, although retained in principle, was loosened in practice to allow for Islamic or even Islamist parties to contest in the elections. More importantly, the religious movements such as the Naksibendis, Nurcus, and Suleymancis surfaced in the public arena.

These developments culminated in a ten-year rule by the Democrat Party, (DP) which assumed power in 1950 on the promise of freeing Islamic piety from the state's stranglehold. Beyond liberating piety, the DP delivered Islamic religiosity into the state institutions nationally, while internationally aligning Turkey with U.S. geopolitical projects in the region. Religion proved instrumental in politics. In turn, the Islamists recognized the usefulness of the state as a change agent for their own aspirations. The DP positioned itself in this nexus of competing objectives by appealing to religiosity. For example, it expanded the reach and competence of the *Diyanet Isleri* by opening hundreds of new religious schools and mosques and hiring thousands of new civil servants for the *Diyanet* offices in the country. It opened a new Higher Institute of Islam in Istanbul. Politically, it also employed a full-scale anti-Communist agenda implying that the future of Islamic faith hung in the balance vis-à-vis the "godless" communist threat. The DP government had the complete support of U.S. administrations. This close cooperation would lead Turkey to house U.S./NATO nuclear missiles, which were later removed during the 1963 Cuban missile crisis.

Throughout the 1950s the DP governed as though it were in a single-party regime. Many in the civil and political sectors regarded the DP's style increasingly "authoritarian." Most significantly, the military officers began to perceive the DP rule as unraveling the architecture of Kemalist Republicanism. In spite of the lingering doubts as to whether the DP's appeal to religiosity was an authentic commitment to Islam or simple electioneering, the military overthrew the DP government in May 25, 1960, and installed a Kemalist junta in power. A military tribunal tried the leading figures of the DP, and tragically three people, including Prime Minister Adnan Menderes, were hanged in October 1960. In 1961, the junta would promulgate a new constitution with both liberal and Kemalist authoritarian tendencies.

At first, the junta tried to resolve the tensions between the two opposing tendencies by anchoring them in a strong commitment to secularism. Ironically, it was the burgeoning commitment to the liberal democratic system in this alignment that allowed for the return of DP-era Islamism into the political arena in the first elections in late 1961. By 1965, the former DP supporters, organized under the *Adalet Partisi* (Justice Party) returned to power with nearly 53 percent of the popular vote. The electoral victory ushered in a new era of Turkish-style conservatism heavily mixing Turkish and Islamic themes and motives. This collusion, harkening back to the early Republican attempts at national engineering as well as invoking the Ottoman Turkish Islam as an inspiration, would transform the Turkish political space into a conservative cauldron in the 1970s and 1980s.

In 1971, the convergence became the ideological fodder for a right-wing military coup. The coup expunged the 1961 constitution of its liberal lineage and set the country on a conservative political flight. The military regime targeted the left, Alevis, and the Kurds. It hanged three charismatic leftist youth leaders in what was perceived as a "payback" for the hanging of the three Democrat Party leaders in the 1960 coup by the "progressive" officers. In the end, this conservative push fell short of its aim to engineer a militarist culture anchored in Turkish nationalism on the one hand and Sunni Islamic orthodoxy on the other. The so-called Turkish-Islamic thesis had limited success thanks largely to the secular-minded Alevi minority. Time and again, Alevis rallied in support of secularist parties, especially the CHP, which from the late 1960s onward had cultivated a Social Democratic left identity in the tradition of European social democratic parties. In the 1970s, Alevis, supporting this shift, nearly produced a social democratic majority for CHP under Bulent Ecevit's leadership in 1977.

Recollecting that the Shia Islamic revolution in Iran was already well under way in the late 1970s, the central role played by the nominally Shia Turkish Alevis in defense of a "secularist and democratic" polity appears even more remarkable in retrospect. Not only did Alevis demonstrate their autonomy from the Shia in Iran, but they also showed their historical capacity to act as a syncretist Islamic population in support of pluralism. However, Alevis suffered the consequences of their choices throughout the 1970s. Many Alevi communities were targeted; hundreds if not thousands of Alevis were killed in orchestrated attacks in Sivas, Tokat, Erzincan, Erzurum, and Maras.[11] Parenthetically, to this day, the massacres remain unaccounted for and continue to haunt Alevi minds. What remains implicated in the refusal to account for them are not merely the political choices of a republic that imposed the Sunni creed of its ruling ancestors on people who did not believe in it, but unfortunately the reputation of Sunni Islam itself, which, when protected from dogmatic machinations, historically inspired fantastic universal achievements and supported countless universal luminaries from al Farabi to Ibn Khaldun to Ibn Rushd. Whether or not the AK Party will speak out for an independent-minded Islam in Turkey remains to be seen.

As experience goes, Turkey is a land of military coups d'état. Every ten years or so, a military intervention rattles the political landscape, for the Turkish military by tradition and by the Constitution sees itself as the protector and overseer of the state. Three full-scale takeovers in 1960, 1971, and 1980 clearly established a pattern. From the 1990s onward, interventions took on softer or more "postmodern" forms such as publicly asking the government to dissolve itself or publishing a midnight statement on the military's website criticizing and warning political centers. The first of these interventions happened in 1998 and succeeded in forcing the resignation of the Islamist prime minister Necmettin Erbakan. The second attempt in 2005 backfired, ultimately enabling the AK Party to beat its opponents easily in the 2007 elections. If the so-called February 28 Soft Coup in 1998 managed to derail the rise of the traditional or dogmatic Islamists, the second subsequent so-called Postmodern Coup of 2005 brought to power the pragmatic and more democratically minded neo-Islamists. Those latter-day Islamists organized around the AK Party have remained in power ever since. However, the grounds for the rise of the Islamist wave were paved by the last of the traditional military takeovers in 1980. Those dynamics are worth examining.

The 1980 military intervention had a different impact on the developments of various political and religious constituencies. The coup proved no exception for the paradoxical status Alevis enjoyed or suffered in Turkey—a part that is considered and treated as a "non-part" even as it plays a significant role in shaping the country. For the Islamists in general, it was a blessing in disguise—again. Led by generals who claimed to have acted to uphold democratic and secular ideals, the 1980 coup nevertheless appropriated the Turkish Islamist vision in its remake of the system. The timing of the coup was of paramount importance to understanding its political objectives. It was an undertaking not independent from the developments in the wider Cold War politics. The global geopolitical context of the coup gave it an externally "predetermined" character. Filtered through the late Cold War geopolitical mind-set, the successful radical Islamic revolution in Iran, the similar stirrings in the Gulf states, Iraq, Pakistan, Afghanistan, and the Sunni Arab world, coupled with the rising tide of left-wing movements in these places and beyond, alarmed the United States and the Western allies. The ideological response introduced in Turkey as well as Pakistan and supported directly or indirectly across the Arab world came to be the so-called moderate Islam. Yet, as we now know, what was cultivated was "moderate" only in the fanciful imagination of Western policy circles. Instead, a rabidly anti-Western Saudi Wahhabi extremism slipped into the efforts and was imported to places like Pakistan and Afghanistan. Ultimately, it blew back on the United States in September 2001.

In Turkey, the so-called moderate Islam, suffused with heavy doses of Turkism and inflected with and practiced as anti-Alevism and anti-Communism, became the state-supported ideology in the 1980s. It recuperated and energized Islamist movements even as it professed to secularism. What it desired was a guided Islamism reminiscent of the deal the Kemalist regime had struck with a majority Sunni society in the founding of the Turkish Republic. What the state got instead was a feisty and recalcitrant Islamic "movement of movements" that had a more ambitious agenda. The new Islamic movement rapidly fueled numerous political and ethical-religious formations ranging from the well-established *Nurcus* to the novel *Fethullahcilar* movement and from the National Salvation Party (MSP) to the Justice and Development Party (AKP). The generals harvested more than they sowed in the immensely self-confident Turkish Islamism. This new Islamism took its cues from the rapidly globalizing world and sprinted for a greater authority in Turkey and a wider voice in the Islamic world beyond Turkey. In the ready-made universal culture of the Islamic Ummah, it is favorably situated to mediate the collective Islamic identities.

Ultimately, the AKP's strong showing in 2002 and 2007, so shortly after it was founded in 2001, owes itself to more than the ideological and practical work accomplished in the trenches in the Republican secular era. More than such a heroic struggle and more than a sudden awakening to contemporary globalism, the AKP phenomenon finds its raison d'être in the rich and textured Turkish Islamic histories as well as the Turkish Republican statism that unwittingly, or not, created the conditions for the AKP's emergence and consolidation. In this way, the AKP makes sense only in relation to a historical prologue in which multiple strands of Islamic traditions and movements, before and during the Republican era, inform the AK Party's vision and position.

For example, the legacy of Jamal al Din Afghani, the foremost Muslim cosmopolitan, inhabits the AKP's Islamist memories. Similarly, Said Nursi, who waged a postnationalist struggle for a modernist planetary Islam, deeply moves and conditions Islamist imaginations. The reformist Gulen movement, which traces its roots to Nursi's ideas, inspires AK Party luminaries governing Turkey in this material world even as they contemplate salvation in the next. At the same time, the Sunni orthodoxy expressed in revivalist forms across the Islamic world energizes the AKP base. The *Naksibendism* with deep historical bonds reaching all the way back to the twelfth century is still a powerful movement in the Turkish Sunni communities. Lastly, the eighteenth-century Wahhabi teachings, which have been exported around the world through Saudi petrodollars and tacit American blessings, echo in the AKP worldview. Finally, framing all these streams of thoughts is the Republican regime. Inescapably, its secularism imposes institutional limitations on the fiercest among the AKP cadres while also compelling them to expand their ideological horizons.

## LAST OF THE SYNCRETIC ISLAMISTS: ALEVI-BEKTASHIS IN TURKEY

A surprising phenomenon among sources that feed the AKP's rise is the Alevi community in Turkey. Nominally Shia, philosophically Sufi, doctrinally syncretic, and ideologically liberal, Alevis have always played a significant, albeit understudied, role in the development of Turkish Islam. Now approximately 15–20 million strong in Turkey alone, Alevism emerged among the nomadic Turkic tribes arriving in Anatolia in the tenth and eleventh centuries. Forming the basis of what later became the Seljuk Turks, the tribes that arrived in Anatolia entered into a world of turmoil. Already under pressure from the Muslim Abbasid Empire, and weakened by the protracted warfare against Mongol-Slavic hordes, the Eastern Byzantine Empire was losing its grip over the Anatolian provinces. As the tribes penetrated deeper into Anatolia (then known as the *Rum* and now as *Anadolu* in Turkish, meaning "mother's bosom"), they encountered populations, particularly the Kurds and the Armenian Christians, interested more in security and welfare than loyalty to an empire in decline. The first contacts with the locals ushered in an era of religious and cultural exchanges. The Turkic tribes, although recent converts to Islam, had retained much of their shamanic beliefs, as demonstrated in the Turkic literature dating back to these times.[12] The Byzantine populations, though mostly Christians, were already familiar with Islam and often chose to negotiate with it rather than to crusade against it.

Although activated through war and conquest, what emerged in these encounters was a mosaic of ethno-religious diversity. Islamic Sufi beliefs, mixing with/in pre-Islamic cultural traits with Islamic, Christian, and Judaic practices, boosted the cross-cultural and religious interactions. As a result, syncretic belief systems, already thriving among Muslims and non-Muslims alike, acquired greater currency. Among the large populations of Anatolian Turks, the Sufi heterodoxy was consolidated into a common stream known as Alevism, which combined Zoroastrianism, Judaism, Christianity, animism, and shamanism within the Sufi Islamic framework. Eventually spread throughout Central and Eastern Anatolia in the eleventh and twelfth centuries, Alevism came to exert significant cultural influence in all but the urban areas populated by the Ottoman ruling classes, the religious ulama and the Ottoman literati.

Alevism became a primary conduit through which the Seljuk and the Ottoman popular Islams initially found expression. For almost 300 years, the Alevi ideals informed the Seljuk and Ottoman "openings" in Anatolia and the Balkans. The syncretic-liberal Alevi doctrine was instrumental in assigning a social character to Ottoman military conquests. Beyond this, Alevi orders had an early humanist thrust. Alevism's broad appeal was augmented by its interpretive esoteric and allegorical approaches to scriptures—Muslim, Christian, or Hebrew—and by its openness to ecstatic experiences and rituals, such as to angelic cults. The radical pull of the Sufi movements attracted one Jalal ad-Din Rumi, whose twelfth-century ruminations today symbolize a distinct humanistic philosophy. Surprisingly, Rumi was not exceptional for his time or more towering than other Sufis, who inspired far greater masses more intensely than Rumi. Ahmet Yesevi, Haci Bektasi Veli, and Ishak Baba were among those radical Sufis who cultivated Islamic ideals into ever syncretic and nonconformist forms and are considered to have clearer paths (*yol*) and deeper understanding (*nefes*). Of these, Haci Bektasi Veli founded an order in the thirteenth century that shaped the Ottoman Empire. The ideals he collected from all directions and resounded and communicated anew in all directions activated and sustained an ethical-political thought system that is astoundingly pluralist even by contemporary standards. What is remarkable is that it is so without sounding heretical, un-Islamic, or even antireligious.

In some ways, this Sufi renaissance within the Alevi communities, which subsequently evolved into the Alevi-Bektashi synthesis, coincides with the decline of Mutazila rationalism and the traditional Sufism in the broad Sunni Islamic world beginning in tenth-century Baghdad. This decline would culminate in the trial of Ibn Rushd in Andalusia in the late thirteenth century. As the Sunni Islamic heterodoxy was consolidated in the Arab world into the Hanefi, Maliki, and Shafi schools, the original Sufi Islam of Farabi and Ibn Sina was pushed into the margins of the Sunni world. The burgeoning of the various strands of Alevi Islam afforded Sufism an existential refuge as well as permissive grounds for its own cultivation into a nonconformist and counter-hegemonic movement within Islam.

All said, historically, the Alevi-Bektashi orientation was negotiated at the fraying edges of the dominant state-society nexus in Islamic histories. It embodied the dynamic instincts of an Islam unafraid of pushing against the boundaries created in its name. It resisted the anxieties engendered upon the closure of the era of *Ijtihad* (free inquiry) in the hands of the Khalif Mutawakkil, who followed jurist Ibn Hanbal into the fold of orthodox religious sciences. Spurred by the shift, the aversion to ijtihad as "free-thinking" or "innovation" in all matters relating to religion suffused into state affairs to emerge as aversion to ijtihad on all matters relating to life. This aversion has since characterized statecraft in Islamic societies and has continued to pressure Islam's political dispositions in conservative directions.

Alevism undoubtedly inherited this dual legacy of openness and suppression. However, in part due to the conservative historical shift Sunni Islam embraced and in part because of the minority position Alevi ideas occupied in the Ottoman legal system, Alevism necessarily emerged as the voice of dissent in support of a pluralist Islam.

It is this historical position that makes Alevism instructive for critical conversations about Turkish Islam historically and in the present AKP era. Alevism has always been simultaneously inside and outside of Turkish Islam. It has been so both self-consciously and due to doctrinal exclusion or excommunication by the Sunni orthodoxy. Alevism came to inhabit this "indistinct zone" in Turkish Islam beginning in the sixteenth century when the Ottoman Empire assumed a decidedly Sunni-Hanefi identity in opposition to its contemporary rival, the Safavid Empire, whose Shah had embraced Shia Islam as the spiritual driving force. With Sunni theology in ascendance in the Ottoman establishment, Alevis came under heavy pressure and withdrew from the empire's public spiritual arena. They came to be that existential part that appeared to play no significant role in the empire—the part that was held in thrall by Sunni Islam, even though Alevis were not strictly Shia either in orientation or in aspiration.[13] Alevis were neither permitted to go their own way nor allowed an unmolested development. As a result, the Alevi culture gradually acquired a guarded character, a secretive existence invisible to the dominant gaze yet forming a mass movement in Anatolia. Marginalized, in the shadows, and threatened, Alevism developed a syncretic "Islamic" identity, forging together distinct Islamic moral-religious ideals. Yet, remarkably, it has always articulated its aspirations within the Turkish political imaginaries. This has continued in the AK party era in the last eight years.

Inscrutable to the Sunni mainstream but neither anti-Sunni nor antireligious, Alevism both challenges and fuels the AK Party phenomenon in present-day Turkey. Along with other indigenous factors, it is part of the reason for the sui generis nature of Turkish Islam, including the AK Party brand of Islam. This link may be obscure to those who try to understand Turkish Islam and the AK Party phenomenon directly, that is, independently of the development of the Alevi socioreligious ideals.[14] There is, however, no doubt that Alevi movements and ideals historically shaped, and continue to shape, the development of the locus of AKP identity, that is, the Sunni orthodoxy from which the AK Party springs. For example, the Alevi-Bektashi support for the Kemalist movement during the Turkish War of Independence was crucial for the success and establishment of the modern Turkish Republic. Ironically, the republican leaders subsequently instated a Sunni preeminence in the Turkish state. Even after being so disenfranchised historically, Alevis continued to support the secular state. Paradoxically, the state cultivated and exploited Alevi fears about a so-called Sunni takeover in order to regiment and control religion's role. Driven by constant anxiety, Alevis acted as a bulwark against both Islamic fundamentalist and Kurdish nationalist challenges to the state. Nevertheless, Alevi attitudes continued to shape the Turkish polity in significant ways. Alevi traditions engendered deeply pluralist cultural and aesthetic sensibilities, not only enriching the country's sociocultural fabric but also expanding and deepening its radical political horizons. Many of the country's artists, writers, and scholars, if they are not Alevis themselves, are definitively influenced by Alevi intellectual traditions. At once indicating their minority status and their cultural capital cultivated from the minority space, Alevi ideals stimulate popular radical imagination. Philosophically, Alevi ideas couched in political and social terminology of "just and equal citizenship" drive progressive movements, inspiring critical faculties among Sunni and Shia circles.

This is where the Alevi tradition is central to the AK Party and the broader Islamic milieu within which the party figures while operating as the governing party of an otherwise constitutionally secular Turkish State. Fully dependent on the Sunni majority politically and ideologically, the AK Party ideology is limited by the Sunni doctrine. Without challenging the Sunni doctrinal lines, the AK Party cannot redefine its identity along the shifting national and global opportunity structures and enable the absorption of modern secular ideals into the party identity. For the AK Party, Alevi traditions and culture create a flexible ground for renegotiating the Sunni orthodoxy without appearing to implicate either the Qur'anic or the Prophetic "truths." That the Alevi intellectual horizons are nominally Islamic enables the AK Party to entertain the prospects for a modern post-Sunni (read: post-sectarian) future without appearing impious in an Islamic sense.

The global crisis in the Sunni world in the post–September 11 era gives a greater urgency to the AKP to pursue a piety that is not fundamentalist, let alone reactionary in orientation. The AKP understands that in Turkey such a pursuit is impractical without engaging with the *open secret* of Turkish Islam—Alevis. Otherwise, every liberalization or democratic opening highlights Alevi frustrations with the political system.

In a purely political instrumental sense, the AKP may simply be aspiring to expand its public support by reaching beyond the Sunni Islamist base. Alevis are the largest untapped electoral group in Turkey for the AK Party, with the Sunni secular urban population coming in a distant second. Whatever the real intent, the more the AKP aims to solidify its base, the more it is entangled with the people whose subordination in terms of theology and politics remains evident. The more the AK Party aims to appeal to the Alevi electoral power bloc, the more this secret is divulged, revealing the privileges the Sunni tradition has enjoyed at the expense of Alevis' right to freedom of religion. It is a dilemma the AK Party is trying to negotiate currently. In December 2008, after several years of internal party discussion, The AKP party initiated an "Alevi Opening" with an eye on the local elections. The initiative promised to be more attentive to Alevi demands such as the official recognition of Alevi Cemevi (worship house), rewriting the educational curriculum, and putting Alevi Dedes (spiritual leaders) on state payroll. Alevi community leaders have been cautious about the initiative, neither embracing it nor dismissing it. The success of the initiative depends on the developments in the near future. Still, we can find some clues as to how the project might unfold by looking at the Islamist/AK Party phenomenon itself, which proved very effective in aligning the majority of the Sunni Muslims with the AKP orientation.

## PIETY INTO POLITICS: THE ROOTS OF ISLAMISTS' RISE TO POWER IN TURKEY

In modern Turkey (and much of the Muslim world) Islamization has first taken roots in the social or civil space via cultural, educational, and social solidarity organizations. The Islamist strategy has been akin to what Antonio Gramsci calls the hegemonic struggle for the hearts and minds of people, that is, the consent of the people. Instead of taking on state institutions frontally or directly, Islamist movements engaged in

## TEXTBOX 4.2. MAJOR DATES IN TURKISH HISTORY AFTER 1980

| | |
|---|---|
| 1980–1983 | The military Coup of 1980, followed by the junta rule that promotes the ideology of "Turkish-Islamic Synthesis" as a measure against radical-left movements. |
| 1983 | Elections held under the junta's long shadow. |
| 1985 | Turgut Ozal, a pious Muslim and a former World Bank bureaucrat, becomes the prime minister and later the president; Turkey embraces globalization and the neoliberal ideology. |
| 1995–2002 | Numerous coalition governments rule Turkey. The openly Islamist Refah Partisi (Welfare Party) increases its role in national politics. |
| 1996 | Necmettin Erbakan, the Welfare Party leader, becomes the prime minister of a center-right coalition. Political Islamism intensifies with demands that go well beyond the bounds or limits envisioned within the Turkish-Islamic synthesis policies. |
| 1998 | "The February 28 Soft Coup" takes place as the openly Islamist Refah Partisi (Welfare Party) is forced to dissolve the government it was leading under pressure from the Turkish military staff. The Welfare Party is closed down by the Constitutional Court and its leaders are banned from politics. |
| 1999 | Recep Tayyip Erdogan, Abdullah Gul, and Bulent Arinc, all former members of the Welfare Party, found the "AK Party" (the Justice and Development Party). |

creative popular struggles through which they repositioned the masses politically. In all of their popular and parliamentary activities, concepts such as "Adil Duzen," (Just/Perfect Order) were used to imply a range of aspirations from the introduction of Islamic Sharia to the founding of an anticapitalist Islamic political and economic union. Against the background of the structural economic crises besetting Turkey plus the political authoritarianism anchored in the Cold War geopolitical maneuverings, popular sentiment swung increasingly in support of the religious parties promising salvation.

The 1980 military coup in Turkey gave a concerted boost to the Islamist movements. Guided by the new American policy of creating and solidifying Islamist militancy into anticommunist fronts, the Turkish junta promoted a stealthy Islamization of the society. On the one hand, it banned the Islamist National Salvation Party and forbade its leaders from active politics. On the other hand, it revived and actively supported an Islamist/ultranationalist agenda under the rubric of the Turkish-Islamic synthesis. Garret Jenkins writes that the junta attempted the most ambitious political engineering in Turkish Republican history since the Kemalist revolution.[15] The junta remained in power for five years. It rewrote the constitution, and radically realigned Turkey's trajectories in a politically conservative direction.

The resulting policies devastated the Turkish left, organized especially among the Alevi and Kurdish communities, and shifted the epicenter of power to center-right and Islamist formations. The shift has been so draconian that no genuine left-wing party has managed to enter Parliament in the last three elections, with the political spectrum spanning between the nationalist and the Islamist formations, or as the political scientist Murat Belge recently put it, between "the right and the other right."[16]

The Islamist political and cultural movements blossomed after the military gave up power in 1985. They permeated the ideational/ideological arena, building and expanding an informal Islamist network society. Ever expanding, the Islamic network gave a coherent form to the society and distributed a definitive content flowing from a singularly authoritative Qur'anic and Prophetic source. The traffic through the networks grew in the permissive environment bequeathed by the military regime. In addition to educational institutions built outside the state's purview, such as preparatory schools and mosques, the social solidarity organizations, Islamist media outlets, and Muslim business associations, such as MUSIAD, together expanded and deepened the Islamist network society. What in effect emerged was a countercultural or counter-hegemonic political movement that is territorially associated with the Turkish Republic yet in everyday life is practically autonomous—transformative ideologically yet not separatist in intent.

## TEXTBOX 4.3. MAJOR DATES IN TURKISH HISTORY AFTER 2002

| | |
|---|---|
| 2002 | The AK Party (the Justice and Development Party) assumes power after an overwhelming electoral victory. Led by Recep Tayyip Erdogan as prime minister, the AK Party initiates a period of political liberalization, particularly aiming to free religion from the stranglehold of the state. |
| 2007 | The AK Party's resounding electoral victory solidifies its single-party rule. |
| 2008 | An "Alevi Opening" initiative emerges as the AK Party's attempt to reach Alevis in Turkey. The opening is met with highly cautious optimism among Alevis. First of its kind in its ambition and intent, its achievements are limited and its future remains uncertain. |
| 2008–2009 | The indictment of the "Ergenekon," a secretive paramilitary organization allegedly comprised of military and civilian ultranationalist elements. The alleged members, including former four-star generals, are put on trial in an unprecedented move in Turkish history. The charges include "conspiracy" to target and to topple what the conspirators referred to as the "Islamist" AKP government. The Ergenekon trials shake the Turkish political system to its core. |
| 2009 | The AK Party gives the green light to the "Kurdish Opening," which proves short-lived in the wake of developments aimed to sabotage the initiative, including a PKK attack on Turkish troops in Tokat resulting in the deaths of seven soldiers. |
| 2009 | Alevis agitate for constitutional changes that would grant them "equal citizenship" on par with the Sunni Islamic creed. |

The Islamic movements have been effective in the use of the various resources at their disposal. Particularly notable has been the rise of the Islamic media. Supported by the newly rising devout Anatolian bourgeoisie, Islamists acquired electronic and print media, which became the primary platform for the dissemination of Islamist visions in everyday life. Televisions stations, newspapers, and magazines controlled by Islamic interests relentlessly raise Islam's profile by articulating Islam's relevance to everyday life. Presented as cultural articulations and not as political challenges to the secular system, Islam-inspired knowledge enters into wider popular circulation. In the seemingly simple universe of questions and answers regarding dress code, dietary rules, and societal norms, a parallel or even a competing Islamist universe of popular and political governance emerges. This process has intensified since the AKP's rise to power in 2002. In what might be called organic Islamization, the AKP era has witnessed an unmistakable Islamic turn in Turkey.

Interestingly, until very recently, this "Islamic turn" represented something less than an "Islamist turn" for people in Turkey. In some ways, the AKP phenomenon and the Islamic resurgence were seen as a liberalizing shift for Turkish politics welcomed by Islamist and liberal sectors alike. Yet, the AKP era proved more complex than many had assumed. Already, some liberal allies, whose support was crucial to the AKP's democratic or moderate Islamist image, have expressed disappointment. Professor Murat Belge suggested: "the social sphere in Turkey is fully conceded to the Shariazation movement."[17] Confirming the observation, a new study released by the Bosphorus University in December 2008 indicates that the Islamist turn narrowed the political and social space for women, secularists, and Alevis.[18] These findings challenge the AKP's central appeal that it is a party for enlarging and deepening democratic pluralism in the country.

The AK Party's performance has been erratic. In some ways, it can be argued that the AK Party betrayed its stated ideal, that is, to merge modern democratic principles with Islamic sensibilities while preserving the secular constitutional order and without becoming an Islamist movement. The AK Party program outlines this project, which in many ways mimics the earlier efforts to relate modernity to Islam without sacrificing Islamic spirituality. The AK Party's inspirations draw upon earlier Islamic reformists such as Afghani and Abduh. However, an important source for the AK Party is Said Nursi, the twentieth-century Islamic Sufi intellectual, whose ideas articulated a counter-hegemonic compass to the Turkish Republic in the second half of the twentieth century. A brief inventory of Nursi's contributions is in order.

## BEDUIZAMAN "THE LIGHT OF TIME" SAID NURSI

Nursi was born in Ottoman Kurdistan in 1876 and came of age as the Ottoman Empire was splintering into various ethnic and religious subsets. Contrary to the Young Turks, who saw Islam as the cause of the decline, Nursi regarded Islam's gradual removal from the official realm as the reason for the Empire's disintegration. Moreover, he regarded Islam as capable of dynamic thinking and conduct. In his Damascus Sermon, Nursi contrasted Islam with the five negative principles of modern civilization.

> 1. [Modern civilization's] point of support is force, the mark of which is aggression. 2. Its aim and goal is benefit, the mark of which is jostling and tussling. 3. Its principle in life is conflict, the mark of which is strife. 4. The bond between the masses is racialism and negative nationalism, which is nourished through devouring others; its mark is collision. 5. Its enticing service is inciting lust and passion and gratifying the desires. But lust transforms man into a beast. . . . However, the civilization the Shari'a of Muhammad (PBUH) comprises and commands is this: its point of support is truth instead of force, the mark of which is justice and harmony. Its goal is virtue in place of benefit, the mark of which is love and attraction. Its means of unity are the ties of religion, country, and class, in place of racialism and nationalism, and the mark of these is sincere brotherhood, peace, and only defence against external aggression. In life is the principle of mutual assistance instead of the principle of conflict, the mark of which is accord and solidarity. And it offers guidance instead of lust, the mark of which is human progress and spiritual advancement.[19]

Yet for all these contrasts, Nursi was not an antimodernist. In fact, he alluded to the historical interactions between Islam and Christianity resulting in the transfer of much useful knowledge from the Islamic world to Europe. That transfer, according to Nursi, had been instrumental to Europe's rise in positive and negative ways. Referring to

Europeans, Nursi wrote, "they have taken from us our elevated morals and a part of our fine character that touches on social life, and they have made them the means of their progress. And it is their dissipated morals and dissipated character that they have given us as their price."[20] His anger was directed more at Muslims, particularly Turks and Arabs, whom he accused of "idleness and laxity" in the face of their duties to past, present and future generations.

> The Europeans are crushing us under their tyranny with the weapons of science and industry. We shall therefore wage Jihad with the weapons of science and industry on ignorance, poverty, and conflicting ideas, the worst enemies of upholding the Word of God. As for external Jihad, we shall refer it to the decisive proofs of the Illustrious Shari'a. For conquering the civilized is through persuasion not through force as though they were savages who understand nothing. We are devotees of love. We do not have time for enmity. Republicanism consists of justice, mutual consultation, and the restriction of power to the law. The Illustrious Shari'a was founded thirteen centuries ago, so to go begging to Europe in the question of laws is a great crime towards the religion of Islam. It is like facing the north while praying. Power must reside in the law. Otherwise, arbitrary rule spreads. The saying "It is Allah Who is the Strong, the Most Firm" must govern the conscience. That is possible through general education and widespread civilization, or in the name of the religion of Islam. Otherwise, absolutism will always prevail.[21]

Nursi's thinking was rooted in his grasp of nineteenth-century globalization attained in the spread of the British Empire. He wrote in 1912: "The world became a single city with the improvement of the transportation facilities. Communication facilities, such as print and the telegraph, also made the world population into population of a single place."[22] Nursi thought that Muslims needed to adapt to the changing world. Islam presented no fundamental obstacle to change. If anything, Islam and its divine source, the Qur'an, were dynamic and transformative in intent, not conservative beyond the commitment to a set of core beliefs and practices. Most importantly, he maintained zealously that Islamic ideals were fundamentally in support of freedom and participatory politics anchored in the Qur'anic injunction of those "whose rule is consultation among themselves."

Nursi thus elevated consultation to a supreme position when he stated:

> The Qur'an orders consultation as a fundamental principle. Just as the consultation of the ages and centuries that mankind has practised by means of history, a conjunction of ideas, formed the basis of man's progress and sciences, so too one reason for the backwardness of Asia, the largest continent, was the failure to practise that true consultation. . . . Firstly, belief necessitates not humiliating others through oppression and despotism and not degrading them, and secondly, not abasing oneself before tyrants."[23]

Nursi's thinking evolved along the shifts in the geopolitics of the Ottoman Empire. Nursi supported the War of Independence under Mustafa Kemal and was not an opponent of the establishment of a modern state. His earlier ideas about constitutionalism and nationalism offer clues to his support for the Kemalist line. "Since in constitutionalism sovereignty belongs to the nation, the nation's existence has to be demonstrated, and our nation is only Islam. For the strongest bond of Arab, Turk, Kurd, Albanian, Circassian, and Laz, and their firmest nationhood, is nothing other than Islam."[24] Nursi issued an ominous warning as to the nature of the modern nation-statism, observing that: "The foundations of an array of states are being laid, due to negligence and strife incited through the revival of the partisanship and tribalism of the Age of Ignorance, which died one thousand three hundred years ago. We have seen this."[25]

Nursi's tone changed once the Kemalist regime was consolidated and "secularism" became the official ideology. His goals took on a more Islamist tone in response, steadily moving away from the earlier internationalist Islamic reform politics to an Islamic Sufi philosophy—at once more elusive in meanings and potentially more radical in implications. Contributing to the process was Nursi's twenty-five-year internal exile at the hands of a regime that considered itself an agent of enlightenment and liberty. In exile, largely in response to the charismatic absolutism (benevolent dictatorship) anchored in the person of the mercurial Mustafa Kemal, Nursi directed much of his writings to a critique of rising modern despotism in Islamic societies in the grasp of European colonialism.

Contrary to the prevalent view that Islam is fundamentally antidemocratic and captures and flattens political agency, Nursi's metaphorical and allegorical writings explored the libratory potentials in Islam as he took on Kemalist modernism. Often, his incisive and politically charged commentary would follow a story with modern subjects including those alienated from Islam because of "science and reason" and those still guided by Islamic principles. Nursi would employ a simple rhetorical device to exhort his readers: "If you have understood the comparison, now look and see the reality."

A perusal of his vast writings demonstrates that Nursi railed not against modernity, reason, science, and technology, nor even the ideology of nationalism for subordinating religion to state. Rather, he saw reason and religion to be of the same unity, necessary for the human person's liberty. In his *Risale-i Nur* collection, specifically in the chapters entitled "Words" and "Flashes," Nursi decries the draconian ways in which religion has been de-linked from and enthralled by reason; where religion appears as "reason's servant" instead of coming into view as its spiritual underpinning. As to Nursi's disdain for nationalism, it is directed at what he calls the "negative nationalism" fashioned around "racialism" of pure ethnic Turks, Arabs, Germans, or the English. Nursi's idea of nationalism is rooted in the Islamic Ummah, which transcends "tribalism" and racialism," and in his opinion, is eminently more civilized than European nationalism. Nursi is particularly critical of "imitation" of European ways in the "Letters" in the *Risale-i Nur*: "You must refrain from succumbing to the stratagem of Europe and the dissemblers who imitate them. . . . Embracing the idea of nationalism, the peoples awakening in Asia are imitating Europe precisely in every respect, and on the way sacrificing many of their sacred matters."[26] Later he states:

> If nationalist patriotism is in effect to slaughter them with an immaterial knife, and give them the idea that "you are being impelled towards everlasting nothingness," and to transform the grave, which they consider to be the gate of mercy, into the dragon's mouth, and to breathe in their ears: "You too will enter there!"—if, while these unhappy elderly people want respect from patriotism, that is what it is, "I seek refuge with God" a hundred thousand times from such patriotism![27]

At heart, Nursi is an Islamist before he is an imam or a politician or a philosopher. Yet his horizon is remarkably inclusive. "Philosophy," he suggests as an example, "should assist religion and the heart, not take its place."[28] Likewise, he does not reject nationalism, but conceives it in Islamic terms as an integration of Muslims worldwide around Islam's core teachings. His choice of an Islamic nationalism is politically self-conscious, justifying within the colonial political economy—"the peoples and tribes of Islam are most in need of one another, and each is more oppressed and more poverty-stricken than the others, and they are crushed beneath European domination." Under these present conditions, he argues, [for Muslims] "to regard one another as strangers due to the idea of nationalism and to consider one another to be enemies is such a calamity that it cannot be described."[29]

In many ways, Nursi's thoughts are reminiscent of the Mutazila philosophers of tenth-century Baghdad and the twelfth-century Andalusian philosopher Averroes than they are an echo of the ijtihad-rejecting al Ghazali and the revivalist Wahhabi. After all, Nursi does not reject philosophy, and he allows for it a significant role in determining meaning and truth. This orientation becomes clear in his hermeneutic approach to the Qur'an that "the phrases of the All-Wise Qur'an are not restricted to a single meaning."[30] Paradoxically, in circles uninformed by history, Islamic or Christian, more often, his ideas are interpreted to endorse an anti-libratory, anti-intellectual dogma akin to the revivalist Wahhabi orientation. The history of the Islamist movements in Turkey is a testimony to the uses and abuses of Nursi's ideas. Especially revealing are its manifestations in politics formed in the 1950s onward.[31] I turn my attention briefly to this history.

## FROM THE NEO-OTTOMANIST "MILLI GORUS" ERA TO THE GLOBALIST AK PARTY REVOLUTION

Nursi's ideas were popular among the masses that brought the Democrat Party to power in 1950. Throughout the 1950s, "Nurcular," as Nursi's followers came to be known, laid the foundations for a populist movement. The already existing networks of religious orders were doubled as Nurcu networks. At the same time, Nurcu networks strived to build the material basis of their movement. They courted sympathetic businesses, as well as started their own enterprises. Tapping into the general piety of the people, both Turkish and Kurdish, they organized educational and social self-help networks. That they could deliver blocs of electoral votes in support of one party or another gave the Nurcu movement real power in the political arena.

Observers suggest that the movement was relatively secretive, which contributed to its success. Yet, I argue that Nurcu activities were more open than secret, known and tolerated by the middle- and low-level authorities who themselves not only had deep sympathies with them, but who also often owed their power to Nurcu support. Even more importantly, the Turkish state's secularist preference for Sunni Islamic doctrine cultivated receptive grounds for the Nurcus. The Nurcu movement's prolific activities ultimately engendered several factions ranging from the conservative Milli Gorus (the National View) to the Gulen movement and finally to the moderate AK Party.

Much has been written about these movements, particularly about the rise of the Milli Gorus movement under the leadership of Necmettin Erbakan in the 1970s. The Milli Gorus and Erbakan era, in turn, produced the AK Party phenomenon led by the trio of Recep Tayyip Erdogan, Abdullah Gul, and Bulent Arinc starting in 1999–2000. A lot has been said about the significance of the Milli Gorus in the rise of the AK Party, which need not be rehearsed here. Nevertheless, it was the Milli Gorus and Necmettin Erbakan that introduced and consolidated Islamist politics in the Turkish public and popular imagination. Within the Sunni Islamic population, the Milli Gorus cultivated an Islamist ideology as an alternative order called the National Order (Milli Nizam). Yet the "national" in the "National Order" was conceived, among other things, more along Nursi's ideas of an Islamic unity than in concert with the modern Turkish nationalism of the Republican era. However, the Milli Gorus movement lacked the broad liberal ideals Nursi and others emphasized in their ideas. Instead, the movement's ideologues picked and chose from a vast amount of work only the reactionary lines, without any consideration to the historical contexts in which the ideas had been formulated. Shaped further by the Cold War dynamics of categorical enmities and polarities, the Milli Gorus developed into an ultraconservative movement congruent with Wahhabist sentiments and revivalist Turkish-Ottoman Islamism. Its singular line of politics was based on what Alev Cinar calls the "defamation of the present"[32] shaped in Republican Turkey.

Just as official nationalism involved an assertion of a founding moment around which a national history was written, Islamists produced their own founding moment around which an alternative history could be written. The war of independence resulting in the establishment of the Turkish Republic is the founding moment for modern Turkey. The Islamists chose to situate their foundational myth in the conquest of Istanbul in May 1453.[33] The conquest, they argued, not only made Islam supreme in the city but also fulfilled Muhammad's prophecy regarding Istanbul.

The Islamist return to this moment well before 1923 was not a modern nationalist reach but an Islamist identity claim staked without announcing its religiosity. It was a refounding move, inserting Ottoman-Turkish history into the Turkish secular national story. This way the Islamists were able to shift the locus of identity to Islam without negating categorically either Turkish ethnicity or Turkish nationalism. Yet as Cinar, too, argued, the distance established between the Turkish Republic and Islamic identity is a form of rejection of the present of republican Turkey in preference for another one altogether. This new present established a chain of references reaching from the Prophetic dream of the conquest of Istanbul through the dream's realization by the Ottoman Turks to Milli Gorus's capture of the Istanbul mayoralty as a reaffirmation.

While tactically a brilliant strategy, ideologically such a formulation proved a poor substitute for an ordering thought in contemporary politics. Nor was it able to exceed the dominant literalism emanating from the Arab world, particularly through the writings of Sayyid Qutb and others. Moreover, it was articulated exclusively as a Sunni discourse and in tacit opposition to Alevi sensibilities. Alevis in turn militated against the Milli Gorus by supporting left and secularist parties. As a result, lines of religio-ideological battles were sharpened, with a succession of Milli Gorus parties such as the Milli Selamet, Fazilet, and Saadet Parties embracing revivalist orientations. Remarkably, these parties, as with the broad Islamist movements they represented, were in part controlled and cultivated in the Turkish republican ideological environment. The control was enacted in cultivation and cultivation necessitated new modes of limitation ranging from actively guiding the trajectories of Islamism to outright bans on movements that went too far. The collapse of the Milli Gorus conservatism attests to this dynamic. When in 1998, the Fazilet Party intensified its drive for Islamism, it was forced out of power in what was called the 28 February Soft Coup. When the Turkish military and political elite accused the party of being a threat to the secular constitutional system, the Fazilet Party simply had to let go the reins. With the limits of allowable politics thus recast and the opportunity structures reordered, the grounds for the AK Party's entry into the political arena were prepared. Coming on the heels of the September 11 attacks in the United States, a moderate Islamist party as an antidote to the virulence of others in Turkey and beyond looked more and more tolerable, even desirable.

There is much speculation yet little evidence that attributes the AKP's rise to power to U.S. influence or interference in Turkish politics. Many point to a very public meeting at the White House between Erdogan and President George W. Bush in 2001 when Erdogan was still banned from politics. An honor often reserved for heads of state, the White House meeting marked the beginning of a mutually beneficial relationship between the United States and the AKP. Whatever the "secrets" involving the meeting, U.S. support for the AKP has been strong throughout AKP's tenure as the governing party. While it is speculative to talk about the terms of understanding between the two sides beyond those shared in public, it is also speculative and unfair to suggest that the AKP has "sold out" to the United States for its own electoral interests. Clearly, a more reliable indicator of the AKP's intentions is the policy pursued internally and abroad. On both fronts, there is no doubt that the AKP has broken from the conservative Milli Gorus ideology. Although the party is still home to many Milli Gorus activists, its leadership has been decidedly neo-Islamist in that it reads the world in more accommodationist and integrationist terms than through a clash of civilizations lens.

The party leadership and the majority of its cadre are more globalist, that is, very well aware that the world is an economically interdependent place. They are also cognizant that cultures, however pious, have to learn to live with globalization's consequences in order to prosper and develop. In part, this ideological shift is a function of the expansion of Anatolian capitalism beyond Turkey's boundaries. Generally conservative by sociocultural disposition, the Anatolian bourgeoisie nevertheless proved adept as they expanded their operations and markets into the Balkans, the former Soviet Republics, and the Middle East. In turn, they supported a shift in political consciousness of the bureaucratic elites, especially at the level of municipalities. It is useful to recollect that Erdogan was the mayor of Istanbul, the largest and economically the most powerful city in Turkey, before he switched to national politics. He, like many AKP politicians, was trained in local politics where he came into contact with and became friends with Anatolian capitalists. Anatolian capitalists, at once increasing in numbers yet still marginal to the state-supported traditional Turkish industrial capitalist class, befriended them back both economically and politically. The support from these circles helps to explain the rise of the AKP as the so-called moderate Islamist party, with which national and global capital could work and which the United States and the West did not need to fear in the post–September 11 era. One could characterize all these developments as a perfect storm that carried the AKP to power.

It is important, however, to be wary of an economic reductionism that attributes most or all of the developments to the shifting alignments of economic forces in Turkey. Certainly, underlying cultural, social, and religious factors played a significant role in the changes. Additionally, geopolitical externalities in the 1970s and 1980s after the military coups also changed the opportunity structures for Islamic-minded politicians. Above all, factors indigenous to historical Islam were crucial in the transformation of thinking as to what Islam is and how it ought to be lived. Among the forces very much energized by Islam's own dynamics were the diverse struggles over philosophy, theology, science, and arts, which I discussed in Chapter 2. These discussions existed since Islam's birth. They grew particularly intense during the nineteenth- and twentieth-century colonial incorporation of the Muslim world into the Western sphere of influence. They reached a climax through Cold War geopolitics and finally exploded into the open with a renewed sense of urgency after the September 11 attacks. Ordinary Muslims around the world began to participate in debates that were previously the preserve of university scholars on the one hand and religious despots and militants on the other hand. New discourses proliferated across Islamic societies, including in Indonesia and Turkey, in ways that are reminiscent of the creative chaos of competing ideas in the early Islamic era.

The new globalism, which promotes novel links and connections across people and places, is doing for today's Muslims what early Islamic cosmopolitanism did for their Muslim ancestors some one thousand years ago: expose them to the sheer differences of the world and compel them to accommodate that world. In Said Nursi's paraphrased words, "Make Islam read the universe anew under conditions not necessarily favorable it its adherents." The cosmopolitanism of Islam in the eighth through the twelfth centuries represented Islamic experiences from the vantage of point of strength and confidence. They hailed from within the empires that ruled much of the known world while actively also learning from various peoples and cultures. Contemporary Muslims in Turkey, Indonesia, and beyond realize that the globalism of which they are inexorably a part is led by a different source, that is, by the West. This time they must learn cosmopolitanism from the vantage point of a relatively vulnerable economic and political position. Yet, this position is not subservience, as in a master-slave relationship. It is not disappearance into the West's cultural or social infinity. Rather, it is deference to knowledge and wisdom no matter the source or the origin, as the Prophet Muhammad stated. What I think attracts Muslims to the new globalism is the realization that historically Levantine Islam and the Christian West have evolved together, even when and if in opposition to each other, and they were thus constitutive of each other's identities. This reading, this sentiment, is found in the AKP ideology as expressed in the party's manifesto as well as in the speeches of the party leaders. The AKP ideology is equally shaped by an economic liberalism of a conservative variety not unlike the Christian Democrats in Germany, for example, or the Tories in England or the Republicans in the United States. Above all, its ideology is materialist while evoking sentimental piety rooted in primarily Islam and secondarily in universal monotheism.

## THE GULEN MOVEMENT'S GLOBAL REACH

Programmatically and sentimentally, the AKP ideology has its echoes in a movement with a meteoric rise in the last two decades. I am referring to the Gulen movement, led by Fethullah Gulen, a Turkish devotee of Said Nursi. The Gulen movement was born in Turkey in the same regimented yet permissive republican grounds. It is now a movement with global reach in that it operates various educational and economic enterprises in Muslim and non-Muslim countries around the world. I was therefore not surprised to see an international Gulen school in the outskirts of Jakarta, Indonesia, in 2008. Gulen educational institutions are active in Turkey, Central Asia, Southeast Asia, Russia, and the Balkans. In Turkey, it operates hundreds of schools, including universities. It has a network of media organizations, ranging from Turkey's largest circulation daily newspaper, *Zaman*, to television stations like Samanyolu and Ebru TV in the United States and magazines such as *Aksiyon* and *Sizinti*. It runs hospitals and social solidarity networks as well as student hostels, which are of paramount importance to the movement. The movement is financed by the businesses owned or operated by people with ideological sympathy to the Gulen organization. An estimated $10–15 billion worth of capital is within the Gulen movement's orbit of influence. A lot has been written on these aspects in both alarmist and effusive ways. Instead of revisiting those arguments, I want to examine the ideas that animate the movement.

Fethullah Gulen is the embodiment of the movement's core ideas. Although once a preacher on the government dole, over the years, Gulen developed his independent following within the concentric circles of Sufi movements in Turkey. However, by his own admission Gulen was not a Sufi himself and belonged to no movement. Yet, he was deeply moved by Said Nursi's ideas. While he refuses to characterize the Gulen movement as a Sufi movement, he readily expresses his admiration for Nursi and regularly invokes Nursi's words in his lectures and sermons. Never a fiery preacher yet a passionate orator, Gulen's knowledgeable and articulate charisma is riveting for his followers, as evidenced in the televised responses to his sermons. Crucially, what makes Gulen a spokesperson for the "moderate" kind of Islam the AK Party is associated with is the ideal of "tolerance" advocated in facing existential differences in the world. Harkening all the way back to the Medina Constitution of the time of Prophet Muhammad, this theme permeates Gulen's rhetoric through and through on every topic. He writes:

> When we mean tolerance, dialogue, respect for everyone, to accept everyone with their positions, we are voicing Prophet Mohammed's (peace be upon him) Medina Document and declaring the realities he expressed in the Farewell Sermon. Hence, we fulfill our obligations and duties. Those who dealt with the issue before us might have been mistaken at this point and walked in a different route through both internal and external reasons and fair or unfair causes. We do not care

about them. If we can, we should fulfill our obligations. Pay attention to the fact that I say obligation and duty. Therefore, do not consider this a virtue. Do not wait for things incumbent upon virtue.[34]

Tolerance as a core ideal works to make possible Gulen's support for economic and political liberalism, including market capitalism and democracy. Democracy emerges as a perfectly acceptable system of governance insofar as it enables the animation of values and objectives Islam, and for that matter Christianity or Judaism, holds dear. Hear Gulen:

When comparing religion or Islam with democracy, we must remember that democracy is a system that is being continually developed and revised. It also varies according to the places and circumstances where it is practiced. On the other hand, religion has established immutable principles related to faith, worship and morality. Thus, only Islam's worldly aspects should be compared with democracy. The main aim of Islam and its unchangeable dimensions affect its rules governing the changeable aspects of our lives. Islam does not propose a certain unchangeable form of government or attempt to shape it. Instead, Islam establishes fundamental principles that orient a government's general character, leaving it to the people to choose the type and form of government according to time and circumstances. If we approach the matter in this light and compare Islam with today's modern liberal democracy, we will better understand the position of Islam and democracy with respect to each other.[35]

Gulen is quick to suggest that this is not instrumentalizing democracy for the purpose of theocracy. He has no interest, he argues, in establishing an Islamic state, for Islam, shaped for a state, in the service of the state, loses its divinity and becomes un-Islamic—possibly a source of oppression:

As Islam holds individuals and societies responsible for their own fate, people must be responsible for governing themselves. The Qur'an addresses society with such phrases as: "O people!" and "O believers!" The duties entrusted to modern democratic systems are those that Islam refers to society and classifies, in order of importance, as "absolutely necessary, relatively necessary, and commendable to carry out." The sacred text includes the following passages: "Establish, all of you, peace" (2:208); "spend in the way of God and to the needy of the pure and good of what you have earned and of what We bring forth for you from earth" (2:267); "if some among your women are accused of indecency, you must have four witnesses [to prove it]" (4:15); "God commands you to give over the public trusts to the charge of those having the required qualities and to judge with justice when you judge between people" (4:58); "observe justice as witnesses respectful for God even if it is against yourselves, your parents and relatives" (4:135); "if they [your enemies] incline to peace [when you are at war], you also incline to it" (8:61); "if a corrupt, sinful one brings you news [about others], investigate it so that you should not strike a people without knowing" (49:6); "if two parties among the believers fight between themselves, reconcile them" (49:9). To sum up, the Qur'an addresses the whole community and assigns it almost all the duties entrusted to modern democratic systems.[36]

Overall, the Gulen movement presents a relentlessly democratic countenance in public discourses. Gulen himself always deploys idioms of pluralism in politics and religion while defending Islam as the privileged source of inspiration at an equal footing with other religious traditions. His main point appears always to be that there is enough room for piety and politics in the world in all their different expressions. The definitive behavior in such a world is ethically self-conscious interactions that enable people to live their ideals while also shaping their overlapping futures together. The Gulen movement's attitude toward Turkey's EU membership is suggestive in this sense, particularly when the Milli Gorus movement has nearly always argued against Turkey's joining of the EU. In an interview Gulen himself addressed the issue:

Some people perceive the joining of Turkey into the EU as an invasion. The foreigners will come and invade our lands. If such thoughts arise from national concerns, we may argue that our national values have blended with our soul to the extent that we cannot tolerate any compromises. As long as they (Europe) accept us as we are, then we can be together; we respect them as they are with their values. If the concern is that our religious values will be devastated [we must remember that], our nation has overcome so many obstacles. We have suffered more than any other nation in the region . . . poverty, remaining aloof to our values, lost identity. Despite all these, thankfully today, we can see that 80-90% of our nation is still firmly attached to its history and the roots of soul and meaning. During the time of the Common Market and the later Customs Union I was always sure and am still sure that our nation would not compromise either their national or their religious values. I am not worried that we are about to lose our lands."[37]

For all his globalist posture, Gulen remains true to the conservative Turkish Islamic synthesis in several respects. Two elements are indispensable to this synthesis. The first is ethno-nationalist, assigning a special role to Turks in Islamic history. The second is sectarian, situating Turkish Islam exclusively in the Sunni traditions. Gulen retains both commitments, and because of that, his attempts to exceed certain theological limitations inhering in fundamentalist movements are compromised. For example, Gulen identifies "tolerance as a responsibility and a duty for Muslims, and not simply a virtue due to its scarcity." Yet when pressed, his Turkish and Sunni-Hanefi roots bubble to the surface to reveal a narrow inflection in his discourse. For a devout Muslim, he is an unabashed Turkish nationalist, unlike Said Nursi, for whom nationalism represented a divisive force within the Islamic Ummah. Gulen, in contrast, gives Turks the place of pride in Islamic history due to their contributions to Islam. "Turkish accomplishments are unmatched by any other nation, including Arabs" is the sentiment that fuels this partiality toward Turks. In fact, as Hakan Yavuz explains, the Gulen movement holds that Arabs, particularly the contemporary Arab nations, have historically undermined the true Islam.[38]

Yet another spectacular limit to Gulen's broadmindedness appears to be his attitude toward the Kurdish issue in Turkey. Basically, Gulen thinks that Kurds suffer no discrimination in the country and that the Kurdish activists owe an apology to the Turkish state and the nation for creating an artificial crisis. Gulen is unforgiving and refuses to see any plight in the Kurdish existence in Turkey. In this sentiment he appears to part ways even with the AKP, which rejects such a position as obscurantism out of touch with the reality. Gulen's abiding commitment to the Hanefi (Sunni) School also works as a limit regarding how he understands and accommodates Alevi Turks and Kurds. He is deafeningly silent on the issue. He utters not one emphatic sentence on the histories of subordination and discrimination against the Alevi-Bektashi people both under the Ottomans and in modern Turkey. He appears preoccupied with his plight alone; an obsession that calls into question his otherwise remarkable accomplishments regarding the dialogue of religions and civilizations.

In this sense, the risk for the Gulen movement's future is clear: as Gulen claims to be the new face on the Islamic horizon, he grows more like those sectarian Ottoman and modern Turkish ancestors who refused to look beyond their own interests. He also repeats those ancestors whose Islam tolerated little theological differences within Islamic horizons. Alevis and Bektashis come to mind as people whose theological differences were for centuries used against them, leading to their marginalization. How people like Gulen treat Alevis continues to be the test case for Turkey's dominant and the newly energized Islamic movements. As it is, the Gulen movement encapsulates both the new and the old, but overall it moves little beyond the kind of political Islam that has been generous and kind only when it was self-serving. Gulen himself remains in the thrall of Ghazali even as he strives to appear like Averroes to the world. If he succeeds in projecting an Averroes-like image—tolerant, open-minded and progressive—it is not because of the merits of his convictions but because of the strength of his movement's infrastructure. Interestingly, his rhetoric, which is genteel and lofty, may yet come back to haunt Gulen and demand that he substantiate it through the movement's actions. One hopes that the rhetoric becomes a habit of the heart rather than remaining an act of the tongue alone.

## FUTURES

Like Gulen, the AK Party, too, has learned to live under suspicion as a party that derives inspiration from Islam yet must never assert it ideologically. In the Islamic world, this dilemma has been in the making since Abbasid Khalif al Ma'mun, one of the most progressive Khalifs, ironically imposed the Mutazila teachings in 833 as the official dogma and targeted those who disagreed with it. Among the many victims of this original thought control in Islam, the first clash of ideals, was the theologian Ibn Hanbal who was imprisoned, tortured, and forced to recant his traditionalist beliefs. However, in a stunning reversal of fortune under Khalif Mutawakkil's rule from 847 to 861, traditionalist ideas were freed from their marginal status and given official standing. By the end of al Ghazali's life in 1111, traditionalism had been organized into a formidable conservative theology and triumphed thereafter in Islamic imaginaries.

However, the original problem in Islam's political movements was left standing. Names of people and the various schools of thought they belong to changed, yet the draconian norm by which ideas or thoughts replaced one another stayed the same. Herein lies the tragedy of Islamic history: instead of appreciation and cultivation of disagreement as a portal to renewal and innovation, the fear of disagreement in politics has been institutionalized across much of the Islamic world.

The AK Party appears to realize this mistake and seems intent to change. As the noted Turkish historian Kemal Karpat states, steady and self-conscious transformation of minds and hearts ought to take place within the AK Party and like-minded organizations such as the Gulen movement before overcoming the heavy burden of history.[39] In April 2010, the AK Party initiated a Constitutional Reform process, aimed at "liberalizing" the military-coup-era constitution. Two dozen articles were revised and approved in the Parliament, to be voted upon in a national referendum in September 2010. Most observers in Turkey and Europe cautiously endorsed the changes, although skeptics still abound in the traditional secularist circles. A recent videotaped scandal involving the leader of the main opposition party in an extramarital affair has unexpectedly strengthened the AK Party's position as representing a serious and principled attempt to reform the country's political system. Winds of change appear unstoppable, but end results are still dependent on how contingencies are negotiated.

Above all, the future of Islam in Turkey remains closely linked to the status of the Alevis, which remains in the balance. Cognizant of the sea change in Turkish politics, Alevis are pressing for political recognition and greater integration into formal institutions of the country. Their current campaign for "equal citizenship" reflects Alevis' belief that they have long been denied full and effective participation in the country's political and cultural life. The AK Party government has been more responsive to Alevi aspirations than any other government. The so-called Alevi *calistays* (workshops) endorsed by the government have been working on policy measures that can be taken, including possible constitutional changes. Preliminary recommendations reported in early 2010 were far from satisfying Alevi expectations. Given this uncertainty,

Alevi skepticism is likely to endure until tangible constitutional changes are actualized in policy and practice.

It is impossible to determine the calculations driving AK Party policies. Multiple factors are likely working together. Undoubtedly, the AK Party's openness toward Alevis enhances its claim to being a democratic liberal movement. This claim also doubles as a shield protecting the AK Party from the Kemalist forces, especially the military. Finally, the openness policy widens the scope of reformist Islamist tendencies within the majority Sunni population. It has the effect of moderating the Sunni-Alevi tensions. As for Alevis, they remain suspicious of the opening. Yet they are also energized by the developments and the resulting opportunities. They have been building up Alevi civil society institutions primarily through a frenzied construction of a network of *cemevleri* (houses of Alevi rituals) around Turkey. A lot of time-honored Alevi traditions are finally emerging into the public view after nearly a century of secretive existence. Alevis are also reinventing some aspects of Alevism, in part because Alevi traditions were retarded by repressive attitudes and in part because of the qualitatively different realities of a globalized world. Where Alevi aspirations encounter and even collude with Sunni Islamic exhilarations, Turkish Islam is proving to be the beneficiary in being renewed.

In a speech in November 2009, Erdogan stressed the imperative of thinking in daring and innovative ways without dismissing historical traditional knowledge in Islamic and Turkish histories. He suggested that the last 200 years have created considerable confusion among Turkish intellectuals, who experienced a great deal of alienation from their own cultural values and ideals. Among others, Erdogan invoked the name of Cemil Meric, who, Erdogan argued, warned against the neurosis of treating all things Eastern with skepticism. This attitude," according to Erdogan, "created a massive gap between intellectuals and people—a gap that is in need of bridging."[40] For Erdogan, the solution is to embrace, not to silence, the multiple legacies that make up present-day Turkey.

Clearly, Erdogan's new discourse represented an unmistakable shift away from the Euro-centeredness that has been the Turkish state's modern obsession. Europeanization as Westernization and Westernization as civilization is no more the dominant trajectory in Turkish (Islamic) imaginaries. However, this shift cannot, and need not, be perceived as a rejection of European modernity, as some people in Turkey argue. Instead, it should be seen as a political reflex aiming to energize the indigenous intellectual forces. For now, many in Turkey, including many Alevis, nominal Sunnis, and liberals, are willing to give Erdogan the benefit of the doubt that he is calling for greater intellectual and artistic dynamism. It is in this spirit that Kemal Karpat regards Erdogan and the AK Party as the prelude to a more dynamic period in Turkish political life. The AK Party, he suggests, will carry the torch as long as its current talents allow for, but will inevitably pass the torch over to new leaders attuned to the rapidly changing global world. In the meantime, whispers that Islam and democracy are antithetical are bound to fuel the familiar suspicions not only in Turkey but also in those Islamic countries in which Turkish experiences resonate. Indonesia, though separated from Turkey geographically, tells us that Turkish stirrings, while unique, are not solitary experiences in the Islamic world. Islam and democracy need not come together in contradistinction but could grow in mutual affirmation. I aim to demonstrate this convergence in the next chapter examining Indonesian Islamic experiences. Due to differing levels of access in Indonesian society and personal interviews with leading political and religious figures, I will discuss Indonesian Islam in a form and style unlike this chapter on Turkey. Relying more on firsthand experiences, I feel, will better bring out the syncretic and pluralist elements of Islam in Indonesia.

# Chapter 5

# Archipelagos of Islam in Indonesia

As the wedding party entered the 300-year-old wooden mosque at the edge of a river delta in the Kalimantan city of Pontianak, Indonesia, the local kids ran circles around us, wanting to take pictures with the "Western" women and men. The adults eyed the occasion with curiosity from a distance. A multicultural and religiously mixed city, Pontianak presented an idyllic yet impoverished setting for a wedding. Nearly half the people of the city are Indonesian Chinese Christians. The other half is composed of Muslims, with the city's environs populated by the indigenous Dayak. Just when I was beginning to admire the wonders of this diversity, I was brought back to the reality beneath the veneer of the happy mix. This blend, I was told by the bride herself, had exploded in violence in 2001, engulfing all three communities. After delivering the reality check, the bride went on having her ceremony in the historic mosque.

At the reception that evening, I sat next to a young Muslim woman dressed in traditional Indonesian attire with a transparent scarf that covered her hair ever so slightly. She turned out to be Yenny Wahid, the daughter of the former president of Indonesia, Abdurrahman Wahid. In the conversation that followed, I had my critical introduction to the turbulent Islamic streams shaping contemporary Indonesia's popular identity. This Indonesia, just like the city of Pontianak, is obscured behind its sheer diversity in ethnicities, cultures, and religions. Divisions are rife, sometimes deep, and occasionally manifested in violence. Paradoxically, the divides also seem to necessitate and work as spans or bridges for the communities of difference. Inhabiting an astoundingly diverse archipelagic country, Indonesians excel in the art of living tentatively in crisscrossing orientations and commitments. Even the country's national motto is meant to reflect this fine and fragile balance: unity in diversity.

My conversation with Yenny raised more questions than answers. Above all, she expressed an abiding concern regarding a new and powerful threat to Indonesia's plural ethnic and religious makeup, that is, the rising tide of Islamist extremism carried by the very same easterly Arabian winds that had brought Sufi Islam to the Indonesian archipelago some 500 years ago. Ever since the fall of the authoritarian but staunchly secular regime of Suharto in 1998, Wahhabi Arab Islam, as she characterized it, was on the rise, a bleak portent for Indonesia's more moderate indigenous Islamic orientation. For certain, she noted, globalization had integrated Indonesia economically into the world. But at the same time, it had also expanded and deepened Indonesia's integration into proliferating networks of Islamic ideologies.

Yet, she asserted, there is still cause for optimism and faith in the Indonesian brand of Islam, which has been an easy-going moderate and tolerant one ever since Islam arrived in the Islands in the hands of Sufi Muslim teachers. After learning of my connection to Turkey, Yenny pointed out that there is a growing interest among Indonesian intellectuals in the Turkish Islamic experiences with democracy and modernity. While I was intrigued by the observation, I thought that the interest in Turkey was likely to be ephemeral. After all, there were vast cultural and geographic distances between Indonesia and Turkey. However, her observation would prove to be correct during my subsequent travels and research work in Indonesia. Over the years, I have met a remarkable array of people with connections to Turkey. Ranging from scholars to students and from activists to politicians, a growing number of Indonesians are interested in the political developments in Turkey. Specifically, they see Turkey as a place in which the state and Islam have not only coexisted but also have converged, as shown in the developments of the last decade.

Most people with interest in Turkey fully understand that the Turkish case is sui generis, that is, unique in terms of the underlying historical developments. However, many also see the Turkish case as a harbinger of similar formations in the Muslim world. They see it as an alternative to the Wahhabi political Islam. For that reason, many in Indonesia, and also in the larger Muslim world, see Turkey as a test case, a possible model for inspiration and imitation. This phenomenon has been noted outside the Muslim world as well. For example, a *Financial Times* report wrote of widespread interests in the Arab world in the Turkish experiences of democracy, pluralism, and Islam. It reported that aspiring Arab democrats were watching the developments in Turkey with both concern and hope.[1] Furthermore, Turkey's neighbors in the region are not the only interested parties. Countries as far away as Indonesia and Malaysia display growing interest in Turkey as a possible model for pluralist Islam.

Yenny is among those Muslim intellectuals interested in theorizing Islam within the polyglot Indonesian fabric without reducing Islam to a simple variable—one of many strands in the fabric—or positioning it as a meta-political hegemonic framework. At the same time, she notes the proliferation of Islamist "grass—or rice—roots" organizations, the diffusion of the discourse of Islam in everyday life, and the expanding and deepening reach of the Islamist networks into national time and space. It is by referring to those novel realities that in our conversation she repeatedly expressed her unease about a deep shift of mood in Indonesia in favor of a literalist Islam fanned by the Wahhabi ideology of the Saudi kingdom. Still, her points of view aside, central to the concerns raised by Yenny and many others was the imperative to regard Islamist discourse seriously as a resurgent field in politics. Hence the fear: Islam has been emerging as a focal point of organizing societal forces not only globally but nationally. Indeed, in Indonesia, an atmosphere of resurgence of Islamic sensibilities is palpable, especially among the youth. Globally inspired and locally enacted, this resurgence is clearly not a mobilization for deeper "modernization or Westernization." At the same time, it is neither antimodern nor anti-Western in the way in which earlier critics had articulated their discontent with the West and modernity. In the 1960s, the Iranian thinker Jalal Ali Ahmad, for example, regarded Westernization as a disease and called it *Occidentosis*. In the 1970s and 1980s, enthralled by the ideas of Sayyid Qutb in his *Milestones*, Muslim Brotherhood in Egypt and in rest of the Arab world turned to jihadism in its militant sense and spawned the latter-day fundamentalism of the brotherhood as a call to combat what Qutb called the new age of ignorance, the modern *Jahiliye*. Facing such calls, Indonesians beg to differ and instead start from their rich and nuanced Islamic histories. It is from this vantage point that I examine Indonesian experiences with Islam.

## ENTER ISLAM: INDONESIAN ISLAM IN THE MAKING

Historically, Islam holds an extraordinary position in society in Indonesia. Introduced to the archipelago relatively peacefully, it acquired flexible qualities. In order to cultivate receptive grounds, from the beginning, it was subsumed within the dominant Hindu-Buddhist Javanese and Sumatran cultures. Although a competitor with the existing civilizational framework, the Islamic message was not articulated as a replacement or an alternative. Instead, it was presented in terms of cultural and spiritual advancement and growth. This attitude continues to remain intact, though it is under greater pressure vis-à-vis the rising tide of literalist Islamic movements. While these movements have grown substantially after the political field was opened to full competition in the post-Suharto era, more traditional Islamist movements such as the Nahdathul Ulama (NU) and Mohammadiyah continue to be dominant. Founded in 1922 and 1912 respectively, these two organizations together claim 80–100 million members and command the religious geopolitics within the country. Their stories, read along an extended historical perspective, remain essential to understanding why Indonesian Islam does not exhibit the radical revivalist elements.

The first Muslims who arrived in Indonesia came as merchants and traders. Historical evidence from China's Tang dynasty records suggests that Muslim merchants were frequenting the Indonesian archipelago as early as the eighth and ninth centuries. These dates coincide with the initial expansion of the Islamic empire under the Umayyads and the Abbasids. While the historical records pertaining to these exchanges remain scant, the first interactions would reach a climax in the thirteenth and fourteenth centuries after the rulers of the Hindu-Buddhist kingdoms began to convert to Islam. Among the first to convert were the princely states along the coast of Maleka in the 1400s, followed by the gradual Islamization of the interiors of Sumatra and Java. That merchants and traders as well as the itinerant Sufis were the pioneers of Islam is significant. By disposition, they were primarily interested in trade and exchange, not conquest. Arriving incidentally in the company of traders, Islam likely appeared not to pose any existential threat to its hosts. Further, in their interactions, Muslims adopted a respectful approach toward the local traditions, beliefs, and wisdom dominated by Hinduism and Buddhism. As a result, from the beginning Islam presented an accomodationist face and availed itself to be "put through an indigenization process."[2]

Two elements were significant in this process. First, Muslim merchants and Sufi masters offered Islam as a message of renewal of the established order as opposed to a challenge to it. The Indonesian Islamic history duly valorizes the pioneers who communicated Islam as a new beginning without threatening the accomplishments of Hinduism, Buddhism, and animism. Of the many figures who played a role in transmitting Islam, nine *walis*, or Sufi masters, are celebrated as the original teachers who spread Islam. Among them are Sunan Gunungjati; Sunan Kudus, or Ja'far Shadiq; Sunan Muria; Sunan Maulana Malik Ibrahim; and Sunan Bonan. Known also as Sheik Maghribi, Sunan Malik Ibrahim, for example, arrived in Java in 1404 and established the first *pesantren* (religious school) on Java. Literally meaning the place of *Santri*, or the devout Muslims, pesantrens became the primary instruments of Islamic acculturation in Indonesia. The Islamic mysticism of the saints proved to be an effective intermediary between orthodox Islam and the highly syncretic Hindu-Buddhist traditions already in practice. Arriving as a devotional system, Islamic ideals rapidly took roots among the people.

Second, European colonialism helped to make Islam more attractive in the eyes of the archipelago's inhabitants. Relentlessly exploitative and often savagely violent toward the natives, European colonial powers quickly alienated those they came into contact with. Inevitably, accompanying the colonial schemes, Christianity was seen as an extension of the conquest, not an addition to the spiritual repertoire of the archipelago. The Portuguese, who first visited the Islands in 1509, rapidly followed it in war and occupied Maleka in 1511. In this light, Christianity appeared to supply a pacifying tail to the colonial enterprise. In comparison with this mode, Islamic proselytizing not only was moderate in temperament, but also sounded libratory by virtue of its historic rivalry with Christianity. It was thus a more appealing option for Indonesians throughout the archipelago. As a result, as the Portuguese expansion in the region deepened, Islam steadily took on an anticolonial identity.

In the ensuing centuries, Islam flourished through the soft power of ideational flexibility and anticolonial image. In the sixteenth century, Aceh became the first formally Islamic kingdom. Contributing to the spread of Islam was the fact that Portuguese expansion in the archipelago continued unabated. For example, as a result of the Portuguese taking Maleka (also known as Malacca) in 1511, many refugees, merchants, and others moved to Aceh, helping its growth as a trading power and as a bulwark against Portuguese colonialism. The developments also gave a boost to Islam's stature. Islam appeared not only as an anticolonial force but, given the dominant political and economic positions occupied by Islamic empires at the time, such as the Ottoman Empire, it was also perceived as the wave of the future. This promise was reinforced when the Achinese Kingdom sought and secured blessings and protection from the Ottomans and the Mughals. The Ottomans would later fund the construction of a major mosque in Aceh in honor of the Ottoman sultan but also as a symbol of the heights of their power in the Islamic Middle East and in Christian Europe. Today, the mosque still stands, and people on both sides still remember its story.

In the end, various elements converged favorably in what is now known as the "Malay culture zone" extending from Maleka to the Moluccas.[3] With Sufi Islam paving the way throughout the zone, the formerly Hindu-Buddhist rulers accepted Islam as their formal religion. At the same time, they inflected it with the Hindu-Buddhist elements already ingrained in the existing cultures. Out of historical necessity and opportunism emerged the Indonesian variety of Islam. The syncretic or hybrid legacy of this Islam still resonates strongly in the modern Indonesian consciousness. Centuries later, in 2008, Indonesia's former president Abdurrahman Wahid would highlight the Hindu-Buddhist-

## TEXTBOX 5.1. PANCASILA: INDONESIAN NATIONAL IDEOLOGY

Pancasila represents the philosophical foundation of the Indonesian state. In Sanskrit, *pancasila* means the "five principles," *panca* meaning "five" and *sila* meaning "principles."

- Belief in the one and only God
- Just and civilized humanity
- Unity of Indonesia
- Democracy guided by the inner wisdom born of deliberations among representatives
- Social justice for all of the people of Indonesia

*Source*: Official site of the Republic of Indonesia, http://www.indonesia.go.id/en/index.php?option=com_content&task=view&id=112&Itemid=1722.

Islamic convergence as a founding legacy for the modern Indonesian identity. Pointing to the fourteenth century Hindu-Buddhist sage Putantenturan's philosophy that Indonesians are one people despite differences among them, Wahid stated: "Our national philosophy of Pancasila comes from this history. You can see that we are used to multi-religious cultures [going back to Hindu-Buddhist kingdoms]. They became example for Indonesia. That is why Islam here is not like anywhere else."[4]

Wahid's point was that Indonesian experiences turned the standard Islam into a deliberative stream unlike any around the Islamic world. As early as the 1910s, Indonesians were debating the meanings of modernity even as they were fighting the Dutch for independence. Instead of rejecting modernity, experienced and viewed inescapably through the Dutch colonial presence, Indonesians cast modernity as an anticolonial ideal for independence. Early modern Indonesian organizations such as the Sarekat Islam, Muhammadiyah, and Nahdathul Ulama, and even the Indonesian Communist Party founded in 1913, were prolific deliberative bodies within and in interactions with each other. The cross-pollination of ideas was manifested in the Islamic modernist Muhammadiyah, established by Ahmad Dahlan in 1912, and the *Saretkat Islam*, led by Tjokraminoto. At some point in their history, these Islamist organizations even harbored left-wing and communist factions, as in the example of Haji Misbach advocating "Islamic Communism" in Surakata.[5]

In the 1920s, leading figures (following Sukarno who led the independence movement and became the first president of Indonesia) were already discussing Islam and rationalization. Recollecting that his grandfather Ali was an actor in this period, Wahid remarked how "from the beginning Indonesians were used to *ijtihad*, or critical thinking." In fact, he noted, out of such independent thinking came the decision of the 1936 NU congress deciding that Indonesian Muslims had no obligation to establish an Islamic state—a faithful move that, in Wahid's opinion, made it easy to accept a secular *Pancasila* identity in the independent Indonesia. "We decided to have a state free from religion in a predominantly Muslim society, thus showing how Islam and democracy can coexist so long as the objective is not an Islamic state."[6]

With a remarkable ease, Wahid puts Indonesian Islam into a historical perspective by suggesting that, while unique, it also reflects the capacity of Islam in general to adjust to local cultures at the same time that it preserves its universal ideals. Put differently, Wahid observed, as a universal religion Islam has historically accommodated five unique cultural responses during its spread around the world originated by the Arabs, who received Islam and set out to spread it by conquest and conviction. The five different varieties were: the Black African Islam, the North African Islam, Turko-Afghan-Persian Islam, South Asian Islam, and finally the Indo-Malay Islam, which is best encapsulated in the Indonesian variant. They are all different from each other even as they aspire to the same universal ideals.

"In order to understand how Muslims really live, we need to look into how they have evolved," was Wahid's call during our conversation. For Wahid as well as other Indonesians, more than any other modern movements, the Muhammadiyah founded in 1912 and the Nahdathul Ulama founded in 1926 embody the contemporary Islamic dynamics in Indonesia. It is argued that since their founding every Indonesian is linked organically to either NU or Muhammadiyah. As these two organizations go, so goes the Indonesian Islam.

## INDONESIAN ISLAM BETWEEN NAHDATHUL ULAMA AND MUHAMMADIYAH

Reflecting the diverse histories of their emergence, both Muhammadiyah and Nahdathul Ulama have remarkably heterological positions regarding the interplay of the sacred and the secular in organizing and regulating political public spaces. The most prominent face of the NU, Abdurrahman Wahid, for example, sharpened his discourse accentuating Islam's liberalism and syncretism not only as being imperative in multicultural and multiethnic Indonesia, but also as being reflective of the nature of original Islam. The Muhammadiyah movement under Amin Rais's influence had a similarly reformist attitude regarding the extent to which Islam should be the regulative societal norm. While not syncretistic, Muhammadiyah is known as a modernist Islamist movement, receptive to the winds of change, come as they may, from around the world.

Both organizations have distinguished histories of struggle and can be said to be responsible for the evolution of Islam in Indonesia in the last century. They were both founded when Indonesia was a Dutch colony in the first quarter of the twentieth century. They remained active during the Japanese occupation of Indonesia in the 1940s. They were instrumental in Indonesian independence in 1954 and the Sukarno era that followed until 1967. They both continued their activities in Suharto's authoritarian New Order Regime, which lasted more than thirty years from 1967 to 1998. Throughout, Nahdathul Ulama and Muhammadiyah were the two constants in Indonesia's turbulent journey from a Dutch colony to independence and from Suharto's authoritarianism to the post-Suharto democratic era. Nahdathul Ulama in rural Indonesia and Muhammadiyah in the cities provided not only gathering places but also thinking spaces. It is through the NU pesantrens and Muhammadiyah modern schools that many Indonesians were educated in both religious and secular subjects. Not surprisingly, many Indonesian leaders had some of their education in either NU schools or Muhammadiyah schools. Today, Muhammadiyah operates dozens of universities and hundreds of primary, middle, and high schools in which Islamic teachings interface with knowledge in arts and sciences. Similarly, Nahdathul Ulama has connections to thousands of pesantren schools where the *kyais* (religious teachers) preserve and advance traditional Islamic education side by side with the secular curriculum introduced by the Indonesian state.

Of the two movements, NU is known as a traditional organization and the Muhammadiyah as a modern movement. Yet, the distinction between the two is both accurate and misleading. The terms *traditional* and *modern* in the Indonesian context connote more than simply the usual meanings of the words *conservative* and *progressive*. For in the NU and Muhammadiyah nexus, what is considered traditional, thus subject to conservation, is not necessarily obsolete or regressive and thus in need of transformation or even elimination. Similarly, modern cannot simply be construed as progressive or libratory, therefore worth endorsing and promoting. In many ways, NU's approach to Islam is more relaxed than the Muhammadiyah's approach. While NU supports an Islam that not only tolerates but incorporates local cultures, customs, and even religions such as Hinduism and animism, Muhammadiyah's modernism is inspired by a methodical approach to Qur'anic and Prophetic traditions "free" from the local superstitions but open to austere influences from without, such as the *Salafist* traditions originating in the Arab Middle East. In that sense, Indonesians find much to celebrate in the NU's hybrid and tolerant orientation while they are also attracted to the Muhammadiyah's disciplined commitment to both modernity and Islam. It can be suggested that these differences were more pronounced in the past, particularly prior to the fall of the Suharto regime in 1998. Since then, both organizations have grown closer in the broad discourse that frames their positions on Islam and society. For example, on the question of whether to incorporate Islamic Sharia into the constitutional order, they emphatically answer "No" for fear that such a change might endanger Indonesia's democratic system and, even worse, splinter the country along religious divisions.[7]

Post-Suharto Indonesia generated new realities—new opportunities as well as novel challenges—which compelled fresh alliances across the political spectrum. Freer and more dynamic politically, but not yet liberated from crushing poverty, corruption, and crony capitalism, Indonesian society has been thrown into what I call "democratic relief." This relief liberated people politically and accorded them agency. How-

## TEXTBOX 5.2. THE MAJOR DATES IN INDONESIAN HISTORY

| | |
|---|---|
| 358–1500 | Hindu-Buddhist kingdoms rule the Indonesian archipelago. |
| 1200–1700 | The Islamic era commences. Muslim kingdoms advance Islam. |
| 1500–1945 | The age of European colonialism |
| 1509–1800 | The Portuguese rule |
| 1600–1942 | The Dutch colonialism |
| 1899–1942 | The national awakening period |
| 1910 | The "*Sarekat Islam*" movement under Tjokraminoto emerges, replacing an earlier Islamist movement. |
| 1912 | Muhammadiyah founded by Kyai Ahmad Dahlan to combat "traditionalism" and ushers in Islamic modernism. |
| 1914 | Indonesian Communist Party (PKI) founded and takes on a militant role against the Dutch rule. |
| 1926 | Kyai Hasjim Asjari founds Nahdathul Ulama (NU). Organized around the pesantren school system, NU competes against Muhammadiyah in defense of traditionalism. |
| 1928 | Indonesia National Party of Sukarno is born of "Perserikatan Nasional Indonesia," led by Sukarno. |
| 1942–1945 | Japanese occupation |
| 1945 | Declaration of Independence |
| 1945–1950 | National revolution |
| 1950–1957 | "Liberal Democracy" era—Sukarno's rise to power |
| 1957–1965 | "Guided democracy" ends in the termination of Sukarno's rule by General Suharto. The PKI (The Indonesian Communist Party) decimated in the takeover. A million people, mostly members of the PKI, are killed. |
| 1966–1998 | Suharto authoritarianism and the "New Order Regime" |
| 1998–Present | Suharto resigns and "Reformasi" era begins. |
| 1999 | Abdurrahman Wahid, "Gusdur," becomes president of Indonesia. |

*Source*: Adopted partially from: *Sejerah Indonesia*, http://www.gimonca.com/sejarah/sejarah.shtml.

ever, it also exposed the limits of popular democratic rule, which demands responsibility for the consequences of the newly found agency, but guarantees no success whether economic or political.

The new democratic era gave free rein to the reasonable or moderate views, but also opened the floodgates for the extremist fundamentalist ideas waiting in the wings. The resurgence of radical Islamist movements, such as *Laskar Jihad*, *Majelis Mujahiddin*, *Hizbut Takrir*, *Jemaah Islamiyah*, and *Front Pembela Islam*, was the most alarming development in the post-Suharto era. Often tied with transnational Islamist jihadi networks, and agitating for the establishment of an Islamic state or for the institution of the Sharia laws, these jihadi movements began to stake claims on Muslims' sympathies. Both NU and Muhammadiyah responded by mobilizing their base against such radicalism in defense of Indonesia's historically syncretic outlook on Islam. The separate yet parallel efforts coalesced, in effect, not in a formal organizational sense, in the common position of "Islam Yes, Islamic State No."

In my interactions, as often as I could, I raised this issue with prominent figures representing both organizations.[8] In response, most neither refuted nor rejected this practical convergence of energies and, in fact, described it as an expected development under the new realities of Indonesia. Despite their differences, organizations such NU and Muhammadiyah, including their leading figures, appear intent in preserving the moderate Islamic outlook in Indonesia. Joining forces with other civil society organizations such as the Liberal Muslims Network or the Pluralism Institute, they (especially the Wahid faction of the NU based through the Wahid Institute) appear determined to expand, deepen, and solidify the gains made through Indonesia's tolerant mix of religions.

This sentiment of determination is widespread among all groups of people. However, determination also betrays the deep sense of alarm people feel but seem reluctant to confess. In some ways, prevalent alarm is due to the shifting of the grounds of Indonesian Islamic identities with the ensuing regime change within and globalization without. Caught in this dynamic vortex, Indonesians themselves are trying to make sense of the changes.

In an article, Abdul Munir Mulkhan makes a compelling case that links the developments in Indonesia with the global process and actors. Reminiscent of my analysis on the integration of the Anatolian Turkish capital and its sociopolitical agents into the global milieu, Mulkhan contends that the majority of the new movements, including the fundamentalist struggles, represent a new social-political phenomenon resulting from the full-fledged arrival of globalization in Indonesia in the post-Suharto era. A new generation of Indonesians is emerging to make their mark on politics across a wide spectrum. Their political commitments range from Islamic fundamentalism to liberal Islamism. They are the "young *santri*," or, the young practicing Muslims. Their commitments, formulated in light of the fresh nexus of local, national, and global interactions, call into question the traditional explanations of Indonesian Islam. Traditionally, the distinction of *santri* (pious Muslim) *abangan* (nominal Muslim) and *priyayi* (elite Muslim with greater Hindu-Buddhist sensibilities) was used to make sense of the largest Muslim nation in the world. This is not the case anymore, argues Mulkhan. It is the young santris who are now shaping the future of Indonesian Islam. Their commitments are channeled via either liberal-syncretistic Islam or fundamentalist Islam. While many operate within traditional organizations like NU or Muhammadiyah, they also join new political Islamic formations. A number of these young santris are deeply involved in extremist organizations, but many others are part of a worldwide Islamic opening or liberalization. "They not only read *salafi* works in Arabic but use other languages to read a wide range of original works in science and technology, philosophy, and the history of the great nations of the world. Their commitment towards the Islamic traditions and their self conformation as pious Muslims does not diminish their desire to become part of the global civilization that is moving to establish its influence in all aspects of human life."[9] All said, much like in Turkey, conditions delivering circumstances beyond the control of any one group or force fuel the anxieties regarding the future of Indonesian Islam.

## PERILS AND PROMISES OF ISLAMIST POLITICS IN INDONESIA: THE RISE AND "DEMISE" OF THE PKS

Among the developments that elicited such anxieties in the last decade is a fairly new political party with Islamist aspirations. Formerly named the Party Keadilan (PK), or the Justice Party, the party is now known as the PKS, or the Prosperous Justice Party. This party's meteoric rise to prominence had been stunning until the election of 2009. After each electoral cycle, with its command of popular vote increasing and its actual capacity for governing the state growing, the PKS, more than any other new party, injected a newly invigorated Islamist discourse into the public space. Its rise terrified the established secular as well as moderate Islamic parties and worried masses of intellectuals and lay people. Given its real and symbolic significance, a brief history of the PKS is instructive in elaborating on Indonesian Islam's character. PKS's predecessor, the Justice Party, was established in 1998 shortly after the Suharto regime collapsed following a thirty-year rule. Emerging in the unprecedented democratic climate in the wake of Suharto's departure, the PK declared its vision to be one of promoting a "democratic" Islam within the secular constitutional order of Indonesia. It expressed its commitment to the Pancasila ideology enshrined in the Indonesian constitution around the six principles: belief in one supreme god, or monotheism; just and civilized humanism; unity of Indonesia and nationalism; democracy; and finally, social justice to be promoted within the democratic framework.[10]

The PK fielded candidates in the first free elections in 1999 and won seven seats in the national Parliament. While small, the party's representation in Parliament catapulted it into the national scene as a new player with a new message, at once "democratic" and Islamic, or Islamic without being antidemocratic. In the elections' aftermath, the PK leaders worked to cultivate the party's democratic credentials while declaring Islam as a tandem inspiration. Interestingly, the then party leaders Hidayat Nurwahid and Zulkieflimansyah later pointed to Turkey's accommodation of the AKP and drew parallels between Indonesia and Turkey.

> The PK is a modern party, and desires to see Indonesia as a modern and democratic country in the future. . . . To realize our aspirations is a journey of a thousand miles. Such a journey begins with a single step, and we have taken that step by establishing the Justice Party as a community of learning and practice. . . . Indonesia's political destiny could be like that of Algeria. But it could also be like that of Turkey where an Islamist party committed to equality and social justice has been elected and has peacefully taken control of the government.[11]

In 2003, the PK merged with Party Keadilan Sejahtera (PKS) or the Prosperous Justice Party and began operating under this name. In the first elections it contested after the merger, the PKS experienced a resounding jump in the popular vote it won, increasing its representation in the Indonesian parliament from 7 seats in 1999 to 45 out of 450 in 2004. In the years following the elections, the PKS has enjoyed a remarkable growth throughout Indonesia. Its visibility increased, its support base widened, and its appeal to the masses intensified. Between the 2004 elections and the 2009 elections, I observed firsthand the ever-present faces of the PKS in billboards, in graffiti, and in huge banners festooning the cities such as Jakarta and Yogyakarta. The party's rising fortunes was the talk of the town among observers, reporters, and ordinary Indonesians. While many expressed doubts and concerns about the PKS's Islamist leanings and its ambiguous positions on the country's secular system, they all accepted that the PKS was gaining ground over and above other more established parties.

On the eve of the 2009 elections, the polls predicted the PKS to receive 12 to 15 percent of the popular vote. A pollster I talked to in the summer of 2008 confirmed these expectations.[12] The PKS leaders cited an even higher 20 percent as their goal. Either way, such results would have made the PKS not only one of the largest parties in the national parliament but also, and more importantly, the kingmaker in the still fragile democratic system. A strong PKS showing would have set the stage for the intensification of creeping Islamization or Shariazation of Indonesia. Yet, the elections produced a disappointment for the PKS, which won only 8.4 percent of the popular vote, a mere 1.5 percent increase from the 2004 elections. Although a blow to the high expectations, the results still placed the PKS as the fourth-largest party, enhancing its position and keeping its program intact.

In retrospect, observing the general feeling in the polls, in the streets and in the Indonesian media in the summer of 2008, whether the PKS would become the premier party of Indonesia politics or not seemed to matter little. It was assumed that the political grounds were shifting to herald a greater role for Islamist discourses and positions in politics and society. The PKS was poised to gather and channel the Islamist demands into policy and conduct using democratic rhetoric as cover. For example, the PKS's constant appeal to the Medina Constitution signed between the Prophet Muhammad and Muslims and the native inhabitants of Medina, including Jews, seriously troubled observers. Many suspected that the PKS was not simply invoking the Medina Constitution as an inspirational document but signaling its views on model government. Amazingly, the popular desire engendered around this issue was always couched as a democratic project: allowing all religions to practice their faith freely. Of course, that the model invoked was theocratic in aspiration was never discussed. It remained hidden behind democratic pretensions.

Although the PKS was careful to deny any affiliation with the ideology of the Egyptian Muslim Brotherhood, it did not shy away from asserting Indonesia's Islamic roots. PKS supporters maintained that the increasing piety should not be seen as a harbinger of puritanism and fundamentalism among Indonesians after years of guided Islam under the Suharto regime. Others contended that the rising piety couldn't be downplayed as a sign of simple religious devotion free from political calculations and aspirations. The uncertainty about the nature of the increasing religiosity dominated the minds of Indonesians.[13] It is worth noting that it is in such a blurry context of the post-Suharto era that the PKS's fortunes had grown in the first place. In 2005, Yenny Wahid had already expressed the concerns that Indonesia had the potential to go down the extreme fundamentalist route if moderate Islamic and secular sectors did not actively defend the country's Islamic traditions. In 2008, prominent intellectuals and politicians were in effect stating the similar fear and offering the same prescription to combat the Islamist winds. The PKS was a heated topic of discussion in both 2005 and 2008, though by 2008, it was seen as major force to reckon with.

Interestingly, the same people also stated that Indonesia has one native or indigenous weapon against fundamentalism and a Wahhabi-style Islamization of the society—the Indonesian society itself with its deep and long traditions of pluralism in culture, ethnicity, and religion. The former president Abdurrahman Wahid summarized this idea succinctly in 2008 in response to a question about why Indonesia's Islamic tradition appears more pluralistic and flexible than other traditions around the Islamic world: "It is not only Islam that is pluralistic but it is also Indonesia." Wahid's message was that beyond the immutable core of Islam, from the Qur'anic regulations such as daily prayers and fasting, Islam is what Muslim communities make of it. Some communities have turned it into a narrowly defined system in terms of prohibitive injunctions. The Saudi Wahhabist dogma is an example of such a limited vision of Islam. Others managed to shape a more syncretic or hybrid Islam in concert with their specific cultural circumstances. Indonesia is an example of such a permissive Islam. However, it is not the only example. Islam in sub-Saharan Africa, known for its integration of a multitude of African traditions, is also a testimony to how people can and do construct Islam into hybrid belief systems. These "vernacular expressions" are not only enthusiastically supported but are also "sources of pride" for the respective communities. This is certainly the case among the majority of Indonesian people.[14] For Wahid, the challenge is to continue to preserve and empower the Indonesian form of Islam that has been democratic in intent and practice. The task is to continue the "education of the people" along these lines—"educating Indonesians about the nexus between democracy and Islam." As much as it heralds tensions, for Wahid, the PKS's rise also presents an opportunity to teach Indonesians about Islam's relationship to democracy historically and in the present.

In this sense, most Indonesian Muslims, like their counterparts in Turkey, appear willing to think Islam anew under global conditions in politics, economics, culture, and religion. Their broadminded and liberal attitude abounds in all walks of life, and it can be readily observed in arenas beyond electoral politics. It is especially strong in the pesantrens (religious schools) and Indonesia's numerous state and private universities.

Pesantrens are different from universities in that they are elementary and secondary educational institutions. As well, their pedigree is more explicitly religious and premodern. Indonesian universities are distinctly modern institutions, which accompanied the rise of the Indonesian state. Yet, for all their differences, I suggest that pesantrens and universities play a remarkably similar functional role of moderation and secularization in Indonesia. Pesantrens broadly moderate the religious knowledge while universities largely secularize it by relating to the modern world. Administratively distinct, yet socially intertwined, both pesantrens and universities play the politically convergent role of supporting a tolerant Indonesian Islam.

This convergence has been more apparent in the post-Suharto era in which the Indonesian civil society has been unleashed through activist and solidarity networks. These networks interact both horizontally and vertically. For example, in contemporary Indonesia, not only do charity organizations network with each other, but also they interact with political parties, activist movements, government institutions, and religious foundations. Similarly, pesantrens and universities operate in this socially and politically networked environment. They not only contribute to the production of knowledge in such an environment, but also become the consumers of knowledge, which is collectively created. Opportunity structures have been altered for all social agents. Pesantrens and universities are key contributors to a sea change in Indonesian realities both as subjects and objects. Lily Zakiyah's pesantren near Jakarta and the Paramadina University in Jakarta were exemplary and instructive. I will discuss them in ways that demonstrate their organic connections across all levels of intellectual activity.

## LILY ZAKIYAH AND PESANTRENS

Lily Zakiyah runs a pesantren in Jombang, East Java. Zakiyah's pesantren represents continuity and change as well as tradition and reform. Historically, pesantrens operated as educational nodes through which Islam was interpreted and communicated to ordinary Indonesians. Although traditionally more numerous in rural communities, pesantrens have also operated in urban centers. From their inception following Islam's arrival in the Indonesian archipelago, they became key to the rise and dissemination of syncretic Islam. For example, Indonesia's foremost defender of syncretic Islam, Abdurrahman Wahid, received his first instructions at a pesantren. As an adult, he founded his own school after he returned to Indonesia from his studies abroad. Throughout their existence, pesantrens functioned not only as educational institutions teaching elementary Islam, but also as social and cultural conduits channeling piety into everyday relations. They played both a moderating and socializing role in disseminating religious knowledge. In moderating religious knowledge, pesantrens helped create the Indonesian brand of Islam—imbricated with and tolerant of other religious influences. In socializing the knowledge of Islam, the schools cultivated Indonesian Muslims' secular political capacity to contemplate and respond to worldwide developments from colonization to globalization.

Lily Zakiyah's pesantren springs from this historical context as a pesantren that is traditional yet atypical. It expands the pesantren tradition in substance and form. It is specifically for the education of children and women. It is set in a lower-class neighborhood. The education is a mixture of religious and secular subjects. Zakiyah is the headmaster. She is a charismatic figure, educated in Indonesia, Canada, Holland, and the United States, and holds a PhD in anthropology. She comes from the traditionalist NU background. Her father and mother were both active in the NU movement yet encouraged Zakiyah and her sisters to get educated. Zakiyah credits her parents for her educational achievements. In our conversation, she recalled how her father shaped her intellectual orientation as an Indonesian Muslim. Her father always insisted that all subjects from engineering to English are Islamic and worth pursuing.

In the pursuit of knowledge, as she puts it, Zakiyah experienced three intellectual "rebirths," each flowing from each other. She situates the first such rebirth in her religious pesantren education. The second rebirth, she remarks, occurred through the Western education she experienced in countries such as the United States and the Netherlands. The third and the most definitive rebirth took place in the confluence of the first two rebirths after returning to Indonesia. It gave rise to an Islamic intellectual identity that spans the promises of the first two births, yet it exceeds their respective limits. Zakiyah characterizes the third birth as "critical piety" or "pious radicalism." "I am a pious critical person; critical of religious dogma as well as of democratic fundamentalism."[15] She elaborates by arguing that when democratic claims are confined to ideological lip service, they become instruments of control by other means, enabling political disempowerment under the name of liberal autonomy of the individual subjects. Similarly, religiosity deprived of historicity in terms of the geographical, ethnic, and cultural differences necessarily impose a dogma without mercy and grace. Zakiyah, too, recalls how the very Qur'anic spirit emphasizes peace (Islam), goodness (Ihsan), and faith (Iman) in what she calls the "beautiful trilogy."[16] Mercy and grace are primary to piety while injunctions and prohibitions are primary to dogma. In the case of democratic fundamentalism, she contends, the danger has always been the imperialism of the West. In terms of dogmatic religiosity, it is the imperialism of the fundamentalist religious authorities that threatens human autonomy, which is essential for success in the circumstances of one's world. We forget, she argues, how

> the Islamic Sharia obtained through *fiqh* is a product of human intellect organized, ordered and limited in *mahdabs* or religious schools of thoughts such the Shafi, Hanbali, Maliki and Hanafi. What are the methodologies by which the rules are achieved in these *mahdabs*? Who makes the rules of methodology? Who, under what circumstances of power and hierarchy, articulates them into rules as if they are without history?[17]

For Zakiyah, as with numerous others I interviewed, religious schools of thought are also always political movements relentless in their pursuit of influence. When they jettison history for the sake of clarity and uniformity, they turn into political ideologies, more dangerous than the secular ideologies in that they cannot be questioned at all. Aceh, Zakiyah remarks, is an instructive case for observing these dynamics.[18] The only province in Indonesia where Sharia laws are applied legally, Aceh demonstrates that "politicians who know nothing of history formulate the Sharia that gets applied. Worse, it is applied only to those ordinary people who have little protection or privilege. The elite escape the Sharia rules even when legitimate grounds exist for their prosecution."[19]

In this way, Sharia turns arbitrary; its sweeping powers come together in devastating ways. Zakiyah is not against Sharia in principle. Rather, she is critical of the Sharia-producing process as well as the normative attitudes at work in the process. "Apply Sharia with wisdom," she demands, adding that wisdom lies in pursuit of certain ethics and justice for the masses and against local and global interests that mercilessly exploit the masses of people. More than anything else, "we need to focus on ethics through education in pesantrens and secular schools." Pesantrens can play a uniquely significant role in making sure that religion is not reduced to "conservative symbolism" in bed with local and global capitalist interests. Instead, it is cultivated as a critical piety in support of libratory ethics and wisdom. Zakiyah points to Saudi-Wahhabi Islam as an example of what is to be resisted. She sees it as an epitome of religion as dogmatic prohibitionism, not for puritanical reasons but for religiosity that makes possible the convergence of Saudi royal interests with the global capitalist interests through the medium of oil.

The religion of symbolism serves as an agent of dominant power relations, as it was historically during most of the reign of the Umayyads and Abbasids, as well as the Ottomans. It does so either by withdrawing religiosity from the political arena altogether or by inserting it into politics as the overriding definitive ideology. Zakiyah's example comes from the politics involving Indonesia's own rich oil resources:

> When Indonesians protested the removal of oil subsidies by the government, the government's retort relied on the economic logic of the markets under the claim that the decision was purely a rational one which had nothing to do with religion and religious ethics. "Indonesia cannot swim against the objective tide of market capitalism if it wants to succeed," the government's argument went. The underlying claim was that religion had nothing to do with market rationalism.[20]

Yet, Zakiyah's point was that the move portrayed religion in a purely symbolic sense. It emptied it of the ethical dimension. Zakiyah suggested that, paradoxically, the Indonesian masses rejected the government's move on religious terms not because they challenged the government's claims on pure economics, but because they perceived it as capitulation to the infidel's system. The logic of the masses simply mirrored that of the government but simply in reverse in that it rested on an Islamic dogma. The government's removal of subsidies was perceived to be against Islam not because it represented a certain economic injustice but because it was seen as the work of nonbelievers. The historic sense of Islamic justice found no expression in a debate reduced to "market forces," being seen as the infidels' machinations to usurp Muslims of their resources. Zakiyah noted that such thinking is what is leading to the rise of radical or fundamentalist Islam in Indonesia. "It is pervasive, it is impossible to avoid." The causes of poverty explained through a crude religious logic is strengthening Islamist fundamentalism.

Zakiyah shares in the sentiment of protest against market fundamentalism and its manifestation in Indonesia. Harkening back to the Suharto years, she argues that "nothing has changed and the current government should be seen as a continuation of the Suharto era's unbridled crony capitalism, the New Order Regime Volume 2, not a break from it."[21] To those who claim Islam is an antieconomical religion, she responds by saying that Islam is not against trade, commerce, or even profit, for the Prophet was a trader. Rather, Islam is against accumulation without a communitarian purpose, or for the sheer purpose of capital accumulation. "Money has to be active; there should be no accumulation of wealth in Islam for the sake of accumulation alone." The clincher comes when she argues that "Islam can be a site of resistance against capitalism" that attempts to remove the divine ethics from the realm of life. It can inject morality into the minds of our leaders.

Zakiyah's second criticism of Sharia has radical implications for the entire Islamic tradition beyond Indonesia. She maintains that "traditional Sharia imposes paternalism in the name of religion, when, in fact, Islam should be seen as one of the earliest attempts in human history to rein in the paternalist dogma." For Zakiyah, gender equality is in the Qur'an, but it is obscured in quotidian affairs because the Qur'anic interpretation has been the "domain of men. Men have interpreted the Qur'an and the Sunnah in societies dominated by paternalist relations." Therefore, it is not surprising that the original Qur'anic efforts to liberate women by according them rights previously unprecedented have been whittled away in Sharia law through the centuries. These interpretations remain dominant today even though the historical orders that gave rise to them have changed significantly with the emergence of positive human and women's rights conventions.

The theme of man governing over women by governing over the Qur'anic hermeneutics was brought up time and again by female scholars I talked with in Jakarta, in the State Islamic University in Yogyakarta, as well as in Banten in West Java. They all stressed this point as a crucial starting place for any critical understanding of gender in the Islamic world. Interestingly, male observers do not discount this claim but seem reluctant to embrace it. Zakiyah's example of the unfairness of the Sharia as opposed to Qur'anic injunctions had to with the question of cleanliness before praying: "in effect there are three degrees of uncleanliness in the Sharia, which are light, medium, and heavy. A baby boy is considered cleaner than a baby girl. But why?" For Zakiyah, these enjoinments are created as knowledge through interpretation anchored in historical paternalism and cannot be founded in the Qur'an. It is at this point in the interview that Zakiyah argued that such rules do not embody the "real Islam, but some variance of the Wahhabi Islam." She thus raises the importance of Islamic historicity understood through the cultural and geographical specificities of Islamic traditions.

Her next example goes to the heart of the popular imagination of Islam within the Islamic world and in the West: the headscarf, known as *jilbab* in Indonesia and *turban* in Turkey and *hijab* in Arab countries. Zakiyah traces the origin of the scarf to a Qur'anic verse demanding modesty:

> Qur'an refers to "modesty." But what is modesty? If I removed my *jilbab*, I am still modest, not arousing sexual desire (*sehvet*). In Saudi Arabia, it would be seen that way, inviting *sehvet*. To be honest, this is also my way for relating to people here. It is unavoidable in these days. Islam is very fair. We have to be fair. In the Qur'an when Adam and Eve committed the original sin, they committed it together, they repented together, and God banished them together. They are never separate. In the Bible, however, the story is different. The cosmic drama is played out differently. Eve tempts Adam, she is the cause of the sin, and she is the temptress.[22]

Zakiyah's point is that the restrictions on women as well as men are culturally induced as opposed to being based on Islam. Zakiyah and like-minded women work to rescue Sharia, and thus Islam, from the control of men trained in the narrowest possible Islamic theology. One such remarkable project is taking shape in Nur Rofiah's work at the Islamic State University Syarif Hidayatullah in Jakarta.

## QUEST FOR INDONESIAN AUTHENTICITY: NUR ROFIAH AND THE UNIVERSITIES

Nur Rofiah is a lecturer of *Tafsir*, or Qur'anic interpretation in the Islamic State University Syarif Hidayatullah Jakarta and the Institute of Qur'anic Science (PTIQ) Jakarta. She received her PhD in theology from Ankara University in Turkey. Her "dream" project involves the reinterpretation of 6,600 verses of the Qur'an from a gendered point of view—a monumental and groundbreaking endeavor in the Islamic world. To start, she has begun working on the verses relating specifically to women's issues. Rofiah's project shatters the stereotypical Orientalist judgment that Islam does not allow or would not allow for such an intellectual inquiry due to its very conservative nature. It also debunks the claims that Muslim women are fundamentally unable to comprehend and challenge the repressive cultural mechanisms in their lives without categorically repudiating their religion. When I met Rofiah for our interview, she was huddled together with six other women in the local Pizza Hut (a lot more upscale than the U.S. outlets), strategizing about their work in the community. If such a scene strikes people in the West and in the Islamic world as strange, even impossible, it is only because they view Muslim women through their own narrow conceptual portals. Muslim women's work is invisible not because women are inactive or incapable but because of the obfuscation—even denial—of their activities as work in the public realm. Their activities are not known because they are not regarded as worth knowing, and thus are not sought after, studied, and analyzed. Refreshingly, women take no heed of these prejudices and go on having their meetings and doing their work.

Rofiah treats the preconceptions about women as an opportunity to foster her own dream, as she explained it. "It is my dream to make Muslim women independent, so that they can learn Islam from their own perspective."[23] To achieve it she and her colleagues start not with broad theological or political questions but with practical everyday challenges such as domestic violence, family health education, and women's labor. They call these "here and now" problems, which enable a critical dialogue about the role Islam plays. This, Rofiah argues, is a question of "effective methodology" for highlighting both the problems and promises in religious discourses and practices. She continues:

> Arabic has big gender bias. In Arabic everything has gender, including trees, which are considered female, and camels are considered male. Everything has gender identity, which gives a different meaning to Qur'anic texts as well. Qur'anic texts contain gender identity that goes unnoticed by ordinary Muslims. What makes matters more challenging is that nearly all *mutafassir* (interpreters and commentators) have historically been men. The women in Islam are identified within a paradigm interpreted by men in every sense. Women see the biases men are unable to contemplate because of their position.[24]

Very often, Rofiah maintains, "it is difficult for men to see that we have problems with the text of the Qur'an, at a minimum with how the text is interpreted. Whatever the reason, most men think that the Qur'anic text is from God since the beginning of time and creation of humans by God." Sensing a self-serving justification in such a position on the side of men, Rofiah states: "I am happy that there are more women doing interpretation in the universities and nongovernmental organizations, including in my own Fatayat NU organization which is part of the Nahdathul Ulama with millions of women members." The "'Here-and-now-problem' approach," Rofiah suggests,

> is successful because it shows how religious beliefs play a role without assaulting religion. On domestic violence, for example, we start from the reality of domestic violence, and then try to show how the Qur'an's intent is against domestic violence since the Qur'an narrows "legitimate" beating of wife or women to a degree that it becomes impossible to stay within acceptable boundaries. We show how it is impossible to beat a person without hurting (the Qur'anic standard for punishment for women). We also work with the ulama that want to get across the same message. It intends to ban beating since it is impossible to beat a woman without hurting. Although we operate under a certain textual limitation, we focus on the interpretation of the text. We receive testimony from women and use this with ulama to support an active ban. So this is how we go from the reality to the religious text in order to change its interpretation.[25]

In parallel efforts, Rofiah and her fellow activists work to produce a literature that challenges the male-dominated classic libraries in Islam. "In many classic Islamic texts, we find interpretations that justify the worst excesses against women in the name of Islam. Textually such practices might be supported, but we believe spiritually that we must disagree." Not surprisingly, she argues, when one studies all the 6,600 verses of the Qur'an, not only does one realize that such overt discrimination against women is in the minority of verses but also there are many verses that prohibit such treatment of women.

Rofiah does not go so far as to question the authenticity of the Qur'an. She still believes that the Qur'an is God's words. "The text is fine," she asserts, but its "interpretation is the problem." "Problems we face have to do with the interpretation. The problem is the bias found in the language of the al Qur'an. It hides the real spirit."[26] This approach is nuanced, albeit potentially dangerous for its supporters.

The question of the authenticity of the Qur'an is never an issue in the Islamic world. Even if a person believes that there is a possibility that the Qur'an is produced (in the process of transcribing from oral collection to written text under the third Khalif Uthman), no one dares to point that out. Rofiah suggests that Muslims accept the Qur'an as the holy scripture and that there is no point in dwelling on the question of authenticity. What is central to successful social movements within Muslim communities is a critical focus on the hermeneutic cycle around the Qur'anic texts. "Open it up!" Rofiah exclaimed, reminding that the most important element in the hermeneutic cycle is human, not the text, nor the context. Even a biased text can be made to bring out different ideas.

Her point is simple but pragmatic. Thus far, the Qur'an in the hands of the conservative ulama and self-serving politicians has worked as an instrument of control. However, hermeneutically, it contains the potential for contemporary Islam to go beyond the dominance of classical traditions. The classical tradition has focused on texts and interpretations that created a conservative literalist Islam. Yet there remains many hadith that would cast a more liberatory light on women's life if they were not kept in the dark by the conservative male ulama. There is much resistance to such an opening, but it is based mostly on familiar refrains that can be done away with. Rofiah gives the attitude of her students as an example:

> Some question my authority. They will ask disparagingly: "Who are you to speak like that, questioning the classical scholars? Classical scholars are better than you." I ask them to name some such scholars. They answer by offering the names of Tabari and such. I ask them to state some of Tabari's opinions. They cannot, for they know nothing of Tabari or other classics. So Tabari is imagined in their minds. I say who knows Indonesia better, Tabari or you? I tell them Qur'anic *tafsir* is about getting directions for our lives, not imposing the text literally on our lives. One needs to understand one's problem first before getting advice from text (methodology of teaching).[27]

Rofiah is emphatic on the significance of experimenting with fresh methodologies, through her "here and now problem" approach, which compels her students to step out of Qur'anic or Sunnah literalism dictated by the classicists or the Salafists with historically traceable preferences and biases in exegesis. Posed with such questions, students, she suggests, realize it is not easy to find answers to "their" "real" problems by starting from a text and only from a text. Pushed in this fashion, they contemplate questions and answers in more empirically accurate ways. Rofiah maintains that this approach ought to be cultivated not only at the universities but also in the grassroots organizations such as NGOs operating independently or under the NU or the Muhammadiyah umbrella. Problems at this level persist, she stated.

> For example, instead of highlighting Women's trafficking, including sexual exploitation and indentured labor, at one point the NU ulama gave priority by fatwa to fighting the ill effects of popular celebrity gossip shows on TV channels. Such a stand conveys the wrong idea that combating the trafficking of women is not of primary importance. Most people in the community think that trafficking is a women's problem only. [As a related issue bearing the elements of such an obsession with texts, Rofiah raises the role of woman as wife in Islamic traditions.] In that thinking, it becomes normal to have the concept of proper wife but not the proper husband; demand obedient wife but not obedient husband.

It is time for women to define themselves, Rofiah asserts. In her words, they "hope to be Muslims without being Arab and hope to be modern without being Western."[28]

Rofiah's experiences with her students are not surprising. If anything, her students' attitudes reflect the broad societal sentiments. A 2009 survey reveals "more than 56 percent of youth in the Greater Jakarta area support Sharia-based bylaws, although nearly 80 percent also support the Pancasila ideology that sets a secular tone for the state and the society."[29] What appears to be a contradiction in the survey paradoxically shows the promise of Indonesian Islam, save the obvious perils of an Islamist putsch. On the one hand, the survey indicates how widespread Islamic sentiments are in Indonesia, especially in Java and Sumatra. On the other hand, it also shows how the sentiments are supple or pliable in the theological sense, tantamount to something less than a purist or a puritanical position. In the end, the results offer "teachable" opportunities.

If ordinary Indonesians often sound contradictory, for instance, supporting Sharia laws yet quickly dismissing the cutting off of hands for theft as strange and out of touch with the times, it is because Indonesians are highly ambivalent about wholesale importation of "other people's Islams." This became evident to me during my visit to a fairly traditional community in Banten in West Java in 2008. During a gathering in a café-restaurant, the community members displayed remarkable patience and maturity as I recalled some the oft-heard critiques of extremist Islamist movements. Given that the area is seen as a potential PKS territory, I expected to hear the usual fundamentalist rhetoric on issues, including the rights of women. Instead, the community members related observations that were less interested in theological or ideological debates and more interested in the practical impact of new developments on their communities. They were especially keen to talk about the politics and economics of overseas migration since many of the local women were migrant workers in places like Singapore, Taiwan, Hong Kong, and the Arab Middle East. More than a hint in their voices suggested that most men perceived women's migrant work to be less than desirable on both religious and familial grounds. At the same time, they were fiercely concerned about the rights of the women abroad and wanted something done. It is this feeling of practical urgency that parties and movements such as the PKS exploit with promises of clean and caring government. Coupled with widespread poverty, pessimism produces puritanism. In spite of the odds stacked against their hope, this community clings to Islam while memorializing their migrant women as hero-victims.

The tact and knowledge of this "conservative" community was further highlighted in their deference to the person who had invited me to the town. Their own Sopi, who, after receiving a master's degree in political science and women's studies in the United States, had come to teach in the local university. While in the United States, Sopi always wore her jilbab and continued to wear it after her return to Indonesia. For her MA studies in the United States Sopi had arrived armed with Sayyid Qutb's traditionalist ideas, but when she returned to Indonesia, she had added Michel Foucault to her repertoire. Just as her wearing the jilbab both in the United States and Indonesia symbolically linked the two countries together, Sopi's syncretic Islam easily bridged traditionalist Sayyid Qutb and postmodernist Michel Foucault on Indonesian grounds. In 2009, she was elected to the regional Parliament as a deputy. Communities such as Sopi's are the sorts of communities that send their children to Rofiah's classes in Jakarta and Siti Ruhiani's classes in Yogyakarta. In these classes and universities they are trained to be able to make sense of the winds of both tradition and change—whether Arab Islamic cultural winds or the winds of the global economic networks. In these cities and islands, the Indonesian cultural zone asserts itself anew in terms unique to Indonesia's syncretic or hybrid characteristics. All that enters the zone is quickly "indigenized." Many *kyais* (Islamic teachers) and intellectuals shape the process, integrating these discussions into the public arena. Of those, Nurcholish Madjid towers above most. Affectionately referred to as Nurcholish, Madjid made outstanding contributions to understanding Islam in Indonesia.

## NURCHOLISH MADJID'S "LIBERATING" ISLAM

No discussion of Indonesian Islam and modernity would be appropriate without engaging the work of the late Nurcolish Madjid. Madjid was a freethinker in the best tradition of ijtihad in Islamic histories. He was a professor of Islamic Studies with a PhD from the University of Chicago. As with several other prominent Indonesian Islamist modernists, he studied with Fazlur Rahman and came to fuse Rahman's modernism into Indonesian syncretism fearlessly. In the end, Madjid was considered a leading Indonesian thinker of Islam without belonging to any particular formal Islamist movement. Reflecting his desire to tread an independent course, he founded the liberal (cum pluralist) Paramadina Mulya University and served as its rector until his death in 2005. Some Indonesians still remain lukewarm to the idea of according him preeminent Indonesian Islamic scholar status because of his perceived unwillingness to take on the Suharto regime in the past. Nevertheless, his overall work is considered to have widened Islamic philosophical and theological horizons and contributed solidly to the rise of the present liberal and/or pluralist Islamic streams. While Madjid preserved a critical distance to formal movements, he had an impact on almost all movements, Islamist or secular. The enduring legacy of Madjid's ideas is manifest in the fact that his thoughts still motivate new insights and directions among Indonesia's political and intellectual masses.

Madjid came to popular attention in 1970 with the unauthorized publication of a private speech he gave, on reforming Islamic understanding. Delivered to a student organization, the speech called for embracing freethinking, or *ijtihad*, as the core of the spirit of the Islamic worldview. He suggested that Indonesian ulama had allowed a certain fossilization of ideas to occur.[30] The focus on the transcendental or pure theological values of Islam blinded Muslims to the temporal and secular challenges of the world. As a result, social and economic justice, one of the core secular drives propelling Islam, has been pushed aside. The net effect has been the impoverishment of Muslim masses both spiritually and materially. Further, Madjid stated, the developmental remedies rooted in sheer political ideologies, whether socialism or capitalism, were ill conceived to begin with due to their preoccupation with societal engineering. He argued that freedom from the general malaise prevailing in the Muslim world cannot be found in the managerial reforms of states and societies through modern instrumental logic alone. Rather, Muslims must commit themselves to the supreme value of the free intellect or open mind as a manifestation of divine will—not as an opposition to it. It is in this sense that Madjid called for a liberalization of Islamic thought. He meant it as a way of "liberating" Islam from the yoke of traditions that parade as Islamic in essence although they represent no more than cultural practices belonging to one temporal context or another. Liberalization (not liberalism) or secularization (not secularism) is not a call for imitation of Western ideologies but a commitment to imperatives of this material world. Like Jamal al Din Afghani or Muhammad Abduh or Fazlur Rahman before him, Madjid's point was that Muslims have an ethical or socio-moral responsibility to take seriously this temporal life rather than deferring all to the celestial life. To others, this was seen as a direct challenge to the Sunnah, which encourages Muslims to pray as if they will die tomorrow and work as though they will live forever. Ultimately, Madjid suggested that ideas determine the social character of people, and they will color and shape their destiny. Given this notion, ideas have to be freed from traditions not found in the Qur'anic and the Prophetic vision.[31]

These positions made Madjid a lightning rod, inviting harsh criticism from Islamist circles but also eliciting some support from liberal Muslim intelligentsia. Although Madjid stated years later that he would have preferred a more stealthy approach, a "*penetration pacifique*," in disseminating the intent of the ideas, his ideas came to be viewed as Neo-Modernist.[32] Madjid gave another speech in 1972 in which he clarified his 1970 speech but still defended the core idea of "desacralizing" worldly matters so that Islam is rescued from the control of Islamist parties or movements with "obsolete and stale ideas." In this fashion, Islam becomes a dynamic force in touch with contemporary realities. Madjid was more true to his *penetration pacifique* strategy in this speech. Instead of a frontal attack on the traditionalists, he constructed an argument on the material and spiritual dimensions of life lived with or in faith. Separate yet contemporaneous, and guided by *ilm* (science) and *iman* (faith) respectively, material and spiritual dimensions of faith are oriented to work "for the good in this world and the good in the hereafter." Iman is not contradictory to ilm and ilm need not discount iman for its endeavors.[33] Committed to freethinking in both spirit and praxis, Madjid's ideas were decidedly neo-Mutazila in dispensation along a thousand-year-old tradition of critical Islamic thought. For Majdid, the Mutazila era contains both the best and the worst of the political tendencies in Islamic history. On the one hand, supported by the Abbasid ruler al Ma'mun, Mutazila ideas gave rise to the Islamic Golden Age. On the other hand, the same ruler imposed the Mutazila ideas as the ruling dogma, thus in effect establishing a sort of dictatorship of rationalism. While the Mutazila ideas were not responsible for undermining actual freethinking, the era itself shows how reason and rationalism can be instruments of repression when married to pure political power. In some ways, in spite of their great achievements in arts and sciences resulting in the Golden Age of Islam, the complicity of Mutazila rationalism in the absolutism of the Abbasid ruler provoked sharper lines of separation between philosophers and theosophists like al Ghazali. Ghazali's masterpiece *The Refutation of the Philosophers* sounded the death knell for the supremacy of the rationalist tradition in the Islamic societies. Ironically, the very Mutazila ideas (of Avicenna and Averroes, for instance) in the hands of contrarian theosophists like Thomas Aquinas and later Martin Luther would give rise to Euro-Christian reformism beginning in the fifteenth century.

In all his work, Madjid's primary concern was the revival of ijtihad in ways that are responsive to the present conditions and circumstances in Muslim societies. For him, there was something ultimately normative in the Qur'anic sense of social justice, economic well-being, and spiritual path. To be responsive to these overriding universal ideals, Islamic societies needed more authentic thinking and autonomous reason. What Madjid proposed was "situational ijtihad," a kind of normative rationalism in tune with its existential contexts but not displaced from or dissonant to Islam's universal sensibilities on justice and welfare. In his own way, Madjid worked to cultivate the conditions for ijtihad in Indonesia—his primary domain of intellectual struggle. Among many works symbolic of his founding influence, two stand out. One is the Paramadina University, which has now grown into a major progressive university. The other, at least for me, is the anthology on select classical Islamic texts under the title of *The Intellectual Treasury of Islam*. In the anthology, Madjid translated essays from Al Arabi, Ibn Sina, Averroes, Al Kindi, Ibn Khaldun, Ibn Taymiyyah, al Afghani, and Muhammad Abduh and commented on each author as practitioners of Islamic ijtihad.[34] What motivated his effort was his awareness that for a variety of historical political reasons, Muslim societies like Indonesia knew little of Islamic rationalist traditions and were not encouraged to ask about them when they needed them the most. Interestingly, most Indonesians, like Turks, do not understand Arabic or realize that the body of classical Islamic texts available in Indonesia, as in Turkey, was limited by omission or commission. For Madjid, Muslim societies rendered ignorant of their histories remained prisoners not to Islam but to a dogma parading as Islam. Whatever such societies achieve is "accidental," not "fundamental," thus not sustainable. Even the famous "tolerant Indonesia Islam," Madjid contended, was an accident of history, having been forged out of necessity in the multicultural and multireligious geography. In this sense Madjid's words resonated in Abdurrahman Wahid's take that it was Indonesia's unique circumstances that demanded tolerance from Islam and not the other way around. By the same token, it was Islam that proved a certain adaptability by taking on hybrid characteristics while expanding throughout the Indo-Malay archipelago. Ultimately, Madjid's struggle was to "plant in the hearts of" Muslims in Indonesia and beyond that Islamic spirit (as manifested in the Qur'an and the Sunnah) that can be comprehended as being defined by tolerance, mercy, and reason. For Madjid, that the spirit of Islam springs from mercy first and foremost and is anchored in compassion, tolerance, and reason is indisputable; it was not an accident but a manifestation of divine design. The foremost *jihad* (struggle) is for *ijtihad* (free thought). All else is afterthought—save one's faith as the only prior thought.

It was in 2004 that Madjid highlighted the accidental tolerance of Islam in Indonesia.[35] He spoke against the background of ethnic and religious violence that had followed Suharto's fall. He seemed pained by the ease with which Indonesians had killed one another faced with the slightest of differences in interests or opinions. Also alarming was the background of rising Islamist radicalism aiming to narrow the field of freedom of thought in the name of authentic Islam. He sensed the shift in mood (as did many others, such as Moeslem Abdurrahman, Jamhari, and Anies Baswedan) in favor of an Islamist discourse. He ended the speech by emphasizing the deep affinity in the Qur'an for justice through tolerance of differences: "I believe this is something Indonesians have to learn. We can discuss this further in the future." Madjid died in 2005 and the future he talked of has arrived. Indonesians are locked up in jihad for the future of ijtihad like their counterparts in Turkey. They are yet writing the latest, not the last, chapter.

## CONTEMPORARY ISLAM AND INDONESIA'S RESISTANCE TO WAHHABISM

What is happening today is in fact dynamic. Multiple streams of Islamic thought are at work through numerous movements and organizations. Some are clearly motivated by a revivalist Islam. Laskar Jihad and Islamic Defense Front represent such formations. Until recently, these revivalist movements have received the lion's share of attention in the media due either to their extreme positions on religious issues or to their sensationalist actions. When Islamic Defense Front attacked nightclubs for example, the media light shone on them as a power to be reckoned with. Ironically, for all the attention they receive, the extremist groups are outnumbered by moderate to progressive movements organized either by NU or Muhammadiyah, or by independent groups. NU's LAKPESDAM, or the Institute for Human Resources Studies, and Muhammadiyah's Young Intellectual Network, or JIMM, reach wide sectors of Indonesian Muslims. They operate nationally through their respective grassroots networks committed to the core ideas of NU or Muhammadiyah. At the same time, reflecting the common concerns regarding the role of religion in society, their mobilizations have in effect had similar objectives formulated around the preservation of pluralistic Islam and promotion of new ijtihad in line with global modernity. Muhammadiyah's Syafi'i Maarif[36] and Wahid agree about that ideational convergence due to the desire to protect the Pancasila state against an Islamic state.

In addition to the NU- and Muhammadiyah-based organizations is a multitude of civil society groups founded to combat the fundamentalist turn in some sectors of Indonesia's Muslims. Among the most prominent are Liberal Islam Network; P3M, or Pesantren and Community Development Association; Emancipatory Islam Network; and Progressive Islam Network. Together, these organizations create a kind of "epistemic community."[37] People as well as their ideas move through the overlapping nodes of the community. A majority of the intellectual and activist figures are mutually aware of each other's agendas and readily interact in different venues. In the big cities, such as Jakarta and Yogyakarta, their overlapping activities lead to a greater fermentation of common ideas and subsequently common positions.

Historically, two organizations paved the way for the constitution of such a geography of scholars. One is the IAIN (Association of Islamic Higher Education), founded at the initiative of the NU in 1960, and the other is the controversial ICMI (Association of Indonesian Muslim Intellectuals), founded in 1990 during the Suharto era. The ICMI was initiated nominally outside of the state structure, but because it had been created under Suharto's watch by his protégé Habibi, it was widely perceived to be beholden to the Suharto regime. However, others suggested that ICMI's compromise with the state enabled Islamic intellectuals to infiltrate state structures and educational bureaucracy, thus influencing the direction of state policies from within. Increased social and administrative mobility led to an increase in political capital for Muslim intellectuals. The IAIN served a similar function in bringing together Muslim intellectuals from modernist, traditionalist, and secular backgrounds. What made it more legitimate as a venue of dialogue across factions was the perception that it was autonomous from the Suharto regime. While complete freedom was never a possibility for any organization during the Suharto era, the IAIN continued to chip away at the regime's edges, thereby enlarging the space for the participation of various Islamic movements in the national discourse. For example, it was IAIN activities in higher education that served as a platform for NU traditionalists to step into the modern political and social arenas.[38]

Existing in a separate but parallel universe of intellectual fermentation, Indonesia's universities double as political organizational spaces. Historically, the Indonesian universities always hosted small but significant intellectual groups interested in broad political, economic, and social issues. However, with Suharto's new order regime in decline in the 1990s, they began to take on a greater role in political society. Particularly crucial was the role they played in linking educated classes with mass organizations like the NU or the Muhammadiyah through conferences, symposiums, and workshops. Although this is a function most universities fulfill around the world, Indonesia's universities are more directly and intensely politicized than their counterparts in the West. Given the large number of State Islamic Universities, private universities operated by Muhammadiyah or the NU-affiliated organizations, or universities operating under secular mandates, the collective political capacity of Indonesian universities to influence public opinion is enormous. The high esteem in which university professors are held only heightens the power of Indonesia's academics. Of course, Nurcholish Madjid was the latest and most celebrated academic who shifted the intellectual debates on Islam and society in ways that reverberated from academia throughout the entire nation. His legacy as an Islamic neomodernist is carried forward by academics spanning both the academic and political worlds.

Take for example, Anies Baswedan, the rector of the Paramadina University in Jakarta.[39] Baswedan enjoys a high profile in the Indonesian public eye that most Western university presidents would not dare dream of. He became a household name after his appointment as the youngest university rector in Indonesia. His profile was further accentuated upon being selected by *Time* magazine as one of one hundred most influential intellectuals in the world in 2007. With these accolades to his name, Baswedan has been using his position to promote a "pluralist and progressive" Islam in Indonesia. He appears on television and in newspapers and meets those such as myself who come for interviews. In our meeting, Baswedan spent nearly two hours analyzing the electoral politics and explaining where Islamist parties fall on the political spectrum. While Baswedan occupies the rector's seat, another (former) Paramadina professor, his fellow Paramadina scholar Yudi Latif, has also emerged as a premier political scholar of Islam and Islamic thought in Indonesia. His *Indonesian Muslim Intelligentsia and*

*Power*, published in English in 2008, catapulted him to international prominence but also solidified his influence as an organic Muslim intellectual, as someone who lives in the community, whose ideas and sensibilities are deeply shaped by the community, and whose life objective is one of serving the interests of the community.

What is remarkable is that Yudi Latif and Anies Baswedan are not exceptional in the Indonesian context. Rather, they represent long historical traditions in which Islamic ideals motivated intellectual involvement in the socio-ethical affairs of the country. M. Syafi'i Anwar, for example, leads the International Center for Islam and Pluralism while also serving as a professor. His high profile in that capacity made him the target of reactionary fundamentalist groups.[40] Abdul Munir Mulkhan is a professor of Islamic Studies in Yogyakarta but he also serves on the Indonesian national Commission on Human Rights.[41] Intellectuals, whether they are university professors, writers, artists, lawyers, or religious teachers, retain close links with political institutions through their educational or popular affiliations. Completing the political circle, very often, the educational institutions or advocacy organizations they are part of foster direct and discrete links with political parties in the hopes of articulating political or philosophical ideas into policy positions or political agendas. In the post-Suharto *Reformasi* era, numerous scholars stepped into the political arena under various party banners.

Together, these organizations and associations create a dense and wide network of community consisting of various nodes of orchestration but without a conductor or a central orchestrator. They strive, on the one hand, to challenge the rising threat of extremist Islamic movements like Jemaah Islamiyah, which bombed a Bali disco in 2002 killing more than 200 people. On the other hand, they move beyond simply reacting to extremism and formulate and communicate Islam through liberal progressive or pluralist lenses. Islamic tenets, originating in the Qur'an and in Prophet Muhammad's exemplary behavior, are refracted through new interpretations in light of the global developments. The main worldview that emerges is one of "diversity is a blessing in Islam" in the tradition of the Qur'anic ethics extolling pluralism: "Had we willed we would have created all human race from one nation. We created many nations so that you may get to know one another." Through this worldview, Islamic modernism is cast as Islamic moderation. The middle way (*wassat*) emerges as the ideal position in negotiating modernity. Islamic modernism conceived as the middle way then proposes that Islamic doctrines should not dictate all aspects of life but function as general aspirational principles for Muslims who wish to follow the faith actively. It is, however, against making the state Islamic and making Islam into a coercive religion demanding and securing worship by the sheer force of the state. The vast majority of Indonesians seem to understand and support this crucial distinction between following their beliefs freely and following Islamic Sharia under the coercion of the state. "Islam Yes, Islamic State No!" is an oft-repeated position showing where even the most devout people stand. Progressive Islam, transformative Islam, emancipatory Islam, pluralist Islam, and tolerant Islam acquire greater substance and power in the society.

The Institute for Islamic and Social Studies (LKiS), for example, published works by the Muslim world's new "Young Turks" like Mohammed Arkoun, Fatima Mernissi, and Muhammad Abid al-Jabiri. The titles of their books are instructive: *Deconstructing Sharia*, *Post-Traditionalism Islam*, and *Islam and Democracy*. LAKPESDAM has published the journal *Tashwirul Afkar* since 1997, taking on difficult and controversial issues of political exegesis (*Fiqh Siyasa*): "Rejecting Arabism"; "Finding Indonesian Islam"; "Challenging Islamic Fundamentalism"; "Islam with Local Characteristics"; "Women's Movements in Islam"; "Towards Pluralistic Islamic Education"; and finally "DeFormulating Sharia."[42] These are breathtaking titles for Muslim communities but have come to be seen as ordinary in the context of Indonesian politics. They indicate the sophisticated analysis to which Islam is subjected but, more importantly, the sophisticated analyses the Islamic worldview allows for and even promotes within the Islamic paradigm. This is what makes Indonesia uniquely similar to Turkey and so different from Malaysia in Southeast Asia and Arab countries in the Middle East. It is also what makes Indonesia a cutting-edge case for understanding if and how an Islamic democratic turn can take place and be sustained without the usual caveats and excuses about "the divine ban here and sacred bar there." If the developments I observed are any indication, Indonesia might yet become a site of a definitive struggle for the freedom of thought in the Islamic world.

Clearly, two fronts have emerged, each vying for the ideological-spiritual hegemony among Indonesian Muslims as well as striving to influence the secular state apparatus. First is the front that encompasses a broad coalition of moderate-modernist Islam around the Pancasila ideology. Muhammadiyah, Nahdathul Ulama, and Liberal Islam Network, among others, uphold this front despite their political and cultural differences. The second front has come to the fore riding post–Cold War religious radicalism, particularly the Wahhabist variety, under the banner of freedom for Muslim believers. The first group is considered "cultural Islamist" while the second group is characterized as "formalist Islamist." The first group is interested in heightening the inspirational role of Islam in society. The second group is driven by a desire to inject, even impose, Islam into the formal state structures. The first front is conscious of its role as the source of new ijtihad, while the latter conceives of ijtihad itself as the source of the decline of Islamic civilization. The first group is historical, revisiting the Islamic past as a political-sociological project. The second group relates to history as a chronological expression of the Qur'an and Sharia. The first group would condemn, and indeed has condemned, the September 11 attacks, as terrorist actions. Yet, the second group openly admired or silently welcomed it. The first group works to remember, that is, reactivate Islamic sensibilities in all their diversity and richness, including both the conservative and critical transformative ones. The second group narrows or imprisons the capacity for political agency or action to a single vision, which is theirs and theirs only. The first front might be characterized as having many faces; the second is clearly authoritarian in intent and ultimately a clear threat to democratic pluralism.

More than any other position, the pro-Sharia position is indicative of the nature of what is at stake in Indonesia. Very often, radical Islamists present the call for Sharia as a struggle for freedom of religion for Muslims. They mimic a rhetoric that is already well rehearsed elsewhere. The argument goes as follows: Muslims have the right to Sharia as the sacred covenant governing their behavior as believers. They wish to introduce Sharia rules among Muslims and for Muslims only as has already happened in Nigeria and the Sudan. Other religious communities have the same right to observe their respective religions. The argument employs a democratic rhetoric of choice and pluralism. It is a powerful appeal that registers as being democratic. However, its "pluralist" appeal obscures its totalitarian intent in at least one crucial way. It obfuscates the fact that the appeal for "Sharia for Muslims" leaves no space for political freedom within the "Muslim" community. All Muslims, whether observant or nominal, come under the purview of the Sharia. They are offered no guarantees for the preservation of political, cultural, and aesthetic pluralities. The "political" in all its dimensions is refracted through, reduced to, and captured by the singular theological line. Uncontested as having divine origins, but administered through human institutions, Sharia becomes an arbitrary interpretative instrument, used and abused politically, even as it is presented to be above politics. To put it bluntly, depending on where and when it is used, heads can fall off, women can be stoned to death, music can be banned, girls can be prevented from having any education, Yoga can be outlawed, or people can be silenced completely. If such examples of abuse seem too un-Indonesian and not likely to happen there, developments in the "autonomous Aceh" clearly disprove this wishful thinking. The Aceh government already gave its blessing to the medieval punishment of stoning men and women to death on account of adultery. Under pressure, the government's defense has been to suggest that it does not intend to carry such punishment out. Having just incorporated the penalty into its legal system, such a defense rings hollow and disingenuous. To top it all off, Aceh's Religious Affairs Office in December 2009 banned performance of the Chinese Lion Dance as offending Islamic sensibilities.

One need not go to Aceh to find troubling signs in the rest of Indonesia. The treatment the Ahmaddiyah sect is receiving at the hands of Indonesian Wahhabists, with the government's inaction to protect the Ahmaddiyah, is indicative of the dangers that would visit pluralism when intolerance comes into fashion as religious obligation. In minds divorced from the idea of Islam as a historical process, other religions come to be seen not as "authentic" expressions of religiosity but competitive world orders to be tolerated when convenient or, when opportune, to be dominated, forced into silence, or forced altogether underground. While the Taliban is a "frontiers" example of what the Wahhabist mentality is likely to produce, the Saudi regime would be a vested and even tamed version. These are not the most attractive choices for honoring Islam.

## FUTURES: ISLAM'S INDONESIAN ODYSSEY

The latest parliamentary elections in April 2009 suggest that the majority of Indonesians are cognizant of the risks of forgoing pluralism in favor of a polity dominated by Islamic Sharia. Indonesians voted en masse for parties that were committed to the Pancasila framework. The top three parties, the Democrat Party, PDIP, and Golkar, are broadly secularist parties. Together they control more than 50 percent of the popular vote. The PKS, in fourth place, represents a disappointment for Islamist electoral aspirations. Electorally, PKS's showing, together with other Islamist parties, indicates the limits of Islamist politics more than the potential for growth or expansion. So long as the Pancasila-oriented parties remain sensitive to the needs of the majority Muslim population, they are likely to consign Islamist electoral movements to a marginal position. As one commentator put it, "The Indonesian masses are generally centrist, unconvinced of the utility of religion playing a supreme role in running the country."[43] Another comment, quoting a shopkeeper in Jakarta, captures the sentiment perfectly: "We are choosing people to lead a country, not to lead a mosque. You can't pray away bad economy, poverty, and unemployment."[44]

This is the pragmatism that Indonesians have demonstrated time and again, particularly since the fall of the Suharto new order regime in 1998. The post-Suharto pragmatism is significant because it came on the heels of fears that Islam, at last freed from Suharto's grip, would rapidly grow and come to dominate the political system. Many observers around the world and in Indonesia genuinely feared that Indonesia might go the way of Pakistan or, even worse, Afghanistan. The fears have been put to rest for the foreseeable future in the demonstrated belief that Indonesian Muslims are pious but not fundamentalist. Or in the words of Moeslem Abdurrahman, Indonesians, especially the middle class, are more likely to practice an "Islamic expressive culture" in their piety than express a desire for a puritanist polity.[45] Islamic piety of the Indonesian variety is a far cry from the religious fundamentalism of the sort articulated in Wahhabi-Arab Islam. In fact, even as the piety increases in the expressive sense, many Indonesians appear to realize that introducing Wahhabist Islam would mean the wholesale importation of religious traditions that are more Arabic than Islamic in nature and intent, and they are distancing themselves from such traditions. Throughout my interactions with Indonesians, this point was raised consistently, although more by women than men, and more publicly by women than men—intellectuals and laypeople alike. Indonesia's female intellectuals and activists are on the cutting edge of this shift in consciousness, aiming to effect practical alterations in behavior in culturally appropriate ways, that is, engendering change without directly confronting Islamic predominance.[46]

Indonesian Muslims, like their Turkish counterparts, hold in high esteem the Arab contributions to Islam. For example, they venerate the Arab as well as Persian Sufi *walis* (saints) who spread Islam to Indonesia. Many of the Indonesian educational institutions, most strikingly numerous universities, are named after these walis. The NU pesantrens teach Arabic language and literature. Unlike in Turkey, many Indonesian intellectuals undergo Arabic-language training, which gives them access to a vast body of Arabic Islamic literature. At the same time, Indonesian geographical and historical-cultural distance from Middle Eastern Islamic history figures definitively in their lives. In many ways, pre-Islamic cultures retain their centrality beneath the surface hegemony of Islam. Islam operates as a tent under which all varieties of religio-cultural practices interact and blend into the uniquely Indonesian Islam. Syncretic in both form and content, Indonesian Islam acquires its own agency, ultimately compelling dissonant ideologies or movements to change.

The Islamist parties appear to be adjusting to the reality that radical Islamist politics is unlikely to take root in Indonesia's archipelagic cultural, ethnic, and religious diversity. The PKS, for example, has reduced its appeal to Islam, and has been busy repositioning itself within the Pancasila tradition of Indonesia. The PKS's transformation into a mainstream party accelerated after a quid pro quo when it entered into a coalition with SBY's Democrat Party in the 2009 presidential elections. In return for supporting the SBY-Boediono ticket, the PKS asked for eight cabinet positions, including the ministries of interior, education, and defense, though it had to settle for two ministerial appointments. While the PKS's showing in the elections fell short of the prediction, it can be argued that its consolidation in the mainstream (or its *penetration pacifique* to use Madjid's words) is deepening. Along with its steady rise, its ability to influence or shape the political agenda is also growing. Other parties are taking note of the shift:

> PPP's (Partai Persatuan Pembangunan) Chairul Mahfiz suggested that the PPP will have to consider whether using Islamic symbols is appropriate moving into the future, particularly given the fact that two other Islamic parties held firm in their share of the votes—Prosperous Justice Party (PKS) and National Mandate Party (PAN)—while at the same time positioning themselves as more open parties, and relying less on Islamic messages when campaigning.[47]

In the end, what is unique about Indonesian Islam is twofold. One factor is rooted in Abdurrahman Wahid's observation that fundamentally Indonesia has always been a syncretic amalgamation in time and space. Pluralism and syncretism are in the nature of Indonesia, shaped by its archipelagic geography and diverse history. The other element is a function of the inherent pluralistic instinct of Islam. The Islamic tenet that there is no coercion in religion, together with the Qur'anic observation that ethnic and religious differences are willed by God, has been at work in Indonesia more than the original Islamic communities in the Middle East. Indonesia's experience with Islam is a testament to the cosmopolitan character of Islam to adapt to different conditions. Recall Said Nursi's words regarding this characteristic flexibility. "Qur'an reads the world," wrote Nursi as he contemplated his time spanning tradition and modernity in Ottoman Anatolia. In the same way, it is possible to suggest that Islam "reads" Indonesia respectfully and creatively to attract it to Islam's way. The fundamentalists who are trying to change Indonesia in the name of an authentic Islam found in Wahhabist histories are seen to violate this very Islamic attitude of a learned interaction that made Islam so attractive in the first place.

Ironically, such an obsession in search of a single and absolute version appears more in line with the modern obsession with categorical and definitive modes. Does not the word "modern" mean a singular measure or mode? To be modern is to fit into a mold understood to reflect a prevalent way of life—rationally ordered in politics, economics, culture, and even religion. Nation-states are the political expressions of such a singular order. National education, military, flags, and anthems flow from this will to conformity that is the cardinal impulse of modernity. Writ global, shopping malls, concentrating and distributing consumerism as conformism, embody the modern economic rationale. And finally, singular-truth orthodoxies of religions appear to fit more comfortably with the modernist monopoly than with the historically anarchic plurality of religious beliefs. The recent attempts by the Indonesian Ulama Council (Majelis Ulama Indonesia MIU) to go after the Ahmaddiyah and the Sufi Tarikat Naqsyabandiyah as well as the various Hindu-Buddhist socio-religious customs exemplify the modern obsession with singularity more than any inherent drive in Islam to restrict pluralism.

For all their claims to eternity, religions, too, adapt to the dominant political and economic relations. However, through such acts, religions run the risk of undermining their own fundamental rhetoric on "truth" and "tolerance." While we know that Islam's tolerance for diversity and difference was never infinite, it was substantial by its theological nature and by the historical necessities of its expansion. By its nature, Islam aspired to pluralism insofar as it positioned itself theologically as the latest religion in the Abrahamic traditions. Given this claim, at the most basic level, it has had to make allowances for the Jewish and Christian faiths in the Islamic framework. By historical necessity, Islam has had to develop pluralist traits in order to expand. In almost every continent, Islam adapted to and absorbed the local traditions into its theological framework. More importantly, it availed itself of the articulation of local customs in Islamic terms. In Turkey, it produced the syncretic Alevism as well as a unique Sunni Islam. In Iran, it engendered Shiism, a marriage of Persian pantheism and Islamic monotheism. In India, it gave rise to Alid Islam, known for its pluralism embracing both Hindu and Islamic values.[48] In sub-Saharan Africa and North Africa, Islam created substantively authentic streams in line with the social and cultural forces at work. In Senegal, a lightly clad Muslim woman presents an ordinary sight, whereas in Algeria or Egypt such an appearance would be quite inconceivable. In Indonesia, Islam folded in with an already distinguished array of existent religious traditions ranging from animism to Hinduism to Buddhism. The gamelan music of Indonesia, with a cast of Hindu-Buddhist figures, continues to animate Muslim imaginaries while in Pakistan, not to mention Afghanistan, music has been on the verge of a complete ban in some regions. All of these manifestations highlight Islam's capacity for flexibility and change even as they might point to its vulnerabilities to extremism of one kind or another.

Abdurrahman Wahid, still one of Indonesia's most recognizable Muslim intellectuals until his death in December 2009, contended that Islam is a forward-looking religion at heart. However, he argued, it cannot be taken for granted. It has to be cultivated in the way of the earliest teachers of Islam. "The education of the masses is a must," he insisted:

> I am well educated in religion. When I came back from abroad, people asked me to teach their children. So my job now is to make Islam modernized in such a way that it would be able to answer the demands of times, for globalization pluralism, tolerance, and this or that.[49]

Islamic histories do not offer ready-made solutions to the present challenges. In any case, that is not history's role. At best, they may tell instructive stories about attitudes Muslim ancestors employed vis-à-vis the challenges and opportunities in their respective lives. For Wahid, all historical experiences are illuminating yet none constitutes a model for emulating, much less imposing, on the rich and diverse universes of Muslim societies around the world. At the same time, some historical experiences remain more inspirational than others in the spirit they deploy. For Wahid, the Andalusian spirit, distinguished by its tolerance of different cultures and its drive to cultivate arts and sciences, is inspirational. Indonesian Islam, with its syncretic, that is, Hindu-Buddhist-Islamic contemplation of spiritual existence, is also inspirational. Like the Andalusian Islam, however, Indonesian Islam, too, is dependent on its followers for relevance and renewal in this temporal world. Wahid concludes: "The Andalusian spirit can be captured through education, without which we have no base. Indonesia is in turmoil now. I have to prepare the community for democracy. One needs courage."[50]

# CHAPTER 6

## RADICAL VANISHING
### *Islam in Global Commonspaces*

The post–September 11 era is pregnant with monumental shifts in Islamic worldviews. At a time when Islam is being played out once more in light of its darker inventories and genealogies, a certain pluralist syncretism informed by more diverse inventories of Islam is stirring cosmopolitan forces into action. There is a shift in several predominantly Muslim countries in terms of substantive and formative attitudes regarding globalization. As I have shown in this book, of those countries, Turkey and Indonesia are remarkably distinctive in their resistance to the literalist and prohibitive orientations popular elsewhere in the Muslim world.

An argument can be made that Islamist movements in Turkey and Indonesia have accommodated, if not embraced, the logic of the global capitalist political-economic system and have grown ever more flexible in ideas as well as in strategies and tactics. They have grown politically flexible precisely as they have asserted their religious convictions and ideals in the political arenas. Rather than seeing globalization as a zone of civilizational clashes, they have opted to see it as a zone of indistinction that is also full of opportunities. Integration within this zone is perceived not only as largely inevitable but also, if operationalized through Islamic sensibilities, as instrumental in reordering political opportunity structures as well as leading to deeper changes in the structures of the global zone.

These attitudes are clearly fluid and flexible. The sense of tension within Islamic communities is palpable, generated between global political and economic pressures and parochial defensive impulses. For many, Islam is an orienting sensibility as well as a regulative ideal through which to rearrange the dominant political orders and conditions, thereby to shift the normative ideals. Comprehended this way, various movements centered on Islam as an autonomous ideal have emerged as political spaces in which the future is contemplated and acted on. While some of these spaces have been cultivated and exploited in total terror and violence by virulent organizations such as the Taliban, others have been supported in the shadows of a bourgeoisie interested in summoning Islam in the service of their ascent from national to international, or protoglobal, capitalists. Still others witnessed the emergence of the "transversalist" movements informed by global political and economic relations through which capitalism operates. In almost every sense there is an insurgent dimension and intentionality to the movements and the spaces they create.

Although this book has focused on Turkish and Indonesian experiences, all Islamic societies are shaped or refracted through a set of tensions endemic in Islamic globalities. At once historical and contemporary in effect, three forms of tension are central and prove instructive in rethinking Islam and politics.

The first tension points to a deep predicament for Islamic societies. Islam has a rich and syncretic history yet lacks a rigorous historiography to record, organize, and communicate its history. Attempts aiming at such a historiography are resisted in the prevailing climate of fundamentalist, literalist, and repressive orientations in the Islamic world on the one hand and the resurgent Orientalist political historiography in the West on the other. The challenge this predicament poses is to think and write about Islam in ways that resist reductionism and obscurantism in political and philosophical senses. In response, in this book, I have striven to take a fresh inventory of Islamic history that recovers and re-sounds the syncretic, transversalist, and pluralist genealogies at the heart of Islamic historical ideals and praxis. For centuries these characteristics were central to the ideals and practices that supported the rise of Islam as a major organizing force. Now often peripheralized in contemporary Islamic horizons, they must be rehabilitated as elements of heterological Islamic histories.

The second tension is energized around the depths of the encounters and interplays between Islam and modernity, and nowadays, between Islam and globalization. While surprising for many, the question of whether modernity is external to Islamic history, let alone to Islamic worldviews, is central to discourses of identity in the Muslim world and in the West. While some ask what went wrong with Islam, others ask what went wrong with modernity. However, to transcend the divide one should ask how it might be possible to articulate Islamic modernities through which Islamic globalism can be examined and considered in contemporary debates. How do we write about political and economic relations and subjectivities without anchoring them in singular historical, civilizational, or geographic origins and sources, whether we are talking about modernity or globalism, the West or the East? It is when Islam's historical confluences and convergences with the Euro-Christian-West are highlighted that one can see how these two civilizations have always been and continue to be deeply internal to and constitutive of each other's identities through political and economic experiences straddling their respective worlds. This is an unbroken civilizational unity in need of resounding.

The third tension is born as political desires clash against economic urgencies locally, regionally, and globally. It concretizes in global capitalist relations of ownership, production, and distribution in debates that otherwise wax purely teleological and metaphysical. Even religious ideals have to contend with economic forces. This tension works as *economic realpolitik*, making corrections to the excessive tendentiousness that is prevalent in civilizational discourse. Revealing the world to be composed of multiple yet intersecting and overlapping spaces—religious, political, economic, and cultural—this tension thus highlights the primary political challenge as one of building critical capacities in the "commonspaces" of the world. Together these tensions fuel the politics of change in Islamic spaces.

Questions around these imperatives proliferate: How, then, are we to study Islam and globalization together without minimizing or negating the gaps and differences that characterize each as a material cultural process and political ideology? How do we view and register normative political tensions that energize Islamic sensibilities into Islamist movements? Can the relations be seen in ways that vitiate the "clash of civilizations" paradigm while retaining the core issues they raise or intimate in terms of Islam's role in globalization (as a major shift in political and economic relations and structures)? The answers can be found in treating Islamist movements as novel critical spaces in which the questions about modernity that the West cannot or might be unwilling to ask can be contemplated and posed. As stated in chapter 2, what early modernity subsumed as the civilizational "part that has no significant part" in political and cultural projects, late modernity is now releasing as political potentiality, expressed both as a repressive turn and a syncretic liberal intentionality. While the first has received the greatest share of attention, it is the latter that is poised to "inject" dialogical rigor into political-economic discourses.

Dialogical thrust works against the overarching historical partiality to modernity as the "measure" of things and peoples around the world. As Derrida put it, a thing's thingness and a people's peoplehood are measured by modernity as the mode. Yet, there is no sufficient measure of the measure itself. Modernity as the measure of things and peoples still remains unaccounted for, let alone sufficiently justified or defended—particularly in the face of global economic and political accelerations that reveal the limits of modernity's central relations, rationalities, and institutions such as sovereignties, borders, territories, nations, and states. While modernity's diffusion has been a geographically extensive reality, the diffusion of its deep reason and rationality has not acquired similarly extensive depth or intensity.

Historically, the diffusion has been burdened because of the proliferating disjunctures between modernity's promises and actual results. As well, it has been weighed down by the growing realization that modernity's normative claim to civilizational authority is itself a "result" of historical struggles. The "modern" has come to be seen not simply as the triumph of a collective Kantian "measure" or "limit" over parochial "infinities" or of "order" over a Hobbesian "anarchy" welcomed around the world, but rather as the hegemony of a culturally specific political-economic calculus imposed on the world. As it is imposed, it is also resisted by communities of impoverished masses and struggling indigenous peoples. Islamic histories are a part of this contentious history of diffusion, and they acquire their relevance at once in a conflictual and cooperative unity or proximity with modernity.

Islam has never either fully internalized or completely rejected the "diffusionist" claims advancing modernity as the privileged narrative of history. As the limits of modern relations, institutions, and subjectivities are revealed in terms of the uses to which they have been put, the histories of capture and ban they have facilitated, sanctioned, and justified, and finally, the narrowness of the future horizons they presently support, Islam is issued forth as a counter-hegemonic political field of militations in thought, imagination, conduct, and policy. However, from the standpoint of liberal secular democracies, the very idea of political Islam remains alarming.

Certainly, the fears regarding intolerant, repressive, and "totalitarian" Islamism emerging as dominant are not unfounded given recent experiences in Iran and Afghanistan as well as Pakistan and Saudi Arabia. Conversely, the so-called moderate Muslims contend that Muslims can and should comprehend democratic and liberal ideals not as alien trajectories to their own civilizations but as part of their own historical development. As shown in chapters 4 and 5, this rhetoric is prevalent in Turkey and Indonesia, for example. Still, to repeat my earlier remarks, Islam's positions or roles in the broader world conditioned by multiple network-based global orders lie not in the easy pronouncement that Islam might support an "alternative" order of one kind or another, but in the possibility that, even through the ontological fears it induces, it might help deepen, expand, and intensify critical spaces for thinking differently about the world's dominant organizing principles and regulative ideals. Strangely, circulated in the global commonspaces, ideological challenges posed by the Islamist resurgence resonate with Emmanuel Levinas's vision of the critical interrogation of modernity as a specific kind of measure that is neither universal nor infinite and, even if desirable, also in need of more extensive inventories of the parts that are held in thrall. This book highlights the potential of "Islamic" movements and politics to perform this critical interrogation through fresh historical inventories. One quality in historical Islam becomes clear as a result.

Islam has a demonstrated history of critical potential. From the beginning of the religion, Islam's normative strength was defined by its willingness to trade in knowledge. What I mean is that for all the conservative waves and movements in Islamic histories, an underlying characteristic of Islam has been openness to difference and disagreement. Disagreement, which was incorporated into the normative character of Islam in its respect for people of the book, in turn supported the development of translational and transitional capacities into a state of the mind and the soul. Respect for knowledge and scholarship has historically remained central in Islamic societies. What has changed from period to period is the dominant meaning of scholarship and learning. Even today, and even in conservative Islamic societies, the place of pride continues to be given to teachers in the broad sense of the word. The Islamic honorifics such as *Hoja* and Imam refer first and foremost to exemplary teachers in arts and sciences rather than to religious leaders. Prophet Muhammad himself secured this place of honor for teachers, stating that "the ink of a scholar is holier than the blood of a martyr." It is this attitude that propelled the first Muslims to open the gates of freethinking, cultivating the grounds for a vibrant and rigorous rationalism exploring the relationship between "human reason and divine revelation." Subsequently developed into an art and science of critical faculties as Islamic *Falasifa*, this attitude is a testimony to the inquisitive spirit in Islamic histories that emerged autonomously from Europe. Prior to the advent of the Renaissance, the Enlightenment, and modernity in Europe, Islamic scholars had already engaged and accommodated the ancient sources through their own self-conscious transversalism, spanning the open geography and richness of the wisdom of distant teachers be they Greeks, Ionians, Hindus, or Persians.

In language, architecture, arts, and sciences, Muslims not only mastered the old knowledges, but also often exceeded their limits, taking them to new horizons. In the course of such engagements, they developed the habits of confident souls and minds that culminated in the spectacular works of Al Farabi, Avicenna, and Averreos. This is crucial to understanding historical Islamic societies. It was the strength of their convictions that enabled Muslims to take leaps of knowledge. In some ways, even the material disintegration following the colonial capture of Islamic regions by Europe failed to do away with the sense of the Islamic "measure" of the world obtained through Islam's paradigmatic yet tolerant political-economic calculus. In another sense, one can argue, as I will later, that the habits of the confident soul continue to lag behind the habits of the subordinated Islamic body. Yet, the failure of the soul to wake up to the capture and control of the body appears also to have translated into relative, almost imperceptible, strength, fueling global political Islams everywhere, both the repressive and progressive versions.

In this light a new line of inquiry is needed in theorizing globalization and Islam—one that comprehends Islam as a pluralist historical material and sociological process on the one hand and "Islamism" as an ideology working to regiment and channel political cultural agencies in the majority Islamic countries on the other. It would show, for instance, that Sharia laws are not divinely rendered but have been interpreted and codified through successive Islamisms in history. Similarly, it would demonstrate that Wahhabi beliefs are a result of the supremacy of a unique line of Islamism in nineteenth-century Saudi Arabia. This distinction ought to instruct inquiries about contemporary Islam and globalization. Islam as well as Islamism occur in globalization's simultaneously permissive and conditioned grounds.

It is worth remembering that the colonial domination of Islamic geographies following the nineteenth century was key for the dormancy of Islamic historiography. The rise of the conservative and often violently imposed political and cultural forces within Muslim communities was even more devastating. As stated earlier, the rise of modern Islamic fundamentalism occurred in the confluence of interests emanating in Islamic and non-Islamic spaces and contexts. That is, Saudi-Wahhabi theocracy converging with Anglo-American geostrategic and economic interests has been the primary fuel for the conservative Islamist status quo. The lesson to be learned is this: it is not simply pure or unadulterated religiosity that conditions religious outlook. As Michel Foucault observed, religious spaces exist side by side, along with, or within economic spaces, geopolitical spaces, aesthetic spaces, and ethnic and cultural spaces, as locations of emplacement and displacement. We need to take seriously and study the complex ways in which religiosity finds its way into politics. It is this point that Edward Said was fond of reminding us through Gramsci: It is not the lack of the infinity of experiences in Islamic histories but the way in which we take inventories of Islamic histories that is definitive of how Islam is perceived today.

This problematization of Islamic histories is at the core of the cognitive orientations in contemporary Islamic movements. As well, they are at the heart of the repercussions the movements engender globally, animating potentially progressive projects on the one hand and narrow repressive political visions on the other. Whatever the resulting projects, programs, and subjectivities, their loci of enunciation are communicated through global networks and inflected with a consciousness of the ever salient global conditions of life. Even the most regressive movements, paradoxically, are globally aware and network-driven. Even the "clash of civilizations" creates global zones of contact, zones in which boundaries turn into transitions and borderizations, ideas and bodies flow and fold into each other's ambit and infinity.

At the same time, a consciousness contrary to the fashionable claim that all that is modern is fast withering into global postmodernities is also very much at work in Islamist politics. Global flows and networks do not supplant the modern, territorial, and nation-statist forms of identity and exchange. Rather, they deepen and intensify them without fundamentally doing away with the central ideas, relations, and subjectivities in which the systems of political and economic exchanges find anchor. Flows and networks are not new identities but channels through which identities are formed and circulated (instantaneously locally and globally, within countries as well as through them) into the political, economic, cultural, and religious commonspaces of the world. They are transnational yet still geographically experienced and culturally mediated. They interlink national polities through novel technologies without negating the relevance or influence of nationalism. Therefore, all that follows or emerges under the rubric of Islam has to be understood as global Islams born in contemporary temporal and spatial tensions.

Earlier in the book, I talked about two acts of vanishing necessary for Islam to renew its radical and cosmopolitan character. The first act makes the diffusionist conceits of the West vanish into history, where the West's debts to Islam and other civilizational life-worlds are contrapuntally accounted for. It was Etienne Balibar who first formulated this idea in an effort to enliven the democratic and cosmopolitan energies in the West. The West, Balibar notes, suffers from a hidden democratic deficit, which goes unnoticed because it remains unacknowledged in the Western claim to be the democratic source for all. In this sleight of the mind can be seen an expression of the democratic deficit that has not been named or acknowledged. This has to stop, Balibar submits, by the "vanishing West" or the West vanishing itself. While admirable, Balibar's call ultimately plays into the same diffusionist conceits feeding the Western sense of manifest destiny instead of chipping away at this destructive delusion. Why do I level such a charge, seeming not to appreciate the gesture? Because in this formulation, the vanishing presents itself as a grandiose gesture, an enlightened act by the modern Western subject who, seeing what must be done for the sake of the world, consciously withdraws from the historical center so that others can shine. But it is this sense of being indispensable to the world's future that has been the fundamental problem, not only for the non-Western world but also for the West itself and the world as a whole. It has led to political, cultural, and economic determinism—capitalism, modernity, development, and "democracy for all." Given these ideological pitfalls, I contend that the West, with all its Christian underpinnings, ought to vanish from the center, primarily for its own sake, for in recognition of the democratic deficit it contains but refuses to come to terms with. Regardless, the Western claim to democratic exceptionalism, sustained and preserved in a thousand different ways, has long been exposed in all but the West not only as absurd but also as unsustainable. Vanishing of the West's secularized Christian anchors must be acknowledged as the recognition of the end of such grandiose historical claims of supremacy, and not be presented as yet another chivalrous charge for the West to undertake. This is the first vanishing act.

The second act makes fundamentalist Islamism vanish into the realm of metaphysics, where it functions as one compass among many compasses and not as the overarching political ideology in the "Muslim World." Metapolitical Islamism has long been instrumentalized as a totally ahistorical ideology. Yet, an Islam that is not afraid of history and resists reducing Muslims to theological creatures alone is being once again cultivated. Put differently, this is an Islam that refuses to go along with the hegemony of juridical Islamism comprised solely of prohibitions, limits, and stoppages occasioned in human hands. When viewed historically, it becomes clear that Islamic identities often escaped the theological prison houses in which political rulers and complicit clergy tried to confine them. Instead, Islam functioned as a space for contemplating worldly challenges and opportunities. Seen in this perspective, Islamic philosophy was not an attempt to capture philosophy and bend it to Islam's iron will, but rather an enabler of philosophy anew via the modes of reflection and enunciation inspired by the Islamic view. Similarly, Islamic arts and sciences were not Islamic in articulating an essential Islam but in being inspired by an intense scientific interest spurred in the Islamic era. It is not surprising, for example, that Islamic cosmopolitan interests spawned an unrivaled experiential culture of travel among Muslims. "The prince of travelers," Ibn Battuta, traveled in part to fulfill the pilgrimage duty (hajj) but also to learn about the world. As a result, Battuta wrote a travelogue that is rich in political and social commentary.

Similarly, the fourteenth-century Islamic scholar Ibn Khaldun's travels were conceived and undertaken explicitly in the service of his studies in what later became disciplines of history, sociology, and ethnology. Ibn Khaldun's Muqaddimah was triggered by a radical critical inquest into the declining state of Arab societies across North Africa and in Spain. The resulting study was a masterpiece of social-historical analysis by an Arab Muslim scholar who, Fatima Mernissi would note, was not afraid of Arab history, of asking tough and honest questions about "what had gone wrong." When Mernissi laments how modern Arabs have grown scared of their history, she highlights, among other issues, the devastating failure of modern Arab and Islamic societies in not having been able to ask penetrating questions and answer them fearlessly for themselves. Indigenous voices repressed or controlled, the field was left to the likes of Bernard Lewis and their stunning displays of twentieth-century Orientalism. The troubling implication that endures in their claims: Arabs cannot represent themselves; they have to be represented.

This historical amnesia, forced violently on Arab Muslims and other Islamic peoples as well as internalized by the masses via the fanciful and heroic story lines of Islamic greatness, is devastating in several ways. First, where are Ibn Khaldun-like figures in modern Islamic societies now? Why can't we ask such questions in the first place? What happens to those who dare raise questions that go to the heart of the system of half-truths and fabrications on which the Arab or other Islamic historiographies rely for their fantasy-heavy historical accounts? What, most importantly, happened to the sort of *Asabiyyah*, that dynamic Arab or Islamic outlook on the world, that enabled Ibn Khaldun, a Muslim administrator-turned-scholar, to develop the critical faculties and knowledge to be able to write such a masterpiece? Why the fear of history?

History is not responsible for how it is narrated, but historiography is. And historiography is always political, never benign or innocent. Mernissi's point is that Arabs retained and cultivated neither the spirit nor the intellectual capacity and courage Ibn Khaldun represented. Multiple factors likely played a role in the downward spiral of Arab-Islamic culture through the centuries: the Ghazalian revolution resulting in the triumph of theology over philosophy was the cardinal factor. Theological sciences' emphasis on knowledge deriving from revelation (*tawhid*) and imitation (*taqlid*) changed the nature of learning in the Islamic imaginary, and has yet to be challenged in modern Islamic history or philosophy. The resulting overconfidence in the superiority of Islam over other religions limited Islamic horizons to theological and juridical lenses. Islamic knowledge (*ilim*) increasingly came to be juridical in nature and less experimental in output. *Ilim* meant not the science of medicine, engineering, chemistry, or astronomy anymore, but more and more the dense interpretive exercises that steadily grew into various Sharia streams. The ossification of Islam's dynamic characteristics in the thrall of worldly empires such as the Arab Abbasid, the Persian Safavid, and the Turkish Ottoman intensified the steady narrowing of the nature of Islamic ilim.

Finally, the pushback by European imperial powers against the Islamic presence in the Mediterranean basin from the sixteenth century onward and the consolidation of European advantages against the Islamic world in the eighteenth- and nineteenth-century capitalist globalization sealed the fate of the once enterprising and experimental Islamic Asabiyyah of which Ibn Khaldun was both a product and a critic. The following twentieth-century encounters with the West were based on unequal political and economic exchanges, and have traumatized Muslims ever since. The West took control of the Islamic world and squeezed it hard for resources; such that the so-called independent Islamic nations that emerged in the twentieth century—Arab or otherwise—were only shadows of proper states in the modern sense of statehood. With their rulers appointed or supported by this or that foreign power, their resources already spoken for by this or that capitalist industry, these states developed only the capacity to repress their own people.

Today, it is difficult to find tolerant let alone liberal democratic states around the Islamic world. Turkey and Indonesia appear as two exceptions but not without strong evidence for concern. In the end, Islamic societies—Arab and non-Arab—still remain afraid of their own Islamic histories, for Islamic pasts threaten to reveal Islam to be different from the theological oppression machine they have constructed it into.

The point, then, is that Islam's future lies not in the renewal of an original immutable essence but in the recognition of Islam's original appeal as a timeless call for progress and change. Islam is characteristically forward looking. In this world and now, it demands more of Muslims than it explicitly expresses in the Qur'an or through the hadith. The Prophet's hadith, "Work for the Hereafter as if you will die tomorrow and work this life as if you will live forever," ought to be seen as an expression of an extranormative commitment to this world. Above all, it demands openness to the infinity of experiences, from having faith in the mystery of creation to making an actual ethical commitment to the world.

It is no wonder that the word "Surah" in the Qur'an opens with the exhortation to be merciful and compassionate in the image of Allah before setting down the respective rules. Hermeneutically, the Arabic words for *mercy* and *compassion* connote a broad swath of sociocultural meanings. They apply to all aspects of social life as religion orders it. And very often Surahs close with the same note on mercy and compassion. Yet, historically, the Qur'anic spirit of compassion and mercy has been reduced to discussions of prohibitions and limits in Islamic Sharia. In the same fashion, whereas the Qur'anic thrust is in support of forever expanding Islamic visions, in actuality, the political tendency has been one of narrowing Islamic horizons. Theology has become too powerful an instrument, capturing and taming Islamic energies in the service of one kind of political Islamism or another. Examples abound in history: the Umayyads, Abbasids, Safavids, the Ottomans, and the Saudi-Wahabis.

Refreshingly, fundamental Islamic ideals escaped full and permanent capture by such movements. Sometimes in cooperation, very often in disagreement, and occasionally by vanishing into the palimpsest of societal fabrics across the Islamic Ummah, they avoided control and supported pluralist Islamic qualities. In vanishing, they injected Islamic sensibilities into the everyday normative fabric. Sufi humanism is a testimony.

In the final analysis, vanishing ought not to be construed as Islam's weakness. It should not be seen as a negation of the totality of political and cultural accomplishments for which Islam is rightly credited. Neither should it be understood as a capitulation to Western modernity as a predominant measure of things. In some ways, Islam has always functioned as a counterplot to presenting modernity not only as the apex of human civilization but also as a purely European project. It continues to play this essentially insurrectionary role in the constant articulation of Islam into the world.

Vanishing should be understood as eschewing universal and essentialist positions and claims. In this way, vanishing figures or functions as a demand, particularly on the West, to shed the conceit that it is the apex of human existence. Vanishing is a democratic pluralist gesture with a rigorous reminder that Islam is inexorably a part and parcel of a global world, of civilizational commonspaces in which it inspires over a billion people. Global commonspaces reveal Islam's interconnections. Political Islams, on the other hand, have to embrace the common, if differentiated, human experiences instead of rejecting them as if they represent or contain little or no value or good or wisdom. Political Islams have to vanish their own conceits regarding other human beings in this world.

It is at such a juncture of double vanishing, of the West's Orientalizing vainglory and the leadership of the Muslim world's complicity with it, that Islamic capacities can reanimate the pluralist reflexes in the world. They can rise anew and exert pressure on the West in the context of philosophical debates on history, community, democracy, and the cosmopolitanism of civilizations. With its Judeo-Christian spiritual underpinning—that historical religiosity contained in its secular depths—the West continues to be Islam's relational counterpart, as Islam shapes the measure of the world in political, economic, cultural, and aesthetic senses.

# NOTES

## INTRODUCTION

1. Nick Cumming-Bruce and Steven Erlanger, "Swiss Ban Building of Minarets on Mosques," *New York Times*, 29 November 2009, http://www.nytimes.com/2009/11/30/world/europe/30swiss.html.

2. Ivan Walson, "Women Take Lead in Building Mosque in Turkey," CNN, 16 July 2009, http://www.cnn.com/2009/WORLD/europe/07/13/turkey.mosque.women/index.html.

3. My translation from: AKP, "Muhafazakar Democracy (Conservative Democracy)," AK Yayinlar, http://www.akparti.org.tr/program.asp?dizin=0&hangisi=0 (accessed 15 October 2009).

## CHAPTER 1. ISLAMIC GLOBALISM UNVEILED

1. For a comprehensive historical and literary study of Orientalism as the cultural ideology of European imperialism in the nineteenth and twentieth centuries, see Edward Said, *Orientalism* (New York: Vintage Books, 1979).

2. Bernard Lewis has been one of the most prolific Orientalist historians of late. He has published dozens of books and many tens of articles in sundry media. The list of publications is too long to fully cite, but in substance and content, Lewis's scholarship, although certainly rich and learned, has nevertheless had the impact of positioning Islam and Muslims as abstracted and distanced objects of study. Here I will list the titles of several of his books, which demonstrate Lewis's enduring pursuit of and mastery over the field of Islamic history in the West. Lewis's authority lies in being one of the few "portals" to Islamic histories. *What Went Wrong? Western Impact and Middle Eastern Response*; *The Muslim Discovery of Europe*; *Cultures in Conflict: Christians, Muslims, and Jews in the Age of Discovery*; *The Political Language of Islam*; *Islam: The Religion and the People*; *The Political Language of Islam*. Fouad Ajami, on the other hand, represents the "Arab" intellectual who is forever striving to internalize and to reproduce the Orientalist view of Arabs, the Middle East, and Islam. In the end, his authority in the subject matter differs in nature from Lewis's in that Ajami's voice is that of a "native interlocutor" who operates as a skeptic-informant. The more Ajami yearns to establish a critical distance from the subject of his work, the more he has to fashion himself in its stereotypical light. Ajami is not nearly as prolific as Lewis, but his ideas continue to influence policy makers especially in the United States. The following books are exemplary of his views: *The Arab Predicament: Arab Political Thought and Practice since 1967* (Cambridge, UK: Cambridge University Press, 1992); *Dream Palace of the Arabs: A Generation's Odyssey* (New York: Vintage Books, 1999).

Finally, my intention in highlighting Lewis and Ajami is not to question their motives, but to contend that their intellectual work plays a greater role in policy and conduct than they acknowledge.

3. Bobby S. Sayyid, *A Fundamental Fear: Eurocentrism and the Emergence of Islamism* (London: Palgrave Macmillan, 2003).

4. Manfred Steger, *Globalism: The New Market Ideology* (Lanham, MD: Rowman & Littlefield, 2001).

5. Said, *Orientalism*.

6. Edouard Glissant, *Poetics of Relation* (Ann Arbor: The University of Michigan Press, 2000) and *Caribbean Discourse* (Charlottesville: University Press of Virginia, 1996).

7. The word "arrowlike" is Glisssant's, found in *Poetics of Relation*, 12.

## CHAPTER 2. HISTORIES UNTOLD

1. An Islamic paradigm spawned attitudes that supported plurality and difference not simply as a form to be tolerated, but as a self-conscious norm to be integrated into the societal fabric. M. J. Thompson, among others, points

out that early on the imperatives of ruling over an expanding political and economic realm under Muslim control helped to cultivate flexible governmental and scientific reflexes. Receiving knowledge in a form that comported with Islamic fundamentals sharpened translational and transitional capacities into a normative character of the mind and the soul. Thus emerged the grounds for a vibrant and rigorous rationalism exploring the relationship between "human reason and divine revelation."

2. Fatema Mernissi, *Islam and Democracy: Fear of the Modern World* (Cambridge, MA: Perseus Publishing, 2002), 114–15.

3. Qur'an, 96:1–5.

4. Qur'an 49:13. This *Ayet* unequivocally expressing such an Islamic position has likely served as a guiding principle since Islam's birth. Another *Ayet* in "Al Maidah" Surah stresses the same Islamic sensibility: "Unto every one of you have We appointed a law and way of life. And if God had so willed, He could surely have made you all one single community: but He willed it otherwise in order to test you by means of what He has vouchsafed unto you" (Qur'an 5:48). Yet another *Ayet* appears to buttress the freedom of religion not simply on religious grounds but also as the political freedom from coercion in matters of faith: "If it had been your Lord's will, they all would have believed—all who are on earth. Will you, then, compel the people, against their will, to believe?" (Qur'an 10:99).

5. The *Medina Constitution* signed by the small Islamic community and Medina's Jewish community before Islam's consolidation highlights this attitude adopted by Islam in the first challenge vis-à-vis existential differences. Although set within the Islamic super-framework, the agreement nevertheless created a "live-and-let-live" arrangement between the communities. This document assumed that the inhabitants of the city of Yathrib (renamed Medinah after the agreement) constituted one community, the Ummah, regardless of their religious differences. Where religious differences mattered, mutual rights and obligations were put in place to make coexistence possible and productive. "Migrants" (Muhammad's followers) and "Helpers" (the natives of the city of Yathrib, including the Jews) together became the "believers and those who followed them, joined them and labored with them. They are one community." F. E. Peters, *A Reader in Classical Islam* (Princeton, NJ: Princeton University Press, 1994), 74. Although this "one community" was not free from tension, its new governing document set out a new direction in intercommunal relations. Indeed, the tensions occasionally erupted into conflict, "within the community, especially with the Jewish inhabitants over commercial, religious and psychological differences." Peters, *A Reader in Classical Islam*, 75. Nevertheless, as the eminent Indonesian intellectual Nurcholish Madjid noted, the idea of the "virtuous city," or the "civilized community (*al Madinah al*

*Fadilah)*" as a multicultural space forever entered into the Islamic imaginary. Nurcholish Madjid, *The True Face of Islam: Essays on Islam and Modernity in Indonesia*, ed. Rudy Harisyah Alam and Ihsan Ali-Fauzi (Ciputat, Indonesia: Voice Center, 2003), 302.

6. Mohammed Arkoun, *Rethinking Islam: Common Questions, Uncommon Answers* (Boulder, CO: Westview Press, 1994), 68.

7. Arkoun, *Rethinking Islam*, 69.

8. As Martin Bernal suggested, these were the times when Egyptian and Greek worlds interacted, and the purge of the Egyptian and Persian traces in Hellenic civilization had to wait for the nineteenth century Orientalists to do the dirty work of expunging history. See Martin Bernal, *Black Athena: The Afroaisatic Roots of Classical Civilization* (New Brunswick, NJ: Rutgers University Press, 1987), 29–35.

9. Majid Fakhry, "Philosophy and Theology: From the Eighth Century C.E. to the Present," in *Oxford History of Islam*, ed. John L. Esposito (Oxford: Oxford University Press, 1999), 271–72.

10. Fakhry, "Philosophy and Theology," 271.

11. Nelly Lahoud, *Political Thought in Islam: A Study in Intellectual Boundaries* (London: Routledge, 2005), 43.

12. Fakhry, "Philosophy and Theology," 273.

13. Natalie Zemon Davis, *Trickster Travels: A Sixteenth-Century Muslim Between Worlds* (New York: Hill and Wang, 2006).

14. Fernand Braudel's work on the Mediterranean as a bridge across the continents gave powerful testimony to historical influences that went in all directions. Martin Bernal went further back in history to show the Afro-Asiatic roots of Hellenic civilization on which the modern idea of the West is based. In short, the Mediterranean, long before the Caribbean, the Atlantic, or the Pacific, created a proto-global civilization hailing across Africa, Europe, and the Middle East.

15. Fakhry, "Philosophy and Theology," 283.

16. Peters, *A Reader in Classical Islam*, 373.

17. Peters, *A Reader in Classical Islam*, 369.

18. Peters, *A Reader in Classical Islam*, 374.

19. Qur'an 59:2, as quoted in Peters, *A Reader in Classical Islam*, 375.

20. Peters, *A Reader in Classical Islam*, 371–72.

21. Hans Küng, *Islam: Past, Present and Future* (Oxford: Oneworld, 2007), 379.

22. Cemil Meric, *Kulturden Irfana* (*From Culture to Knowledge-Light*) (Istanbul, Turkey: Insan Yayinlari, 1986), 193–96.

23. Küng, *Islam: Past, Present and Future*, 380.

24. Anthony Black, *The History of Islamic Political Thought* (New York: Routledge, 2001), 74.

25. Black, *The History of Islamic Political Thought*, 74.

26. Black, *The History of Islamic Political Thought*, 74.

27. Black, *The History of Islamic Political Thought*, 74–75.

28. Ian Almond, *Sufism and Deconstruction: A Comparative Study of Derrida and Ibn 'Arabi* (New York: Routledge, 2004), 2–3.

29. Almond, *Sufism and Deconstruction*, 4–5.

30. Omar A. Farrukh, *The Arab Genius in Science and Philosophy* (Washington D.C.: American Council of Learned Societies, 1954), 93.

31. Farrukh, *The Arab Genius in Science and Philosophy*, 107. Farrukh writes: "Undoubtedly the comprehensive study of time and space in Kant's famous 'Critique of Pure Reason' is a proof of his Supreme genius. But the credit, which belongs to Kant, is that of full application, rather than that of origination and definition, for the original conception goes back to the two great Arab Philosophers, Ibn Hazm and Ibn Rushd. It is Ibn Rushd who said: 'Time is something to which is given the sense of movement by memory. . . . Time is something to which memory only gives the impression of movement through a sense of prolongation. If time were known to have an independent existence, then this action of the memory would be a true action, related to reason, rather than to the imagination. . . . But time has no reality.'"

32. For such a study discussing Ibn Hazm's work as an anticipation of Immanuel Kant's criticism of pure reason, see Lenn E. Goodman, *Islamic Humanism* (New York: Oxford University Press, 2003).

33. If as Mashhad Al Allaf argues in the *Essence of Islamic Philosophy*, ICC Classics Series (St. Louis, MO: Author, 2003), 201, al Ghazali's thoughts on "method of doubt" bear striking similarities to Descartes' method in *Meditations*, and we know that al Ghazali's work was available for Descartes to read in Latin translations, it is incumbent on us to highlight Ghazali's ideas as well. The aim is not to argue that Ghazali's ideas influenced or begot Descartes' ideas, or even anticipated them independently some 400 hundred years before Descartes. Instead, it is to assert Ghazali as a historical authentic subject. Likewise, as Farrukh reminds, the skeptic Muslim philosopher and poet Al-Ma'arri's *Epistles of Forgiveness* (*Risalat Al-Ghufran*) evidently inspired Dante's Divine Comedy—so deeply ingrained in Western popular imagination as a great literature. Al-Ma'arri's (973–1057) skepticism was shaped by his rationalism. He wanted reason to anchor all human endeavors. Yet he also realized reason's limits vis-à-vis religion. "Things so confuse mankind," he wrote, "that Reason's self is shackled when she tries to face them fair." (Farrukh, *The Arab Genius in Science and Philosophy*, 90–91). Al-Ma'arri emerged into public view with his

poetry collection entitled *Unnecessary Necessities* (*Luzum ma lam yalzam*) or commonly known as the *Luzumiyat*—"Necessities." His penetrating skepticism evolved further in his *Risalat al Ghufran*. Risalat solidified Al-Ma'arri's place in Islamic intellectual annals but not in Western chronicles. *Humanistic Text*, a collective writing project, contends that Al-Ma'arri's rationalistic critique and skepticisms "remind us of Xenophanes, Carvaka and Lucretius and does not appear in Western thought until the Enlightenment." How then do we not know al Ma'arri while celebrating Dante as a literary genius? What is to account for this gap in knowledge—history or historiography?

34. Herein lies a significant point: even in its drift from rationalist philosophy to theology and theosophy, the accumulated Islamic knowledge found prolific channels that came to be critically important for the development of ethico-social and moral-political systems in Europe. Sufism was the latest of interactive venues, which emerged in the Muslim world when philosophy was under pressure.

35. The expressions, "power of networks" and "networks of power" are inspired by Manuel Castells, *The Rise of the Network Society* (Oxford, UK: Wiley-Blackwell, 2010), 500.

36. My translation of Rumi's poem entitled "Gel!" ("Come!"), available at: http://siir.1turk.net/siir/896 (accessed 10 December 2009).

37. Ismet Zeki Eyupoglu, *Butun Yonleriyle Haci Bektas Veli* (*Haci Bektas Veli: A Comprehensive Study*) (Istanbul, Turkey: Ozgur Yayin Dagitim, 1989).

38. Madjid, *The True Face of Islam*, 29, 153.

39. My translation of the poem entitled "Dunya Ustunde Kurulu Direk," available at: http://www.cs.rpi.edu/~sibel/poetry/poems/pir_sultan_abdal/dunyanin_ustunde_kurulu_direk.html (accessed 10 August 2009).

40. Dina Le Gall, *A Culture of Sufism: Naqshbandis in the Ottoman World, 1450–1700* (Albany: State University of New York Press, 2005). Daphna Ephrat, *A Learned Society in a Period of Transition: The Sunni "Ulama" of Eleventh-Century Baghdad* (Albany: State University of New York Press, 2000).

41. Madjid, *The True Face of Islam*, 170–71.

42. Shaikh Badruddin of Simawna, *Inspirations on the Path of Blame* (Brattleboro, VT: Threshhold, 1993).

43. Arkoun, *Rethinking Islam*, 76

44. Arkoun, *Rethinking Islam*, 76. Also Mohammed Arkoun, *The Unthought in Contemporary Islamic Thought* (London: Saqi Books, 2002).

45. Arkoun, *Rethinking Islam*, 79. In modern India, Subaltern Studies historians shattered some of the myths of the unthinking natives. Muslims are yet to initiate their own subaltern project and sustain it across the Islamic world. Unlike their fundamentalist coreligionists who network into an ideological web the world of ethnically and culturally disparate Islamic societies from Al-

geria to Afghanistan, the precious few movements of critical and unorthodox forces have remained disjointed, unable to challenge the conservative Islamist status quo.

46. Humorous as it may sound, it is this claim to supreme control that enabled some in modern Turkey to attribute Ottoman heritage to President Barack Obama through his "Ottoman" great-grandfather who, as claimed, had found his way to Kenya from the Ottoman province of the Sudan.

## CHAPTER 3. ISLAMIC INTELLECTUAL LEGACIES

1. Assaf Hussain, "The Ideology of Orientalism," in *Orientalism, Islam and Islamists*, ed. Assaf Hussain, Robert Olson, and Jamil Qureshii (Brattleboro, VT: Amana Books, 1984), 8.

2. See M. Siddik Gumus, *Islam's Reformers* (Istanbul, Turkey: Hakikat Kitabevi, 2005).

3. For this critical reading of Iran's history in the eighteenth and nineteenth centuries, I borrowed greatly from: Hamid Dabashi, *Islamic Liberation Theology: Resisting the Empire* (London and New York: Routledge, 2008). These cases are instructive regarding the uses and abuses of religion in politics. From the Mughals, we can learn how Islam inspired an empire in starkly different directions under two different rulers—liberal and enlightened under Akbar and repressive and intolerant under Aurangzeb. From the Safavids, we learn that religion ossified into a state ideology not only loses its own moral direction but also halts progress.

4. Khayr al-Din al Tunisi, *The Surest Path*, trans. from the original Arabic with introduction and notes by Leon Carl Brown (Cambridge, MA: Harvard University Press, 1967), 75–78.

5. al Tunisi, *The Surest Path*, 78.

6. Dabashi, *Islamic Liberation Theology*, 98–99.

7. Shariati, *Man and Islam* (Houston, TX: Flinic, 1981), 41.

8. Edouard Glissant, "Creolization in the Making of the Americas," *Caribbean Quarterly* 55, no. 1 (March–June 2008), available at http://findarticles.com/p/articles/mi_7495/is_200803/ai_n32280290/?tag=content;col1.

9. Ali Shariati, *What Is to Be Done: The Enlightened Thinkers and an Islamic Renaissance* (Houston, TX: The Institute for Research and Islamic Studies, 1986), 49.

10. Shariati, *Man and Islam*, 41.

11. Shariati, *What Is to Be Done*, 48.

12. Shariati, *What Is to Be Done*, 48.

13. Cemil Meric, "Leaves" ("Yapraklar"), in *Magaradakiler* (*Those Who Live in the Cave*) (Istanbul, Turkey: Iletisim Yayinlari, 1997), available

at http://cemilmeric.net/arsiv/meric2/Kimdir/yapraklar.htm. All translations from Turkish are mine.

14. Meric, "Leaves."

15. Meric, "Leaves."

16. Meric, "Leaves."

17. Meric, "Leaves."

18. Cemil Meric, *Bu Ulke (This Country/This Ideal)* (Istanbul, Turkey: Otuken Yayinevi, 1975), 80. All translations from Turkish are mine.

19. Meric, *Bu Ulke*, 96.

## CHAPTER 4. CROSSROADS OF GLOBAL ISLAM AND ISLAMISM IN TURKEY

1. Adopted from Doug McAdam, *Political Process in the Development of Black Insurgency* (Chicago: University of Chicago Press, 1982).

2. My translation from the AK Party official website, "Muhafazakar Democracy (Conservative Democracy)" downloaded originally in 2008 but is no longer electronically available: http://www.akparti.org.tr/program.asp?dizin=0&hangisi=0. I retain a copy in my archives. A new party program is available in Turkish at http://www.akparti.org.tr/siyasivehukuki/parti-programi_79.html and in English at http://eng.akparti.org.tr/english/partyprogramme.html.

3. International Press Institute, World Congress Report and 56th General Assembly, Istanbul, 2007, 45, available for downloading at http://www.freemedia.at/events/congress/.

4. International Press Institute, 46.

5. "Muhafazakar Democracy" (Conservative Democracy), 2004.

6. Erdogan's statement is available in English: http://eng.akparti.org.tr/english/chairman.html.

7. See Karen Barkey, *Empire of Difference: The Ottomans in Comparative Perspective* (Cambridge, Cambridge University Press, 2008), 160–61.

8. Barkey, *Empire of Difference*, 161.

9. Kadir Cangizbay, *Cok Hukukluluk, Lailik ve Laikrasi* (*Rule of Law, Laicite, and Laikrasi*) (Ankara, Turkey: Liberte Yayinlari, 2002), 114–17.

10. Cangizbay, *Cok Hukukluluk*.

11. I was a teenager in the city of Sivas when such an attack occurred. In coordinated assaults, several predominantly Alevi neighborhoods were targeted by mobs assembled from Sivas and from other provinces. The neighborhood I lived in was destroyed, neighbors killed or wounded, and for months thereafter, soldiers patrolled the streets.

12. See the *Dede Korkut Hikayeleri*, in which Early Turkish shamanism and Islamic monotheism encounter and fold in each other. Turkish national education curricula draw liberally on these and other ancient pre-Islamic folk tales and fashions them effortlessly with the Later Islamic motifs.

13. This conceptualization of part/non-part and the condition of being held in thrall is inspired by two works: Giorgio Agamben, *Homo Sacer: Sovereign Power and Bare Life* (Stanford, CA: Stanford University Press, 1998); and Etienne Balibar, "Outlines of a Topography of Cruelty: Citizenship and Civility in an Era of Global Violence," *Constellations* 8, no. 1 (2001): 15–29.

14. Occasionally, particularly in foreign sources, this approach takes on an absurd dimension resulting in the claims that 99 percent of Turkey's population is composed of Sunni Muslims.

15. Garret Jenkins, *Political Islam in Turkey* (New York: Palgrave Macmillan, 2008).

16. Murat Belge, "Türkiye`nin solu yok ama iki tane sa tarafı var!" ("There is no left in Turkey only two rights!"), *Tum Gazeteler*, available at: http://www.tumgazeteler.com/?a=4392000 (accessed 2 December 2008).

17. Belge, "Türkiye`nin solu yok ama iki tane sa tarafı var!"

18. Binnaz Toprak et al., "Turkiyede Farkli Olmak: Din ve Muhafazakarlik Ekseninde Otekilestirilenler" ("Being Different in Turkey: People Othered along Religion and Conservatism"), Bosporus University Study (January 2009), available at: http://www.docstoc.com/docs/3284017/ (accessed 14 October 2009).

19. Said Nursi, "The Damascus Sermon," in *Risale-i Nur Collection*, translated by Sukran Vahide (Istanbul, Turkey: Sozler Nesriyat A.S., 1996), available at the website Risale-i Nur Kulliyati, http://www.risaleara.com/, 48. Nursi expresses the same ideas in nearly identical words in his "The Words," on pages 341 and 342. See Said Nursi, "The Words," in *Risale-i Nur Collection*.

20. Nursi, "The Damascus Sermon," 24.

21. Nursi, "The Damascus Sermon," 35.

22. Ahmet Kuru, "Globalization and Diversification of Islamic Movements: Three Turkish Cases," *Political Science Quarterly* 120, no. 2 (2005): 262.

23. Nursi, "The Damascus Sermon," 56–57.

24. Nursi, "The Damascus Sermon," 56.

25. Nursi, "The Damascus Sermon," 37. As opposed to the "negative nationalism" of Europe, Nursi highlights the virtues of Islamic nationhood. See "The Rays," in *Risale-i Nur Collection*, 317 and 411.

26. Said Nursi, "The Letters," *Risale-i Nur Collection*, 287.

27. Nursi, "The Letters," 373.

28. Nursi, "The Letters," 288.

29. Nursi, "The Letters," 286.

30. Nursi, "The Letters," 291.

31. Examples of scholars' ideas supporting various political movements abound in the nineteenth and twentieth centuries. Carl Schmidt's and Martin Heidegger's ideas were at work in Nazi Germany's political and cultural milieu. Heidegger was even a member of the Nazi Party. Schmidt's ideas have long been implicated for allegedly inspiring some proto-Nazi ideas. Mikhail Bakhtin's ideas circulated across political movements that were Fascist beyond nationalism. Edward Said already demonstrated in *Culture and Imperialism* how scholarly ideas, say, of John Stuart Mill, Jean-Jacques Rousseau, and Jules Herman, among others, helped construct and justified the philosophical and cultural architecture of European colonialism. Nevertheless, these are also figures considered to be transformative, even progressive, in their impact on Western thought. Said Nursi's ideas can be treated in the same way. They, in all their rich depth and breadth, have been summoned in the service of various political formations. Islamists have been at the forefront, while leftists have been suspicious of their religiosity. Yet, the attitudes are changing in this regard. Just as AK party ideologues draw on Western scholars to justify greater liberty for piety, leftists and secularists are taking a fresh look at Nursi's ideas to invoke an Islam with a broad and liberal horizon.

32. Alev Cinar, *Modernity, Islam and Secularism in Turkey: Bodies, Places, and Time* (Minneapolis: University of Minnesota Press, 2005), 22.

33. Cinar, *Modernity, Islam and Secularism in Turkey*, 122–29.

34. Fethullah Gulen, "An Analysis of the Tolerance Process," 26 February 2006, available at http://en.fgulen.com/recent-articles/1942-an-analysis-of-the-tolerance-process.html (accessed 5 January 2010). The website is excellent, with a sea of information that includes Gulen's writings, speeches, and interviews; full reports from symposiums and conferences on the movement; as well as news reports published about the world.

35. Gulen, "An Analysis of the Tolerance Process."

36. Fethullah Gulen, "A Comparative Approach to Islam and Democracy," 4 February 2002, available at: http://en.fgulen.com/recent-articles/1027-a-comperative-approach-to-islam-and-democracy (accessed 2 January 2010).

37. Fethullah Gulen, in an interview with Mehmet Gundem, "Has Fethullah Gulen Organized a Secret Mob within the Security Department and Armed Forces of Turkey?" 9 January 2005, available at: http://www.fethullahgulen.org/press-room/mehmet-gundems-interview/1909-has-fethullah-gulen (accessed 5 September 2009).

38. Hakan Yavuz, *Islamic Political Identity in Turkey* (Oxford: Oxford University Press, 2003), 196–99.

39. Devrim Sevimay, interview with Kemal Karpat, "Tarihci Kemal Karpat: AKP Yeni Donemin Sadace Baslangici, Yeni Liderler Gelecek ("Historian Kemal Karpat: AKP Represents Only the Beginning of a New Period, New Leaders Will Emerge)," *Turktime*, 1 June 2009, available at: http://www.turktime.com/haber/TARIHCI-KARPAT-AKP-YENI-DONEMIN-SADECE-BASLANGICI-YENI-LIDERLER-GELECEK/56654 (accessed 18 November 2009).

40. *Yeni Safak*, 7 November 2009, "Our Intellectuals are Withdrawing to Their Own Polarized Positions" ("Aydinlarimiz Kendi Kutuplarina Cekiliyor"), available at: http://yenisafak.com.tr/Politika/Default.aspx?t=07.11.2009&c=2&area=4&i=221624 (accessed 28 November 2009).

## CHAPTER 5. ARCHIPELAGOS OF ISLAM IN INDONESIA

I dedicate this chapter to Kyai Haji Abdurrahman Wahid, who passed away on December 30, 2009. Affectionately known as "Gusdur," Wahid was the President of Indonesia from 1999 until 2001. Legendary for his commitment to "pluralist ethos" as being definitive of Indonesia's historical character, Wahid has had a larger-than-life impact on Indonesia's political and cultural life in the last 30 years. I had a chance to interview him in Jakarta in August 2008. I also dedicate the chapter to the memory of Paramoedya Ananta Toer, the novelist extraordinaire, who wrote for the World even though he was writing about Indonesia.

1. Roula Khalaf, "Turkey Tests Islamist Appetite for Democracy," *Financial Times*, 14 May 2007, available at: http://www.ft.com/cms/s/0/e93e7470-0236-11dc-ac32-000b5df10621.html.

2. M. Syafi'i Anwar, "Islam, Universal Values and the Challenges of Globalization: Towards a Dialogue of Civilizations," in *Islam and Universal Values: Islam's Contribution to the Construction of a Pluralistic World* (Jakarta, Indonesia: International Center for Islam and Pluralism, 2008), xvii.

3. Bruce B. Lawrence, "Eastward Journey of Muslim Kingship," in *The Oxford History of Islam*, ed. John L. Esposito (New York: Oxford University Press, 1999), 426.

4. Interview with Abdurrahman Wahid on 14 August 2008, Jakarta, Indonesia. The interview was conducted in English, taped, and later transcribed.

5. "Sejarah Indonesia, An Online Timeline of Indonesian History," available at: http://www.gimonca.com/sejarah/sejarah.shtml (accessed 25 September, 2008 and 10 December 2009).

6. Interview with Abdurrahman Wahid.

7. Based on interviews with numerous members of NU and the Muhammadiyah, including Abdurrahman Wahid and Amin Rais respectively.

8. Some of the people I interviewed on the record or informally are: Prof. Ryaas Rasyid, the president of the Partai Demokrasi Kebangsaan (PDK); Prof. Bahtiar Effendy of Syarif Hidayatullhal State Islamic University, Jakarta; Din Siyamsuddin, chairman of the Muhammadiyah as well as the deputy president of the Indonesian Ulamas Council; Abdurrahman Wahid, former Indonesian president and former chairman of Nahdathul Ulama; M. Syafi'i Anwar, executive director of International Center for Islam and Pluralism (ICIP); Anies Baswedan, rector of the Paramadina University in Jakarta; Lily Zakiyah Machfudz, director of the Center for Pesantren and Democracy (CePDeS); Drs. Siti Ruhaini, Siti Syamsiyatun, and Alimat Qibtiyah, all of the State Islamic University Sunan Kalijagan, Yogyakarta; Dr. Mocthar Pabottingi at the Indonesian Institute of Sciences, Center for Political Studies; Nur Rofiah of Institut PTIQ (Institute of Qur'anic Sciences) at the State Islamic University, Syarif Hidayatullah; Abdul Munir Mulkhan, former governing board member of the Muhammadiyah, member of the Indonesian National Commission on Human Rights, and a participant in the Liberal Islam Network; Dr. Muhammed A. S. Hikam, former Indonesian technology minister and parliamentarian; Rizal Namli, former Indonesian economics minister, and Rizal Sukma, the executive director at the CSIS, Jakarta; Professor and Rector H. M. Amin Abdullah of State Islamic University Sunan Kalijagan, Yogyakarta; and Dr. Jamhari, vice rector at the State Islamic University, Syarif Hidayatullah, Jakarta. I also talked with journalists and reporters, in addition meeting with everyday Indonesians and students at various universities—State Islamic as well as the Catholic University in Jakarta.

9. Abdul Munir Mulkhan, "A New Socio-Cultural Map for Santris," in *A Portrait of Contemporary Indonesian Islam,* ed., Chaider S. Bamualim (Jakarta, Indonesia: Universitas Islam Negeri Syarif Hidayatuallah Jakarta, 2005), 39–40.

10. For a discussion of the PK's history, see Elizabeth Collins, "Dakwah and Democracy: The Significance of Partai Keadilan and Hizbut Tahrir in Indonesia," paper presented at the annual meeting of the American Political Science Association, Philadelphia, PA, 27 August 2003, available at: http://www.allacademic.com/meta/p62309_index.html (accessed 2 January 2010). The current reincarnation of the PK is the PKS, the Prosperous Justice Party. For the PKS's mission and vision statement, which substantially qualifies the commitment to Pancasila along its Islamist "*da'wah*" (missionary) aims, see PIP PKS in North America, http://pk-sejahtera.us/index.php?option=com_content&view=article&id=8&Itemid=25. In Indonesian, see http://www.pk-sejahtera.org/v2/index.php.

11. Hidayat Nurwahid and Zulkieflimansyah, "The Justice Party and Democracy: A Journey of a Thousand Miles Starts with a Single Step," *Wilson Center, Asia Program Special Report*, Vol. 110 (April 2003), 22.

12. Interview with M. Qodari, the executive director of Indo Barometer, 15 August 2005, Jakarta, Indonesia.

13. From my recorded and informal interviews with various Indonesian observers, ranging from scholars to laypeople.

14. Martin Van Bruniessen, "Liberal and Progressive Voices in Islam," in *Reformist Voices in Islam*, ed. Shireen T. Hunter (Armonk, NY: M.E. Sharpe, 2009), 190.

15. Interview with Lily Zakiyah Machfudz, the founder and director of the Center for Pesantren and Democracy Studies (CePDeS). The interview was conducted in English at the pesantren in Jombang, East Java, Indonesia, 16 August 2008.

16. Lily Zakiyah Munir, "General Introduction to Islamic Law," available at: http://www.lfip.org/laws718/docs/lily-pdf/Introduction_to_Islamic_Law.pdf.

17. Interview with Lily Zakiyah.

18. See Lily Zakiyah Munir, "Sharia and Justice for Women," available at: http://www.lfip.org/laws718/docs/lily-pdf/Sharia_and_Justice_for_Women.pdf.

19. Interview with Lily Zakiyah, 16 August 2008. For Zakiyah's published view on Aceh, see: "Islamic Fundamentalism and Its impact on Women," available at: http://www.lfip.org/laws718/docs/lily-pdf/Islamic_Fundamentalism_and_Its_Impact_on_Women.pdf.

20. Interview with Lily Zakiyah.

21. Interview with Lily Zakiyah.

22. Interview with Lily Zakiyah.

23. My Interview with Nur Rofiah in Jakarta, Indonesia, 15 August 2008. Interview was conducted in English.

24. Interview with Nur Rofiah.

25. Interview with Nur Rofiah.

26. Interview with Nur Rofiah.

27. Interview with Nur Rofiah.

28. Interview with Nur Rofiah.

29. *Jakarta Post*, "Young Back Sharia-Based Bylaws: Survey," 6 May 2008, available at: http://www.thejakartapost.com/news/2008/06/04/young-back-shariabased-bylaws-survey.html (accessed 25 September 2008).

30. Van Bruniessen, "Liberal and Progressive Voices in Islam."

31. Ideas summarized from the Madjid speech entitled "The Necessity of Renewing Islamic Thought and the Problem of Integration of the Ummah," in Nurcholish Madjid, *The True Face of Islam: Essays on Islam and Modernity in*

*Indonesia*, ed. Rudy Harisyah Alam and Ihsan Ali-Fauzi (Ciputat, Indonesia: Voice Center, 2003), 315–22.

32. Ann Kull, *Piety and Politics: Nurcholish Madjid and His Interpretation of Islam in Modern Indonesia* (Lund, Sweden: Lund University, 2005), 61.

33. In "Reinvigorating Religious Understanding in the Indonesian Muslim Community," in Madjid, *The True Face of Islam*, 323–36.

34. Kull, *Piety and Politics*, 112–13.

35. Nurcholish Madjid, "Islam and Tolerance in Indonesia," in *Islam and Universal Values: Islam's Contribution to the Construction of a Pluralistic World* (Jakarta, Indonesia: International Center for Islam and Pluralism, 2008), 38.

36. Interview with Syafi'i Maarif on 12 August 2008 in Yogyakarta at the Muhammadiyah headquarters.

37. Muhamad Ali, "Moderate Islam Movement in Contemporary Indonesia," in *Islamic Thought and Movements in Contemporary Indonesia*, ed. Rizal Sukma and Clara Joewono (Yogyakarta, Indonesia: Center for Strategic and International Studies, 2007), 195.

38. Abdul Munir Mulkhan, from the unpublished review of his essay Mulkan passed on to me in hard copy, 4.

39. Interview with Anies Baswedan on 13 August 2008 at the Paramadina University campus in Jakarta.

40. I had a lunch meeting with M. Syafi'i Anwar and Prof. Bahtiar Effendy in Jakarta on 16 August 2008. Conversation was not taped. Anwar himself related some of the threats against him, which are also reported in the national and international media. Included in the campaign of threats and harassment directed at him was the accusation that he worked for the CIA. He was clearly worried about the rising tide of Wahhabist Islamism in Indonesia. At the same time, he also vowed to continue his educational-political work in defense of pluralism.

41. Interview with Abdul Munir Mulkhan on 12 August 2008 at his home in Yogyakarta. The interview was conducted in Indonesian through an interpreter and taped.

42. Ali, "Moderate Islam Movement in Contemporary Indonesia," 206.

43. See Indonesia Matters, "Islam on the Political Map," available at: http://www.indonesiamatters.com/4905/political-map/ (accessed 5 June, 2009). This is a fascinating, mostly liberal, discussion board and news outlet on Indonesia. The language of discussion is English and discussions are generally very well informed.

44. Indonesia Matters, "Islam on the Political Map."

45. Interview with Moeslem Abdurrahman on 14 August 2008 in Jakarta, Indonesia.

46. The three women scholars I met in Yogyakarta embodied this dynamic process. They were Drs. Siti Ruhaini and Siti Syamsiyatun and the lecturer Alimat Qibtiyah—all of the State Islamic University Sunan Kalijagan, Yogyakarta. They were extremely instructive in their analyses of the issues as they related to the role of Islam in society. Interestingly, they stated how Islamic discourse can be and is being employed to combat some of the basic socioeconomic and sociocultural problems, such as widespread poverty, domestic abuse, and educational differentials between men and women. Highlighting such societal problems in a religious light, they argued, also enabled them to highlight the problems' extra-religious dimensions. An excellent example, they offered, was the state support preserving religio-cultural practices that condition the field of opportunities for women in the society. Arguing that they are not always heard or listened to properly, all three women also expressed a certain dissonance with their counterparts in the West in terms of the methods and pedagogies of social and political activism. (Based on my interview on 12 August 2008 in Yogyakarta, Indonesia.)

47. Indonesia Matters, "Islam on the Political Map."

48. For an extensive analysis of "Alid" Islam in Southeast Asia, see Akbar Ahmad, *Journey into Islam: The Crisis of Globalization* (Washington, DC: Brookings Institution Press, 2007).

49. Interview with Abdurrahman Wahid.

50. Interview with Abdurrahman Wahid.

# BIBLIOGRAPHY

Ahmad, Akbar. *Journey into Islam: The Crisis of Globalization*. Washington, DC: Brookings Institution Press, 2007.

Ajami, Fouad. *The Arab Predicament: Arab Political Thought and Practice since 1967*. Cambridge: Cambridge University Press, 1992.

———. *Dream Palace of the Arabs: A Generation's Odyssey*. New York: Vintage Books, 1999.

Ali, Muhamad. "Moderate Islam Movement in Contemporary Indonesia." In *Islamic Thought and Movements in Contemporary Indonesia*, ed. Rizal Sukma and Clara Joewono. Yogyakarta, Indonesia: Center for Strategic and International Studies, 2007.

Ali, Tariq. *The Clash of Fundamentalism: Crusades, Jihad, and Modernity*. London: Verso, 2003.

Almond, Ian. *Sufism and Deconstruction: A Comparative Study of Derrida and Ibn 'Arabi*. New York: Routledge, 2004.

Al-Mulk, Nizam. *The Book of Government or Rules for Kings (The Siyar al Muluk or Siyasat-nama)*. Translated from Persian by Hubert Darke. London: Routledge and Kegan Paul, 1978.

An Naim, Abdullahi A. *Islam and the Secular State: Negotiating the Future of the Shari'a*. Cambridge, MA: Harvard University Press, 2008.

Anwar, M. Syafi'i. "Islam, Universal Values and the Challenges of Globalization Towards a Dialogue of Civilizations." In *Islam and Universal Values: Islam's Contribution to the Construction of a Pluralistic World*. Jakarta, Indonesia: International Center for Islam and Pluralism, 2008.

Arabi, Ibn. *Sufis of Andalusia (The Ruh of al Quds and al-Durrat al-Fakhirah)*. Translated by R. W. J. Austin. London: Allen & Unwin, 1971.

Arkoun, Mohammed. *Rethinking Islam: Common Questions, Uncommon Answers*. Boulder, CO: Westview Press, 1994.

———. *The Unthought in Contemporary Islamic Thought*. London: Saqi Books, 2002.

Atasoy, Yildiz. *Turkey, Islamists and Democracy: Transition and Globalization in a Muslim State*. London and New York: I. B. Tauris, 2005.

Bamyeh, Mohammed A. *The Social Origins of Islam: Mind, Economy, Discourse*. Minneapolis: University of Minnesota Press, 1999.

Barkey, Karen. *Empire of Difference: The Ottomans in Comparative Perspective*. Cambridge: Cambridge University Press, 2008.

Bernal, Martin. *Black Athena: the Afroasiatic Roots of Classical Civilization*. New Brunswick, NJ: Rutgers University Press, 1987.

Black, Anthony. *The History of Islamic Political Thought*. New York: Routledge, 2001.

Cangizbay, Kadir. *Cok Hukukluluk, Lailik ve Laikrasi (Rule of Law, Laicite, and Laikrasi)*. Ankara, Turkey: Liberte Yayinlari, 2002.

———. *Hickimsenin Cumhuriyeti (Nobody's Republic)*. Ankara, Turkey: Utopya Yayinevi, 2000.

Charfi, Mohamed. *Islam and Liberty: The Historical Misunderstanding*. London: Zed Books, 2005.

Cinar, Alev. *Modernity, Islam and Secularism in Turkey: Bodies, Places, and Time*: Minneapolis: University of Minnesota Press, 2005.

Collins, Elizabeth. "Dakwah and Democracy: The Significance of Partai Keadilan and Hizbut Tahrir in Indonesia." Paper presented at the annual meeting of the American Political Science Association, Philadelphia, PA, 27 August 2003. Available at: http://www.allacademic.com/meta/p62309_index.html (accessed 2 January 2010).

Davutoglu, Ahmet. *Alternative Paradigms: The Impact of Islamic and Western Weltanschuungs on Political Theory*. Lanham, MD: University Press of America, 1994.

Dabashi, Hamid. *Islamic Liberation Theology: Resisting the Empire*. London and New York: Routledge, 2008.

Demant, Peter R. *Islam v. Islamism: The Dilemma of the Muslim World*. Westport, CT: Praeger, 2006.

Ephrat, Daphna. *A Learned Society in a Period of Transition: The Sunni "Ulama" of Eleventh-Century Baghdad*. Albany: State University of New York Press, 2000.

Esposito, John L. *Oxford History of Islam*. Oxford: Oxford University Press, 1999.

Eyupoglu, Ismet Zeki. *Butun Yonleriyle Haci Bektas Veli (Haci Bektas Veli: A Comprehensive Study)*. Istanbul, Turkey: Ozgur Yayin Dagitim, 1989.

Fakhry, Majid. "Philosophy and Theology: From the Eighth Century CE to the Present." In *Oxford History of Islam*, ed. John L. Esposito. Oxford: Oxford University Press, 1999.

———. *A History of Islamic Philosophy*. New York: Columbia University Press, 2005.

Farrukh, Omar A. *The Arab Genius in Science and Philosophy*. Washington, DC: American Council of Learned Societies, 1954.

Glissant, Edouard. "Creolization in the Making of the Americas," *Caribbean Quarterly* 55, no. 1 (March 2008): 268–75.

———. *Poetics of Relation*. Ann Arbor: The University of Michigan Press, 2000.

———. *Caribbean Discourse*. Charlottesville: University Press of Virginia, 1996.

Goodman, Lenn E. *Islamic Humanism*. New York: Oxford University Press, 2003.

Gulen, Fethullah. "An Analysis of the Tolerance Process," 26 February 2006. Available at: http://en.fgulen.com/recent-articles/1942-an-analysis-of-the-tolerance-process.html (accessed 5 January 2010).

———. "A Comparative Approach to Islam and Democracy," 4 February 2002. Available at: http://en.fgulen.com/recent-articles/1027-a-comperative-approach-to-islam-and-democracy (accessed 2 January 2010).

———. "Has Fethullah Gulen Organized a Secret Mob within the Security Department and Armed Forces of Turkey?" interview with Mehmet Gundem, 9 January 2005. Available at: http://www.fethullahgulen.org/press-room/mehmet-gundems-interview/1909-has-fethullah-gulen (accessed 5 September 2009).

Gumus, M. Siddik. *Islam's Reformers*. Istanbul, Turkey: Hakikat Kitabevi, 2005.

Hidayat, Nurwahid, and Zulkieflimansyah. "The Justice Party and Democracy: A Journey of a Thousand Miles Starts with a Single Step." *Wilson Center, Asia Program Special Report*, Vol. 110, April 2003.

Husain, Mir Zohair. *Global Islamic Politics*. New York: Longman, 2003.

Hussain, Assaf. "The Ideology of Orientalism." In *Orientalism, Islam and Islamists*, ed. Assaf Hussain, Robert Olson, and Jamil Qureshii. Brattleboro, VT: Amana Books, 1984.

Jenkins, Garret. *Political Islam in Turkey*. New York: Palgrave and McMillan, 2008.

Karpat, Kemal. *The Politicization of Islam: Reconstructing Identity, State, Faith: Community in the Late-Ottoman State*. Oxford: Oxford University Press, 2001.

Khalaf, Roula. "Turkey Tests Islamist Appetite for Democracy," *Financial Times*, 14 May 2007. Available at: http://www.ft.com/cms/s/0/e93e7470-0236-11dc-ac32000b5df10621.html.

Khaldun, Ibn. *The Muqaddimah: An Introduction to History*. Translated from Arabic by Franz Rosenthal. Princeton, NJ: Princeton University Press, 1967.

Koprulu, Mehmed Fuad. *Islam in Anatolia after the Turkish Invasion (Prolegomena)*. Translated by Garry Lesier. Salt Lake City: University of Utah Press, 1993.

Kull, Ann. *Piety and Politics: Nurcholish Madjid and His Interpretation of Islam in Modern Indonesia*. Lund, Sweden: Lund University, 2005.

Küng, Hans. *Islam: Past, Present and Future*. Translated by John Bowden. Oxford: Oneworld, 2007.

Kuru, Ahmet. "Globalization and Diversification of Islamic Movements: Three Turkish Cases." *Political Science Quarterly* 120, no. 2 (2005): 253–74.

Lahoud, Nelly. *Political Thought in Islam: A Study in Intellectual Boundaries*. London: Routledge, 2005.

Lawrence, Bruce B. "Eastward Journey of Muslim Kingship." In *The Oxford History of Islam*, ed. John L. Espositio. New York: Oxford University Press, 1999.

Le Gall, Dina. *A Culture of Sufism: Naqshbandis in the Ottoman World, 1450–1700*. Albany: State University of New York Press, 2005.

Madjid, Nurcholish. *The True Face of Islam: Essays on Islam and Modernity in Indonesia*. Edited by Rudy Harisyah Alam and Ihsan Ali-Fauzi. Ciputat, Indonesia: Voice Center, 2003.

McGinnis, Jon, and David C. Reisman, *Classical Arabic Philosophy: An Anthology of Sources*. Indianapolis, IN: Hackett Publishing, 2007.

Meric, Cemil. "Leaves" ("Yapraklar"). In *Magaradakiler (Those Who Live in the Cave)*. Istanbul, Turkey: Iletisim Yayinlari, 1997.

———. *Bu Ulke (This Country/This Ideal)*. Istanbul, Turkey: Otuken Yayinevi, 1975.

———. *Isik Dogudan Geli: Ex Oriente Lux (The Light Comes From the East)*. Istanbul, Turkey: Pinar Yayinlari, 1984).

———. *Umrandan Uygarliga (From Umran to Civlization)*. Istanbul, Turkey: Iletisim Yayinlari, 1996.
Mernissi, Fatema. *Islam and Democracy: Fear of the Modern World*. Cambridge, MA: Perseus Publishing, 2002.
Mulkhan, Abdul Munir. "A New Socio-Cultural Map for Santris." In *A Portrait of Contemporary Indonesian Islam*, ed. Chaider S. Bamualim. Jakarta, Indonesia: Universitas Islam Negeri Syarif Hidayatuallah Jakarta, 2005.
Nursi, Said. "*Risale-i Nur Collection*. Translated by Sukran Vahide. Istanbul, Turkey: Sozler Nesriyat A.S., 1996. Available at Risale-i Nur Kulliyati, http://www.risaleara.com/.
Peters, F. E. *A Reader in Classical Islam*. Princeton, NJ: Princeton University Press, 1994.
Rippin, Andrew, and Jan Knappert. *Textual Sources for the Study of Islam*. Chicago: University of Chicago Press, 1990.
Saed, Abdullah. *Islamic Thought: An Introduction*. London and New York: Routledge, 2006.
Safa, Peyami. *Asir Avrupa ve Biz (20th-Century Europe and Us)*. Istanbul, Turkey: Otuken Yayinlari, 1976.
Said, Edward. *Orientalism*. New York: Vintage Books, 1979.
Sait Halim Pasa, "Buhranlarimiz" ("Our Crises"). In *Butun Eserleri (Complete Collection)*, ed. N. Ahmet Ozalp. Istanbul, Turkey: Anka Yayinlari, 2003.
Sayyid, Bobby S. *Euro-Centrism and the Emergence of Islamism*. London: Palgrave Macmillan, 2003.
"Sejarah Indonesia: An Online Timeline of Indonesian History." Available at: http://www.gimonca.com/sejarah/sejarah.shtml (accessed 25 September 2008 and 10 December 2009).
Shaik Badruddin of Simavna. *Inspirations on the Path of Blame*. Brattleboro, VT: Threshold Books, 1993.
Shakland, David. *The Alevis in Turkey: The Emergence of a Secular Islamic Tradition*. London: RoutledgeCurzon, 2003.
Shariati, Ali. *Man and Islam*. Houston, TX: Flinic, 1981.
———. *What Is to Be Done: The Enlightened Thinkers and an Islamic Renaissance*. Houston, TX: The Institute for Research and Islamic Studies, 1986.
———. *On the Sociology of Islam*. Translated by Hamid Algar. Berkeley, CA: Mizan Press, 1979.
Steger, Manfred. *Globalism: The New Market Ideology*. Lanham MD: Rowman & Littlefield, 2001.
Stauth, Georg. *Politics and Cultures of Islamization in Southeast Asia: Indonesia and Malaysia in the Nineteen-Nineties*. New Brunswick, NJ: Transcript, 2002.
Toprak, Binnaz, et al. "Turkiyede Farkli Olmak: Din ve Muhafazakarlik Ekseninde Otekilestirilenler" ("Being Different in Turkey: People Othered along

Religion and Conservatism"). Bosporus University Study (25 January 2009). Available at: http://www.docstoc.com/docs/3284017/ (accessed 14 October 2009).

Tunisi, Khayr al-Din al. *The Surest Path*. Translated from the original Arabic with Introduction and Notes by Leon Carl Brown. Cambridge, MA: Harvard University Press, 1967.

Van Bruniessen, Martin. "Liberal and Progressive Voices in Islam." In *Reformist Voices in Islam*, ed. Shireen T. Hunter. Armonk, NY: M.E. Sharpe, 2009.

Yavuz, Hakan. *Islamic Political Identity in Turkey*. Oxford: Oxford University Press, 2003.

*Yeni Safak*. "Our Intellectuals are Withdrawing to Their Own Polarized Positions" ("Aydinlarimiz Kendi Kutuplarina Cekiliyor"). 7 November 2009. Available at: http://yenisafak.com.tr/Politika/Default.aspx?t=07.11.2009&c=2&area=4&i=221624 (accessed 28 November 2009).

Zakiyah Munir, Lily. "General Introduction to Islamic Law." Available at: http://www.lfip.org/laws718/docs/lily-pdf/Introduction_to_Islamic_Law.pdf.

———. "Sharia and Justice for Women." Available at: http://www.lfip.org/laws718/docs/lily-pdf/Sharia_and_Justice_for_Women.pdf.

———. "Islamic Fundamentalism and Its impact on Women." Available at: http://www.lfip.org/laws718/docs/lily-pdf/Islamic_Fundamentalism_and_Its_Impact_on_Women.pdf.

Zemon-Davis, Natalie. *Trickster Travels: A Sixteenth Century Muslim Between Worlds*. New York: Hill and Wang, 2006.

# INDEX

# ABOUT THE AUTHOR

**Nevzat Soguk** is professor of political science at the University of Hawai'i, Mānoa, specializing in international relations theory, international organizations, and comparative politics. Most broadly, his research is guided by an interest in critical international relations theory, especially those aspects centering on the state, the global, and transnational processes of governance, and international migration. He published *States and Strangers* (1999). His numerous articles have appeared in diverse journals such as *Alternatives*, *Global Society*, *International Politics*, *Theory and Event*, *Review of International Affairs*, *Millennium*, and *New Political Science*.

CPSIA information can be obtained at www.ICGtesting.com
261677BV00002B/8/P
9 780742 557505